Maryland and Delaware

Off the Beaten Path®

Help Us Keep This Guide Up to Date

Every effort has been made by the author and editors to make this guide as accurate and useful as possible. However, many things can change after a guide is published—establishments close, phone numbers change, and facilities come under new management.

We would love to hear from you concerning your experiences with this guide and how you feel it could be improved and be kept up to date. While we may not be able to respond to all comments and suggestions, we'll take them to heart and we'll also make certain to share them with the author. Please send your comments and suggestions to the following address:

The Globe Pequot Press
Reader Response/Editorial Department
P.O. Box 480
Guilford, CT 06437

Or you may e-mail us at:
editorial@globe-pequot.com

Thanks for your input, and happy travels!

OFF THE BEATEN PATH® SERIES

Maryland and Delaware

FOURTH EDITION

by Judy Colbert

Guilford, Connecticut

Cover and text design by Laura Augustine
Cover photo by Corel
Maps created by Equator Graphics © The Globe Pequot Press
Art on page 136 by M. A. Dube; all other art by Carole Drong, rendered from photographs by Judy Colbert.

Library of Congress Cataloging-in-Publication Data

Colbert, Judy.
Maryland and Delaware : off the beaten path / Judy Colbert. —4th ed.
p. cm. —(Off the beaten path series)
Includes index.
ISBN 0-7627-0458-6
1. Maryland Guidebooks. 2. Delaware Guidebooks. I. Title. II. Series.
F179.3.C65 1999
917.5204'43—dc21 99-28880
CIP

Manufactured in the United States of America
Fourth Edition/First Printing

Dedicated to Ben and Rockzana,
the newest travelers

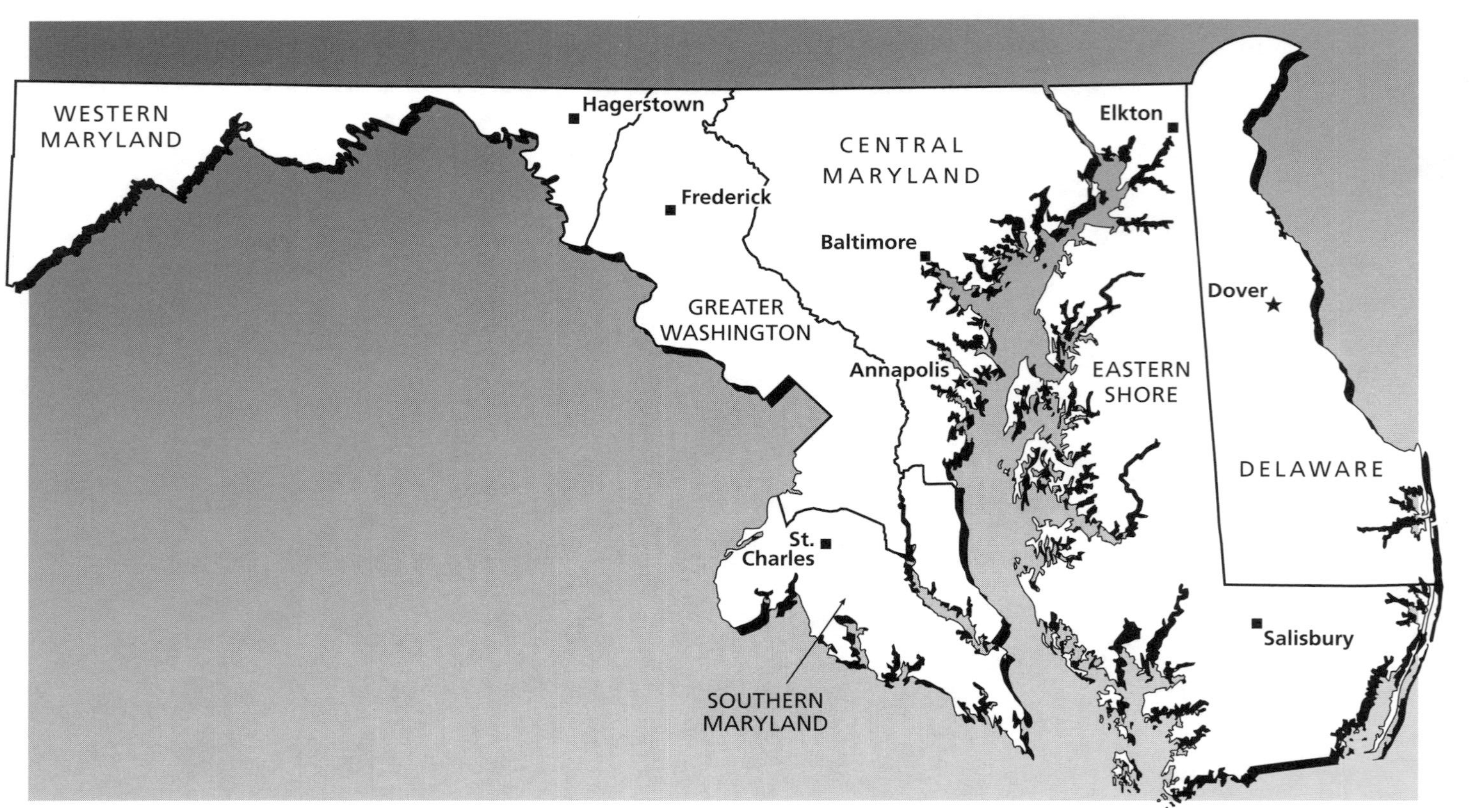
WESTERN MARYLAND
Hagerstown
Frederick
CENTRAL MARYLAND
Elkton
Baltimore
GREATER WASHINGTON
Annapolis
Dover
EASTERN SHORE
DELAWARE
St. Charles
Salisbury
SOUTHERN MARYLAND

Contents

Introduction

Welcome to *Maryland and Delaware: Off the Beaten Path,*® fourth edition, where you'll find some of the best food, the most unusual attractions, the friendliest people, the most incredible history, the most wonderful scenery and natural resources, and the best way to spend a few hours off the interstate.

Maryland is often called America in Miniature because the state goes from the seashore (the Atlantic Ocean and the Chesapeake Bay) on the east to the mountains (the Appalachians) on the west. The mountains are not high compared to the Rockies (Backbone Mountain in Garrett County is the tallest, at 3,360 feet), but they provide fair downhill and excellent cross-country skiing. The seashore is among the finest in the East. In one day you can go from one to the other and theoretically ski in the morning and the afternoon; snow skiing one direction, water skiing the other. About the only clime we don't have here is desert, yet there are sand quarries.

Maryland is also called the Free State (road signs say KEEP THE FREE STATE LITTER FREE), and if you ask residents, they'd probably cite the freedom of worship advocated by the state's founders. Others might point to Maryland's alliance with the northern states during "the war" and its intolerance of slavery (at least in some parts of the state). These historical facts are true, but the name dates from 1917, when the state opposed prohibition on the grounds that it was a states' right issue.

Not everything in Maryland, however, is miniature. The National Aquarium in Baltimore is one of the world's largest. The collection at the Walter's Gallery, also in Baltimore, is world renowned. Maryland also has the nation's largest white oak tree (see Talbot County), one of the nation's largest hydroelectric generating stations at Conowingo (see Cecil County), the largest colony of African black-footed penguins in the United States (Baltimore City Zoo), one of the largest and finest public libraries in the U.S. at the Enoch Pratt Free Library (Baltimore City), and the largest wooden dome in the country built without nails (Annapolis). Well, the list continues, but you get the idea.

As with other places around the country, the demand for telephone numbers has increased exponentially in the past few years. Maryland has four area codes divided in an overlay pattern. Generally, (301) and (240) codes are for the western, suburban Maryland (around Washington, D.C.), and southern Maryland counties. Similarly, (410) and (443) are for Annapolis, Baltimore, and Eastern Shore areas. All local calls require the entire ten-digit number (area code and phone number). Only long-distance calls require the number 1 before the ten-digit number. The area code for Delaware is (302), and you needn't dial it for local calls.

I hope you enjoy reading and using this book as much as I enjoy discovering *Maryland and Delaware: Off the Beaten Path®*.

Fast Facts about Maryland

Maryland Tourism

Maryland Office of Tourism, 217 East Redwood Street, Baltimore 21202; (800) 543–1036, (410) 767–3400, or www.mdisfun.org.

Allegany County Convention and Visitors Bureau, Western Maryland Station Center, 13 Canal Street, Cumberland 21502; (301) 777–5905 or (800) 50–VISIT.

Annapolis and Anne Arundel County Conference and Visitors Bureau, 26 West Street, Annapolis 21401; (410) 280–0445, info@visit-annapolis.org or www.visit-annapolis.org.

Baltimore Area Convention and Visitors Association, Legg Mason Tower, 12th Floor (written queries), 100 Light Street, Baltimore 21202; (410) 659–7300. Visitors Center at the Constellation Pier, Inner Harbor (walk-in queries); (800) 282–6632 or www.baltimore.org.

Baltimore County Convention and Visitors Bureau, 435 York Road, Towson 21204; (410) 583–7313, (800) 570–2836, info@visit.bacond.com or www.visitbacond.com.

Calvert County Department of Economic Development, 175 Main Street, Calvert County Courthouse, Prince Frederick 20678; (301) 855–1880 (DC), (410) 535–4583, (800) 331–9771, cced@chesapeake.net or www.co.cal.md.us.

Caroline County Economic Development Commission, 218 Market Street, Denton 21629; (410) 479–0660 or (410) 479–2230.

Carroll County Office of Tourism, 224 North Center Street, Room 100, Westminster 21157; (410) 857–2983 or (800) 272–1933.

Cecil County Tourism, 129 East Main Street, Room 324, Elkton 21921; (410) 996–5303 or (800) CECIL–95.

Charles County Tourism, P.O. Box B, La Plata 20646; (301) 645-0558, (301) 870–3000 (DC), (800) 766–3386, tourism@govt.co.charles.md.us or www.govt.co.charles.md.us.

Dorchester County Tourism, 203 Sunburst Highway, Cambridge 21613; (800) 522–TOUR, (410) 228–1000, dtourism@shorenet.net or www.shorenet.net/tourism.

Tourism Council of Frederick County, Inc., 19 East Church Street, Frederick 21701; (301) 663–8687 or (800) 999–3613, fredtour@erols.com or www.co.frederick.md.us.

Garrett County Chamber of Commerce, 200 South Third Street, Oakland 21550; (800) 800–5557, (301) 334-1948, GCTourism@garrett.ncin.com or www.gcnet.net/gctourism/gct.html.

Discover Harford County Tourism Council, Inc., 224 North Washington Street, Suite 8, Havre de Grace 21078; (410) 939–3336, (800) 597–2649, harfordmd@dpnet.net or www.harfordmd.com.

Howard County Tourism, P.O. Box 9, Ellicott City 21041; (410) 313–1900, (800) 288–TRIP (288–8747), hctc@clark.net or www. howardcountymdtour.com.

Kent County Tourism, 400 South Cross Street, Suite 1, Chestertown 21620; (410) 778–0416 or www.kentcounty.com.

Conference and Visitors Bureau of Montgomery County, 12900 Middlebrook Road, Suite 1400, Germantown 20874; (800) 925–0880 or www.cvbmontco.com.

Trivia

The state sport is jousting, the oldest equestrian sport in the world, with men and women competing. Like other sports and competitions, jousting originated as a test of a man's occupational skills. In Maryland, the challenge in jousting is not to toss a man off his horse, but to spear a series of metal rings while riding on a horse.

The 80-yard course has three arches from which rings are suspended; in each round, the size of the rings decreases. These are not huge rings to begin with: the largest ring is $1^3/_4$ inches in diameter and the smallest is $^1/_4$ inch.

There are numerous jousting tournaments throughout the year. The schedule usually starts in April and continues through to the Maryland State Championship and the Nationals in October. Events may take place in Hagerstown, Frederick, St. Mary's City, Easton, Denton, Trappe, Port Republic, Lily Pons, Clear Spring, Chestertown, and Havre de Grace. Each tournament has its pageantry and fun, its food and its partying. Usually there is an admission charge, which often is used to benefit a charitable organization. Write to the Maryland Jousting Tournament Association, 328 Bush Chapel Road, Aberdeen 21001 for a schedule of events.

Ocean City Office of Tourism/CVB, 4001 Coastal Highway, Ocean City 21842; (800) OC–OCEAN or www.ocean-city.com.

Prince George's County Conference and Visitors Bureau, Inc., 9200 Basil Court, Suite 101, Largo 20774; (301) 925–8300 or visitor_info@co.pg.md.us.

Queen Anne's County Office of Tourism, 425 Piney Narrows Road, Suite 3, Chester 21619; (888) 400–RSVP, (410) 604–2100, tourism@qac.org or www.qac.org.

St. Mary's County Division of Travel and Tourism, P.O. Box 653, Governmental Center, Washington Street, 2nd Floor, Leonardtown 20650; (301) 475–4411 or (800) 327–9023.

Somerset County Tourism, P.O. Box 243, Princess Anne 21853; (410) 651–2968, (800) 521–9189 or www.skipjack.net/le_shore/visitsomerset.

Talbot County Conference and Visitors Bureau, Chamber Building, 210 Marlboro Avenue, Suite 3, Easton 21601-1366; (410) 822–4606, (888) BAY–STAY, talbot@baystay.org, or www.talbotchamber.org.

Hagerstown/Washington County Convention and Visitors Bureau, Elizabeth Hager Center, 16 Public Square, Hagerstown 21740; (301) 791–3246, (800) 228–STAY or (301) 791–3175 (TTY/Voice).

Wicomico Convention and Visitors Bureau, 8480 Ocean Highway, Delmar 21875; (410) 548–4914, (800) 332–TOUR, wicotour@shore.intercom.net, or www.co.wicomico.md.us/tourism.

Worcester County Tourism, 105 Pearl Street, Snow Hill 21863; (410) 632–3617, (800) 852–0335, econ@ezy.net, or www.skipjack.net/le_shore/visitworchester.

Other Web Sites and Information

Maryland Department of Natural Resources, www.gacc.com/dnr

Farmers Markets, www.mda.state.md.us/market/fmd.htm

Maryland Fall Foliage Hotline, (800) LEAVES 1

Maryland Welcome Centers

The welcome centers offer maps, local traffic conditions (major road construction), brochures about the area and the rest of the state, and assistance in planning your trip.

All welcome centers are open daily from 9:00 A.M. to 5:00 P.M. except

Thanksgiving, Christmas day, New Year's day, and Easter. The eateries at the Chesapeake House are open for extended hours, with the Burger King open twenty-four hours a day.

Trivia

The state's official fossil, the four-ribbed snail, is of an extinct invertebrate that ranged in size from microscopic to 3 or 4 inches in diameter. Fossils can be found at the Cliffs of Calvert, in the Choptank and St. Mary's areas.

Youghiogheny Overlook Welcome Center, I–68 East, mile marker 6 (east of West Virginia state line), Friendsville, (301) 746–5979.

I–70 West Welcome Center, I–70 West, mile marker 39 (just east of the Washington County/Frederick County line), Myersville, (301) 293–4161.

I–70 East Welcome Center, I–70 East, mile marker 39 (just east of the Washington County/Frederick County line), Myersville, (301) 293–2526.

U.S. 15 Welcome Center, U.S. 15, 1 mile south of Pennsylvania, Emmitsburg, (301) 447–2553.

I–95 South Welcome Center, I–95 South, mile Marker 37 (just south of Route 32), Savage, (301) 490–2444.

I–95 North Welcome Center, I–95 North, mile marker 37 (just south of Route 32), Savage, (301) 490–1333.

Chesapeake House Welcome Center, I–95 North/South, mile marker 97 (includes fast-food restaurants, gift shop, and country market), Perryville, (410) 287–2313.

State House Visitors Center, State Circle, Annapolis, (410) 974–3400.

Crain Memorial Welcome Center, U.S. 301 North, 12480 Crain Highway (just north of the Govenor Nice Memorial Bridge), Newburg, (301) 259–2500.

Eastern Shore Welcome Centers, U.S. 13 Welcome Center, U.S. 13 North, 144 Ocean Highway (just north of the Virginia state line), Pocomoke City, (410) 957–2484.

Bay Country Welcome Center, U.S. 301 North/South, 1000 Welcome Center Drive, Centreville, (410) 758–6803.

Bicyclists are prohibited from riding on Maryland Transportation Authority toll facilities, including bridges, tunnels, and approach roads. Understanding that this can be an *oops* in your travel plans, the Authority offers the following services as a courtesy to bikers:

At the Chesapeake Bay Bridge (William Preston Lane Jr. Bridge) bike transportation is by a private, professional service, for a fee, and must be arranged prior to your arrival. Call (410) 974–1355.

At the Thomas J. Hatem (US Route 40, Susquehanna River) and Harry W. Nice (US Route 301, Potomac River) bridges Authority personnel will transport bikes and bikers across the bridge for the normal toll fee when time, personnel, and equipment permit. Call (410) 575–6650 for the Hatem Bridge and (301) 259–4444 for the Nice Bridge.

Major Maryland Newspapers

The Capital, 2000 Capital Drive, Annapolis, (410) 268–5000 (main editorial number); (410) 268–4800 (circulation); (301) 261–2200 (Washington, D.C., number).

Washington Post, 1150 Fifteenth Street, Washington, D.C., (202) 334–6000 (editorial); (202) 334–6100 (circulation); www.washingtonpost.com.

Baltimore Sun, 501 North Calvert Street, Baltimore, (410) 332–6000; www.sunspot.com.

The Star Democrat, 29088 Airpark Drive, Easton, (410) 820–6505; mail@stardem.com.

Public Transportation

Amtrak, (800) USA– RAIL, www.amtrak.com.

Baltimore Washington International Airport (BWI), (800) 435–9294, (410) 519–0000, (301) 261–1000, or www.bwiairport.com.

Fast Facts about the Old Line State

Area (land): 10,455 square miles (27,077 square kilometers), 42nd in size

Capital: Annapolis

Largest city: Baltimore

Number of counties: 23, plus Baltimore City

Highest elevation: Backbone Mountain, 3,360 feet (1,024 meters)

Lowest elevation: Sea level, along the Atlantic Ocean

Greatest distance from north to south: 124 miles (199 kilometers)

Greatest distance from east to west: 238 miles (383 kilometers)

Coastline: 31 miles (50 kilometers) of Atlantic Ocean coastline, 3,190 miles (5,134 kilometers) of Chesapeake Bay coastline.

Population: 4,798,622 (1990 census), 14 percent increase over 1980, nineteenth among states. Density is 459 persons per square mile (177 persons per square kilometer).

Population distribution: 81 percent urban, 19 percent rural

Median family income: $45,034 (1989)

Statehood: April 28, 1788 (seventeenth state)

Nicknames: The Old Line State, the Free State, America in Miniature

State flower: Black-eyed Susan

State tree: White Oak

State motto: *Fatti Maschii, Parole Feminine* (Manly deeds, womanly words)

State bird: Baltimore Oriole

State fossil shell: Ecphora gardnerae

State dog: Chesapeake Bay retriever

State reptile: Diamondback terrapin

State fish: Striped bass

State crustacean: Chesapeake Bay blue crab

State insect: Baltimore checkerspot butterfly

Trivia

Minute quantities of gold have been found along the Potomac, near Great Falls, and in the Piedmont regions. If you'd like to try your hand at panning, or at least see where some gold has been mined, stop by the Chesapeake and Ohio (C&O) Canal Park and Great Falls Tavern Museum, near the intersection of MacArthur Boulevard and Great Falls Road. Park in the C&O Canal parking area and follow the unmarked trail to the Maryland Gold Mine, which was worked until the 1920s. No one has become rich with Maryland gold, but one can try. For more information about the history of gold finds in the state and rules and regulations about prospecting, write to the Maryland Geological Survey, 2300 St. Paul Street, Baltimore 21218.

State dinosaur: Astrodon

State boat: Skipjack

State song: "Maryland, My Maryland"

Climate Overview

Maryland enjoys, if that's the word, hot and humid summers, with temperatures and humidity sometimes in the 90s, and cold and snowy winters, with an average of 16 inches of snow a year in the Baltimore–Washington, D.C. corridor, although in 1997–1998, there was only $^{1}/_{10}$ of an inch of snow, while a few years earlier there were 70 inches of the white stuff (if this is Friday it must be snowing, or if it's snowing, it must be Friday).

Trivia

The Maryland flag was adopted in 1904. The red and white section is the coat of arms of the Crossland family, the first Lord Baltimore's relatives on his mother's side. The black and gold design is the coat of arms for the Calvert family, Lord Baltimore's relatives on his father's side.

Keep in mind, of course, that there's more likely to be snow in the mountainous western part of the state (they get the second-most snow on the Eastern seaboard, next to Vermont, on average) and almost snowless on the Eastern Shore. Summer temperatures will be ten to twenty degrees cooler, usually, in the mountains than at the beach.

Actually, the weather can be quite pleasant most of the year, and the state at least has its share of seasons, with beautiful spring blossoms, showy summers, fall foliage, and winter wonderlands. The Chesapeake Bay is large enough to create its own weather systems.

Famous Sons and Daughters of Maryland

Karen Allen, movie actress

Benjamin Banneker, astronomer, essayist, surveyor

Henry Blair, inventor

Eubie Blake, musician

John Wilkes Booth, actor, assassin

James M. Cain, author

Charles Carroll, American revolutionary

John Carroll, clergyman

Samuel Chase, jurist, lawyer

Bosley Crowther, movie critic

Stephen Decatur, Naval hero

John Dickinson, patriot, lawyer

Frederick Douglass, statesman and abolitionist

Jimmie Foxx, baseball player

Robert "Lefty" Grove, baseball player

Alan Frank Guttmacher, physician

Dashiell Hammett, author

John Hanson, politician, farmer

Frances Ellen Watkins Harper, author, orator, social reformer, and suffragist

Matthew Henson, explorer

Alger Hiss, public official

Johns Hopkins, merchant, banker, philanthropist, founder of hospital bearing his name

Judy Johnson, baseball player

Al Kaline, baseball player

Francis Scott Key, poet, attorney

Barry Levinson, film producer

Thurgood Marshall, Supreme Court Justice

Charles Wilson Peale, portraitist

Emily Post, journalist, etiquette expert

Babe Ruth, baseball player

R. Sargent Shriver Jr., diplomat, director of the Peace Corps

Upton Sinclair, writer, social critic

Dr. Helen Taussig, pediatric cardiologist

Harriet Tubman, abolitionist, organizer of the Underground Railroad

Leon Uris, author

John Waters, film producer

Fast Facts about Delaware

Delaware Tourism

Bethany-Fenwick Chamber of Commerce, P.O. Box 1450, Bethany Beach 19971; (302) 645–6838.

Brandywine Valley Tourist Information Center, Route 1, Longwood Gardens 19348; (800) 228–9933 or (610) 388–2900.

Delaware Office of Tourism, 99 Kings Highway, P.O. Box 1401, Dover 19903; (302) 739–4271 or (800) 441–8846, www.state.de.us.

Delaware State Visitor Center, 406 Federal Street, Dover 19903; (302) 739–4266.

Greater Georgetown Chamber of Commerce, P.O. Box 1, Georgetown 19947; (302) 856–1544.

Greater Milford Chamber of Commerce, P.O. Box 805, Milford 19963; (302) 422–3344.

Greater Seaford Chamber of Commerce, P.O. Box 26, Seaford 19973; (302) 629–9690.

Greater Wilmington Convention and Visitors Bureau, 100 West Tenth Street, Suite 20, Wilmington 19801; (800) 422–1181.

Kent County Convention and Visitors Bureau, 9 East Loockerman Street, Suite 203, Dover 19901; (800) 233–KENT.

Lewes Chamber of Commerce and Visitors Bureau, 120 Kings Highway, Lewes 19958; (302) 645–8973.

Milton Chamber of Commerce, 104 Federal Street, Milton 19968; (302) 684–2504.

New Castle Visitors Bureau, P.O. Box 465, New Castle 19720; (800) 758–1550 or (302) 322–8411.

Rehoboth Beach–Dewey Beach Chamber of Commerce, P.O. Box 216, Rehoboth Beach 19971; (302) 227–2233.

Smyrna Visitors Center, 5500 North Kings Highway, Smyrna 19977; (302) 653–8910.

Sussex County Convention and Tourism, P.O. Box 240, Georgetown 19947; (302) 856–1818.

Major Delaware Newspapers

Newark Post, 153 East Chestnut Hill Road, Newark 19713; (302) 737–0724.

News-Journal, 950 West Basin Road, New Castle 19720; (302) 324–2700.

Philadelphia Inquirer, 440 North Broad, Wilmington 19801; (302) 654–6033.

Public Transportation

Philadelphia International Airport (215) 492–3000.

Amtrak, (800) USA– RAIL, www.amtrak.com.

Salisbury/Ocean City Regional Airport, (410) 548–4827.

Fast Facts about the First State

Area (land): Delaware ranks Forty-ninth in the nation, with a total area of 1,982 square miles.

Capital: Dover

Largest city: Wilmington

Number of counties: 3

Highest elevation: 447.85 feet above sea level, in New Castle County

Lowest elevation: Sea level, along the Atlantic Ocean

Greatest distance from north to south: 96 miles

Greatest distance from east to west: 35 miles

Coastline: Almost 300 miles

Population: 700,000 (1994), Forty-sixth among the states

Population distribution: 73 percent urban, 27 percent rural, density of 34.5 persons per square mile

Statehood: December 7, 1787

Nicknames: The First State, Small Wonder, Blue Hen State

Trivia

According to the Graduate College of Marine Studies at the University of Delaware, there are as many as sixty-two species of shark roaming the eastern waters of North America, including the Delaware and Maryland coasts. Typical mid-Atlantic sharks include the Common Hammerhead shark, the Atlantic Mako shark, the Sand shark, the Smooth Dogfish shark, the Spiny Dogfish shark, and the Sandbar shark.

State flower: Peach blossom

State tree: American Holly

State motto: Liberty and Independence

State bird: Blue Hen chicken

State song: "Our Delaware"

State bug: ladybug

State fish: the weakfish (aka sea trout, gray trout, yellow mouth, yellowfin trout, and tiderunner)

State beverage: Milk

State mineral: Sillimanite

State colors: Colonial blue and buff

Climate Overview

Delaware's climate is moderate year-round. Average monthly temperatures range from 75.8 to 32.0 degrees. The average temperature in the summer months is 74.3 degrees. About 57 percent of the days are sunny. Annual precipitation is approximately 45 inches. Temperatures along the Atlantic Coast are about 10 degrees warmer in winter and 10 degrees cooler in summer than the rest of the state. The average growing season varies from 170 to 200 days.

Famous Sons and Daughters of Delaware

Richard Allen, religious leader

Valerie Bertinelli, actress

Joseph Biden, U.S. Senator

Robert Montgomery Bird, author

Emily Perkins Bissell, social reformer

Annie Jump Cannon, astronomer

John Clayton, U.S. Senator

F. I. DuPont, inventor

Pierre DuPont, industrialist

Dallas Green Jr., professional athlete

Henry Jay Heimlich, developer of the Heimlich Maneuver

John P. Marquand, novelist

John Bassett Moore, attorney

Howard Pyle, illustrator

Jay Saunders Redding, teacher

Judge Reinhold, actor

Caesar Rodney, politician

Christopher Short, professional baseball player

Edward Robinson Squibb, founder of Squibb Pharmaceuticals

Estelle Taylor, actress

The prices and rates listed in this guidebook were confirmed at press time. We recommend, however, that you call establishments before traveling to obtain current information.

Western Maryland

Western Maryland's three counties—Garrett, Allegany, and Washington—are a combination of farmlands, rugged mountains, sedate streams, and white-water rivers.

The products of farms and iron furnaces needed to be transported to customers between Wheeling, West Virginia, and the East Coast. So through this territory came the National Pike, which now is Alternate Route 40. It was the first road across the country funded by the federal government. This was long before President Eisenhower dictated there would be a national system of interstate highways. Along the road are many of the original mile markers, white metal (although they look like stone) obelisks that stand about 3 feet high.

Garrett County

Perhaps Garrett County is best known for ***Deep Creek Lake,*** the largest lake in Maryland (all Maryland lakes were made by humans). In 1925 a dam 1,300 feet long and 62 feet high was constructed to provide hydroelectric power, and the lake resulted. It is fed by Deep and Cherry Creeks, seven stream runs, and two glades.

Just 13 feet from the shores of Deep Creek Lake is the ***Lake Pointe Inn,*** a fine bed-and-breakfast inn with sweeping views of the lake and mountains. The oldest house on the lake, it dates from the late 1800s, although it enjoyed a restoration in 1995. Each of the nine rooms has individually controlled heat, telephone with a private number, private bath, and down comforter and pillow. One room is handicapped accessible. Enjoy an evening by the stone fireplace in the Great Room or a lazy afternoon on the wraparound front porch. A light dinner is available upon request (give at least three days notice), for an additional charge.

Trivia

The Garrett County Chamber of Commerce, knowing how to promote their county's treasures, has two brochures available. So, if fishing is your passion, obtain their Fly Fishing in Western Maryland *brochure, which includes information about the rivers, streams, and Deep Creek Lake, and what lures to use and when.*

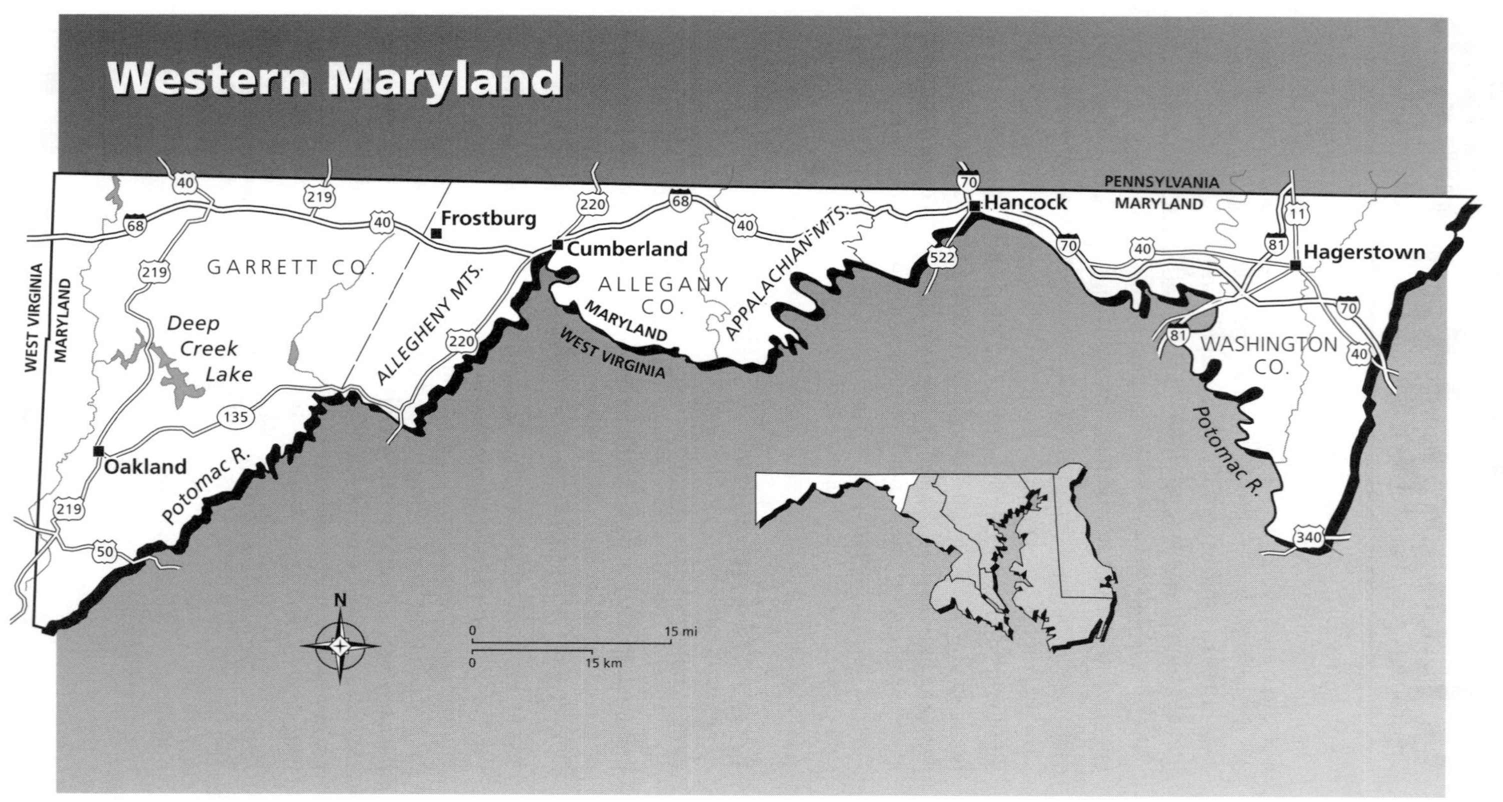
Western Maryland
PENNSYLVANIA
MARYLAND
WEST VIRGINIA
MARYLAND
Frostburg
Cumberland
Hancock
Hagerstown
Oakland
GARRETT CO.
ALLEGANY CO.
WASHINGTON CO.
ALLEGHENY MTS.
APPALACHIAN MTS.
Deep Creek Lake
Potomac R.
Potomac R.
MARYLAND
WEST VIRGINIA
40
219
68
40
219
220
68
40
70
70
40
11
81
70
81
40
522
220
135
219
50
340
N
0
15 mi
0
15 km

Judy's Favorite Attractions in Western Maryland

Antietam Battlefield

LaVale Toll Gate House

Sideling Hill Exhibit area

Washington County Museum of Fine Art

Western Maryland Station Center

Rafters on the ***Upper Youghiogheny River*** (or Upper Yough, pronounced "yock") fight their way over Gap and Bastard Falls and through rapids with names like Charlie's Choice, Rocky III, Cheeseburger, and Meat Cleaver. In the 9-mile ride there are twenty Class IV and V rapids (the top of the scale being class VI) and a downhill drop of 100 to 120 feet per mile. These rapids can provide some tough but exhilarating times; an experienced guide is a necessity.

When the White Water Canoe/Kayak World Championships were held in the United States for the first time in 1989, they were held on nearby Savage River, another popular rafting place. Then, in 1992, the river was the site of the canoe and kayak team Olympic trials.

Other recreational pastimes in Garrett County include water sports, skiing (downhill and cross country), hiking, camping, golfing, horseback riding, hunting, and mountain biking. The mountains in this area receive the second-largest annual snowfall in the East (after the White Mountains of New Hampshire), which makes for good downhill skiing at Wisp (Deep Creek Lake) and extraordinary cross-country skiing.

Within the more than 70,000 acres of public land, Garrett County has cleared and marked trails in Germany State Park, 6 miles of maintained trails around Herrington Lake, and an additional 6 miles of primitive trails. Deep Creek and Swallow Falls State Parks have marked hiking trails that are suitable for cross-country skiing. Ski rentals are available at Herrington Manor and New Germany State Park.

Trivia

On October 14, 1790, Col. Elie Williams and Gen. George Washington met at the spring house in Williamsport (in Washington County) to discuss the possibility of the town being the new capital of the United States. The idea was dismissed because the Potomac River was not navigable by large ships.

In La Vale you will find the only remaining tollhouse (circa 1836) in Maryland.

The ***La Vale Toll Gate House*** shows life as it was when the National Road (Route 40) came this way. There's a neat sign showing the tolls for various animals, pedestrians, and wagons. This is the only remaining toll gate on the National Road in Maryland. The furnishings are fascinating as well, and be sure to ask about the "courting candle."

The House is at 14302 National Highway, La Vale,

Trivia

Garrett County has the state's highest mountain (Backbone, at 3,360 feet), the longest waterfall (Muddy Creek Falls, at 52 feet), and the largest lake (Deep Creek, with a length of 12 miles and a 65-mile shoreline).

and is open Friday through Sunday from 1:30 to 4:30 P.M., May through August, and on Sunday only in September. Call (301) 729–3047 for more information or an appointment.

Paralleling the Potomac River to Cumberland was the Chesapeake and Ohio Canal. The canal was part of George Washington's dream of a water system that would unite the Atlantic with the Ohio River. The canal is now a National Historical Park. The 184½-mile towpath is used year-round by hikers, cyclists, and nature enthusiasts who enjoy seeing the restored aqueducts and canal locks and communing with nature.

Railroads superseded the canal as an efficient means of transportation. Today I–81, I–68, and I–70 provide the lifelines connecting this part of the state with the rest of the country. The geographic features that isolated western Maryland for so many years also made it attractive to vacationers; residents from Washington, D.C., and Baltimore traditionally have come here to escape the summer heat. Here you will find traces of Amish and Scottish culture, of hardy stock and friendly people. You will note some wealth, both in property and in cultural heritage. As yet, you will not find hundreds of thousands of tourists. You will find hospitality, tranquillity, perseverance, a dedication to remember the "old ways," and beautiful mountain scenery.

Reportedly it also has the only town in the country named ***Accident.*** The story is that George Deakins was given a land grant for 600 acres in western Maryland in 1751 by King George II. Deakins sent two engineers on separate missions to find his paradise. By accident, each selected the same plot, starting at the same tall oak tree. Deakins called this plot "The Accident Tract," and the name endures; locals wouldn't have it any other way. Most noted by visitors are the Accident Garage, the Accident Fire Department, and the Accident Professional Building.

Trivia

If you'd like to see the historical marker for the 3,360-foot highest point in the state on Backbone Mountain, take Route 50 east of Red House and you'll be at the crest of the Alleghenies.

The ***Drane House***, built in the late eighteenth century, just east of Accident, is one of the few original frontier plantation homes remaining in this area. A key to Accident's past, it has been restored and is open for free tours upon request. Call the Accident Town Hall, Monday, Wednesday, and Friday, at (301) 746–6346.

Vacationers have been seeking respite in Garrett County for hundreds of years, and traces of that history can be found throughout the county. The Shawnee Indians summered here. People from the sun-baked, humid cities of Washington and Baltimore came here to enjoy the cool mountain climate as early as 1851. That is when the Baltimore and Ohio Railroad ran its line to Oakland, which would become the county seat. The train no longer stops in Garrett County, but the Oakland station, an outstanding and picturesque Queen Anne structure built in 1884, remains.

Oakland is the county seat, so you're most likely to find a variety of interests addressed here.

The ***Oakland Post Office Mural*** was created by Robert Gates in 1942; it portrays a buckwheat harvest. Gates also did the mural in the Bethesda Post Office, which depicts the Montgomery County Farm Woman's Cooperative Market.

Trivia

The town of **McHenry** *was settled about 1805 by Col. James McHenry, aide to Gen. George Washington, signer of the Declaration of Independence, and the man for whom the Baltimore fort was named.*

About 10 miles out of Oakland is the Nature Conservancy's ***Cranesville Sub-Arctic Swamp***, covering more than 500 acres (plus more in West Virginia). Although open to the public during daylight hours, the conservancy likes you to call ahead of time to tell them you'll be wandering along their boardwalks. The number is (301) 656–8673.

This natural phenomena is a remnant of a boreal forest that produces growth normally found in arctic regions. So, you geologists, biologists, and nature lovers can see many rare species of flora and fauna. Although the ice sheet or glaciers of the last Ice Age (15,000 years ago) didn't reach this far south, they did lower the temperatures here, making this area a suitable habitat only for northern or colder clime plants and animals. They stayed this far south, even though the colder weather retreated north, because of a natural phenomena known as a frost pocket, due to the cool air in the high mountains.

Among the plants you'll find here are the tamarack or larch (*Larix laricina*) and the tiny, round-leaved sundew, an insectivorous plant. Additionally, this is the only significant site in Maryland where you can see creeping snowberry (*Gaultheria hispidula*). There are nineteen different plant communities, from shrubby wetlands to hardwood forest, in Cranesville.

One of the animals you might see is the northern water shrew (*Sorex palusyris punculatus*), and among the state-rare breeding birds are the golden-crowned kinglet, alder fly-catcher, Nashville warbler, and the saw-what owl.

In 1965, Cranesville Swamp became one of the first National Natural Landmarks to be designated by the National Park Service. It's open to the public for photography, nature study, birding, and walking, with four color-coded marked trails (with interpretative signs) through the woods to a 1,500-foot boardwalk. The trails start from either the drive into the swamp or from the parking lot, and all trails lead to the boardwalk. Please stay on the trails and the boardwalk so you don't take a chance of harming the plants.

Pets, even on a leash, are not allowed, nor is smoking or all-terrain vehicles. Remove nothing except your trash. Camping and fires are not allowed, either.

Do wear sensible shoes, sunblock, insect repellent, and socks pulled up over your pants' cuffs to protect against chiggers, mosquitoes, ticks, poison ivy, or poison sumac. Please bring field glasses and a good field guide to help you enjoy your visit.

Understand that the roads into the swamp are not paved. So, although the swamp can be gorgeous under a snow cover, you may need a four-wheel drive vehicle to get there.

Grover Cleveland and his bride, Frances Folsom, stayed in the three-story, fourteen-room "Cottage Number Two," now "Cleveland Cottage," near the ***Deer Park Hotel*** for their fifteen-day wedding trip in 1886. The Deer Park Hotel was built in 1873 by the Baltimore and Ohio Railroad when John W. Garrett (for whom the county was named) was company

Trivia

The 317-foot, one-lane, wooden-plank bridge crossing the North Branch of the Potomac River, linking Green Spring, West Virginia, with Oldtown, Maryland (about 15 miles southeast of Cumberland), was one of the last privately-owned toll bridges. The bridge, constructed in 1937, was closed in 1995 because, according to Allegany County Public Works officials, "the deteriorated structural condition" of the Maryland-side abutment and evidence of pier decay. Without the 50-cent toll bridge, those who want to travel be- tween the two areas face an additional 40-mile commute. The bridge remains open to pedestrians.

president. None of the hotel's main structure remains because it was razed in 1942, but some of the foundation is still visible. About 5 miles east of Oakland, on Route 135, turn south on Deer Park Hotel Road and proceed 1/2 mile, then drive east on the loop at Pennington Cottage to reach the hotel.

Trivia

Presidents Grant, Garfield, Harrison, and Cleveland attended services in the St. Matthew's Episcopal Church in Oakland. (301) 334–2510.

Solomon Sterner opened the ***Casselman Hotel*** in Grantsville in 1824 to take in travelers from the National Pike. As is usual with restaurants, inns, and hotels along the pike, this one is on the north side, or the side that westbound travelers would be on.

When the nearby ***Casselman Bridge*** was built in 1813, it was the largest single-span, stone-arch bridge in America. Gracefully curving 50 feet above the river, it was constructed so that the Chesapeake and Ohio Canal could travel beneath its span. The canal never came this far, but the bridge carried traffic for 125 years. It is now closed to motorized traffic, but the Casselman River State Park has a picnic area and a scenic spot to enjoy for a few minutes or a few hours. Yes, it is on the National Register of Historic Places. (301) 895–5453.

East of Casselman Bridge is ***Penn Alps,*** home to numerous crafters who work in log cabins that have been brought here from the surrounding countryside. The shops in ***Spruce Forest Artisan Village*** are open from late May through late October.

Trivia

There are more than 200 Yoders listed in the phone book in Maryland (and that doesn't include Yoders who have married and changed their names), and now there's talk about constructing a "Yoder House" in Grantsville, Maryland, made of "Yoder Stones." In other words, it will be built with stones collected from the foundations of old Yoder homesteads in the area and perhaps other stones of Yoder importance. A group of Yoders have a plan for such a structure to be built among other houses in the Spruce Forest Artisan Village, next to Penn Alps. Ideas include using it for an information center, a museum of local Yoder facts and relics, and perhaps as home to award-winning bird carver Gary Yoder, who has been a longtime mainstay feature at the artisan village. The "Miller House" in the Spruce Forest came about in generally the same way as the proposed "Yoder House." For more information about this nonprofit, 503C organization, write to Yoder House Project, 177 Casselman Road, Grantsville 21536.

Trivia

Garrett has one other "first" honor. In 1989 Frank "Doc" Custer sent 3,200 of his white-pine and balsam-fir Christmas trees to the Bahamas. This was the first time that a Maryland grower had exported trees outside the United States. Custer planted his first tree in 1956, and his Mountain Top Tree Farm, outside Oakland, is one of the largest tree farms in the state. As you drive around the county and spot perfect trees for your next holiday season, remember it may be going to Nassau to brighten up the holidays for someone who misses snow and cold weather.

Penn Alps is on Route 40 in Grantsville. The artisan village phone number is (301) 895–3332.

Garrett County has drawn even more artistic talent with the relocation of Mark and Laura Stutzman, who operate Eloqui illustration studio. You've seen Mark's work on numerous McDonald's packages *(Batman, Jurassic Park),* but he's best known for designing the Elvis Presley postage stamp for the "Legends in American Music" series. Look for activities sponsored by the Garrett Lakes Arts Festival, and you'll probably find both Mark and Laura in attendance.

About a mile east of Grantsville, still on the National Pike, is the ***Fuller-Baker Log House***. The house is representative of those constructed on the Allegheny frontier, except that it is large enough to have been a tavern. It is believed to be the only remaining log tavern on the National Pike between Cumberland and Wheeling. Maryland's first governor, Thomas Johnson, owned the property when the house was built in 1815, but it is named for two other longtime residents. The first was Henry Fuller, who came to the area in 1837 to work as a stonemason. The Bakers were also early settlers and owned the house at a later date. The house in now on the National Register of Historic Places.

About 20 miles east of Oakland is the ***Baltimore and Ohio Viaduct*** at Bloomington. It was opened in 1851 to connect the port of Baltimore with industrial Wheeling and the Ohio Valley. The multispan, stone-and-concrete bridge carries the railroad across the North Branch of the Potomac River. A Confederate raiding party schemed to demolish the viaduct but was driven away by Union troops before the bridge could be blasted. Blasting holes drilled by Capt. John H. McNeill and his McNeill's Rangers are still visible on the bridge. The Baltimore and Ohio Viaduct is on Route 135, just west of the Garrett and Allegany county line.

There is such an interesting blend of history here, from Native American to Civil War, and such an interest in genealogy, that you might want to spend a few hours at the ***Garrett County Historical Museum,*** with its exhibits portraying the history of the county's residents. There's a large genealogy library here, too.

There is no admission fee to the museum (contributions are accepted, though), which is located at 107 South Second Street. It's open daily, but the hours vary by day, so call first. (301) 334–3226.

For additional information contact Deep Creek Lake—Garrett County Promotion Council, 200 South Third Street, Oakland 21550, or call (301) 334–1948. The e-mail address is GCTourism@gcc.cc.md.us.

Allegany County

Outdoor enthusiasts enjoy Allegany County and Cumberland, the county seat. Within the county borders are Rocky Gap State Park, Dan's Mountain, and Green Ridge State Forests, and the C&O Canal National Historical Park, where people can hunt, boat, fish, camp, and explore history.

Cumberland is considered the ***mibster capital*** of the country. For some reason the marble players of this town far surpass the players from other towns. A recent world champion was a twelve-year-old from Cumberland. If it has been a while since you played, or if you have never tried your hand at it, visit Constitution Park. In addition to the Little League baseball field, picnic groves, swimming pool, wading pool, playground, railroad caboose, 1937 fire truck, army tank, horseshoe pits, and courts for basketball, tennis, shuffleboard, volleyball, and badminton, there are two game areas with three marble rings each. Games and tournaments are held regularly at the park; six national marble champions have played and practiced here on their way to victory.

Constitution Park is off Williams Street in the southeast area of Cumberland. From Maryland Avenue turn left on Williams Street to reach the park entrance. Call (301) 759–6440.

A brochure is available to help you walk through the ***Victorian Historic District of Cumberland***, beginning at the east bank of Will's Creek and extending to the western property line of 630 Washington Street. The brochure highlights the architectural details and historical importance of about three dozen buildings. One of these is the History House Museum, which has eighteen rooms available for touring and features Victorian furniture, antiques, and displays pertaining to Allegany County's history.

There is also a brochure available on the Fort Cumberland Walking Trail, which highlights the site of the 1755 fort with plaques on its history.

The trail passes by George Washington's headquarters, a cabin that he used when he served at the fort as an aide to Gen. Edward Braddock during the French and Indian War. Another brochure, this one entitled *Walking Tour of Historic Downtown Cumberland,* highlights the architectural gems in the Downtown Pedestrian Mall area.

The Western Maryland Station Center, which was in service from 1913 until 1976, now houses the ***Transportation & Industrial Museum,*** dedicated to the history of the railroads and canals that made this area a major transportation and industrial center in the nineteenth century. The center also houses the Allegany County Visitors Bureau, the Allegany Arts Council and Gallery, the Western Maryland Scenic Railroad, and the C&O Canal National Historical Park Visitors Center.

Exhibits in the museum highlight the railroad, the National Pike (the first federal toll highway constructed across the country), the C&O Canal (a full-size lock is included in the exhibits), and such local industries as brewing and distilling, iron making, glass making, tire making (Kelly–Springfield), and mining. Mercantile establishments and the local First and Last Chance Saloon are represented as well.

The Allegany Arts Council has twenty-four arts organizations actively involved in choral singing, theater, cinema, photography, crafts, instrumental music, and visual arts. Classes are scheduled regularly, and a gallery exhibits works that are for sale. The Canal Visitors Center has an interpretive display in the station, where photographs, models, and artifacts are exhibited.

Trivia

The **Our Fathers House Log Church** *is among the last log churches in the eastern United States still in use. Reportedly, the church was constructed for $50. (301) 334–1948.*

The Transportation and Industrial Museum, 13 Canal Street, is open Tuesday through Sunday from 10:00 A.M. to noon and 2:00 to 4:00 P.M. The Allegany Arts Council and Gallery is open Monday through Friday from 9:00 A.M. to 3:00 P.M. and the telephone is (301) 777–5905. The C&O Canal National Historical Park Visitors Center is open Tuesday from 11:00 A.M. to 4:00 P.M., Wednesday through Saturday from 10:00 A.M. to 5:00 P.M., and Sunday 1:00 to 4:00 P.M.

The Allegany County Visitors Bureau is open May through October 9:00 A.M. to 5:00 P.M. daily, November through April 9:00 A.M. to 8:00 P.M. Monday through Friday, and 10:00 A.M. to 4:00 P.M. on weekends. Call (301) 777–5905.

The romance of early-twentieth-century steam railroading is with us once more on the ***Western Maryland Scenic Railroad,*** where passengers take a 17-mile ride combining mountaintop scenery and rich transportation history. The Western Maryland features a locomotive built in 1916 by the Baldwin Locomotive Works for the Lake Superior & Ishpeming Railroad, based in Michigan. It is a Consolidation 2-8-0 used from 1916 to 1956 for switching and freight hauling in Michigan's Upper Peninsula. It was on display at the Illinois Railroad Museum from 1971 until it was purchased by the WMSR in 1992.

As the train steams its way up the 2.8 percent grade on the westward trip from Cumberland to Frostburg, it travels along old Western Maryland Railway and Cumberland and Pennsylvania Railway rights-of-way. Riders view many memorable sights, including the famous Cumberland Narrows (a natural 1,000-foot breach in Will's Mountain known as the "Gateway to the West"), an iron truss bridge, Bone Cave, and Helmstetter's Horseshoe Curve.

Other interesting sights along the way include the 1,000-foot Brush Mountain Tunnel, the Allegheny Front, Victorian architecture, the C&O Canal, Buck's Horse Farm, and the frontier town of Mt. Savage (where America's first iron rails were produced). At the Frostburg terminus you can get a close-up view of the engineer and fireman in blue-and-white overalls and the locomotive turntable, which reverses the engine for the return journey.

At the other end, in Frostburg, is the Old Depot Center complex, which now features a restaurant, an ice-cream parlor, a bakery, and the ***Thrasher Carriage Collection***. This collection offers more than fifty examples of early nineteenth- and twentieth-century horse-drawn vehicles. Built by the finest manufacturers, the vehicles include a Vanderbilt family sleigh and the formal coach used by Theodore Roosevelt at his inauguration. Call (301) 589–3380 or 777–5905.

The rail trip takes about three hours, including a ninety-minute layover in Frostburg. A special dining car has been dedicated as the Gov. William Donald Schaefer Special for the governor who was credited with inspiring state, local, and private development of the scenic railroad.

The train runs weekends only in April, November, and December and Tuesday through Sunday from May through October. There's an expanded schedule in October for fall foliage viewing. Ticket prices are $14.75 for adults, $13.25 for seniors, and $9.50 for children ages two to twelve. Prices may vary in October.

Charter trips and special events such as dinner trips or trips featuring murder mysteries, dinner theater, or dancing are scheduled periodically. Private parties for weddings, birthdays, business meetings, school outings, and other events also may be booked. Write to Western Maryland Scenic Railroad, Western Maryland Station, Canal Street, Cumberland 21502, or call (800) TRAIN–50 or (301) 759–4400. Visit the WMSR on the Internet at www.wmsr.com.

One of the sights you will see on the railroad excursion, or on a drive through Mt. Savage, is the ***Mt. Savage Castle***. This National Historic Landmark in stone, built in 1874, is a replica of the Craig Castle in Scotland. At the height of its grandeur, the castle was owned by industrialist Andrew Ramsay, a Scot who was renowned for his production of ceramic glazed brick, which can be found throughout the building. He also planted the rare trees and abundant flowers that overflow the estate.

The castle's twenty-eight rooms, nine bathrooms, carriage house, and terraced gardens have been restored to their former elegance and furnished with antiques by William and Andrea Myer. Bob and Lisa Miller now own and operate the castle as a bed and breakfast with six elegantly furnished sleeping rooms. Four rooms have private baths; two rooms share a large main bathroom.

A full breakfast is provided for overnight guests, and high tea is served

Mt. Savage Castle

at 4:00 P.M. Weather permitting, both are served in the outside courtyard or porticoes. In keeping with the Scottish tradition, croquet and putting can be enjoyed on the grassed terrace. Tours, receptions, parties, conferences, and other special events may be booked at the castle. Privacy is assured by the 20-foot stone wall that surrounds the grounds. The address is 15925 Mt. Savage Road, The Castle, Mt. Savage 21545. Call (301) 759–5946.

The ***Mt. Savage Museum & Historical Park*** is an 1800s ironworks house built to house laborers and where Cardinal Edward Mooney was born. Mooney (1882–1958) was the archbishop of Detroit from 1937 until 1946, when he was named a cardinal. There's no admission fee to the museum, located at the Mt. Savage Historical Park, and the hours vary, so call first. (301) 264–4175.

Just as the railroad and the canal played an important part in the area's development, the National Pike has a claim to fame. You can drive to the top of either side of the ***Cumberland Narrows*** for an unparalleled view, on a clear day, of Cumberland and the surrounding countryside. To reach the eastern wall of the Narrows, take Will's Mountain Road off Piedmont Avenue to the parking lot of Artmor Plastics, park, and walk about 2 blocks. To reach the western wall, take exit 41, the Sacred Heart Hospital exit, off I–68. Go through the traffic light and up the hill to Bishop Walsh Road, where you will turn right to the high school. Drive to the back of the school, where the road ends, and walk through the woods, past the water tower, to the edge—about a five-minute walk. This is not a prepared path and it is not handicapped accessible.

Westvaco Paper Company at Luke spreads over three counties and two states—Allegany and Garrett in Maryland and Mineral in West Virginia. The town is named for William Luke, who founded the paper company on this site in 1888. The company manufactures more than 1,200 tons of high-quality, coated, white printing papers each day. The products are used for such magazines as *Forbes, Town and Country, Good Housekeeping, Fortune,* and Disney and National Geographic Society publications.

A ninety-minute tour allows visitors to view the papermaking process from pulpwood to cooking to the finished rolls and sheets. Call (301) 359–3311 to arrange a tour. The company prefers about two weeks' notice.

When you are driving from the Oakland area of Garrett County to Luke, you will have several miles of a very steep downhill grade on Route 135 where trucks are cautioned to drive no more than 10 miles an hour. If you are caught behind one of these trucks, slip into low gear (in the car and in your mind) and spend a little time looking at the beautiful countryside—something you would not be able to do if you were rushing through at 55 miles an hour. That is why you are off the beaten path, isn't it?

The ***Lonaconing Iron Furnace*** was erected about 1836 by the George's Creek Coal and Iron Company and produced iron for the next twenty years. When the furnace was constructed, it was unique in several respects. It was 50 feet high and 50 feet square at the base—a daring departure from contemporary furnaces, which were 30 feet high and 30 feet square. Moreover, it was the first furnace built in this country that

Lonaconing Iron Furnace

successfully used coke fuel at a time when all furnaces were using the less-efficient charcoal.

The furnace was built against a hillside because it was fed from the top. The site was chosen because the necessary iron ore, coal, wood, clay, limestone, sandstone, and water were readily available, although transportation to the marketplace was not convenient. Castings made here included stoves, farming implements, and dowels for the C&O Canal lock walls.

Today the furnace is the backdrop for a pleasant town park in Lonaconing, where you can stop to lunch at the picnic tables or enjoy the play equipment. A sign notes the location of the former Central School, and a bronze plaque honors Robert Moses "Lefty" Grove, a native son who was elected into the Baseball Hall of Fame in 1947. Lauded as the greatest left-handed pitcher of all time, he played for the Philadelphia Athletics from 1925 to 1933 and the Boston Braves from 1934 to 1941.

The furnace is located on Route 36, 35 East Main Street, in Lonaconing. (301) 463–6233.

For additional information write to the Allegany County Visitors Bureau, Mechanic and Harrison Streets, Cumberland 21502, or call (301) 777–5905 or (800) 508–4748.

Washington County

Washington County—the first county to be named after George Washington—was founded on September 6, 1776, just months after our country itself was born. In a Civil War battle fought at Sharpsburg, along Antietam Creek, more than 23,000 casualties were suffered.

Since 1989 an annual remembrance of the battle at ***Antietam*** has been held the first Saturday in December; it is signified by 23,100 luminaries placed every 10 feet along 4½ miles of roadway, in the fields, along Bloody Lane, and around some of the monuments erected on the battlefield. It takes 400 volunteers to set the lights, starting at 3:30 P.M. About 3,000 cars drive through to look at the candles, starting about 5:30 P.M.; the candles burn about ten hours. The luminaries are paid for by corporate sponsors, and the drive is free, but a donation is requested.

The idea for the candles came from the Rest Haven Cemetery, which had previously placed a luminary at every grave site. Borrowing the idea, Hagerstown residents lit luminaries every night for the two weeks prior to Christmas. One night it was the north side of town, another it was the south side, and so it continued throughout the area. Band members of the high schools sold 81,000 lights in the neighborhoods.

The newest monument, the first to be erected since 1967 and probably the last ever, is a tribute to the ***Irish Brigade*** that fought on Bloody Lane. More than 500 men were slaughtered or wounded in this battle, but they had never been formally recognized. The campaign to have this monument erected helped cause the creation of the Adopt-a-Monument National Battlefield program.

Budget cuts have reduced the funding of preservation and rehabilitation programs for the 103 monuments, and more than half of them have major sculptural elements, statues, carved reliefs, and ornamental embellishments. Now people and groups can donate time, supplies, or money to support the park or a specific monument or marker. Contributions, small enough to buy a paintbrush or large enough to paint, repair, and seal a War Department tablet for about $250, are readily accepted.

Trivia

The Washington Monument, in the state park of the same name, was the first monument honoring George Washington (as opposed to the first **architectural monument** *dedicated in Washington's memory—that's in Baltimore). Built of local stone by the citizens of Boonsboro in 1827, there's a great view of the valley below after a short climb. (301) 791–4767.*

For more information about the Adopt-a-Monument program, write to P.O. Box 158, Sharpsburg 21782; or call (301) 432–7648.

Washington County parks rate with the best and include the ***C&O Canal National Historical Park,*** the Appalachian Trail (37 miles), Fort Frederick State Park, Washington Monument State Park, Pen Mar County Park (and at least eight other county parks), and Hagerstown City Park.

Hagerstown, the county seat of Washington County, is also the home of the ***Hagers-Town Town and Country Almanack,*** which has been printed since 1797. The weather forecasts generate the most interest, and people swear by them. In fact, a folk tale has it that the book called for snow on July 4, 1874, and that it did snow on that date. Research indicates that the almanac did not predict snow, and the minimum temperature for that day was said to have been in the high sixties—not too conducive to snow.

A favorite base of operations of mine is the ***Beaver Creek House Bed and Breakfast,*** just south of Hagerstown, operated by Don and Shirley

Day. The house was built in 1905 and the rooms are filled with family antiques and memorabilia. The white-brick home with dark shutters is huge, yet warm and friendly, with a great wraparound porch where you can sit on a swing and watch the scenery not go anywhere. Particularly pleasing are sunrises over the Blue Ridge Mountains, should you be up that early. Guests in any of the five centrally air-conditioned guest rooms (each with private bath) may have breakfast on the screened porch, in the courtyard, or in the dining room, and share afternoon tea in the parlor.

The bed and breakfast is located at 20432 Beaver Creek Road, Hagerstown 21740. Call (301) 797–4764 or visit the Web site: www.bbonline.com/md/beavercreek.

Airplane and airport food don't exactly enjoy a stellar reputation, but you're sure to change your mind when you stop at ***Nick's Airport Inn*** on US 11 at the airport. In fact, many people fly their private planes here just to enjoy the tasty offerings. Fresh seafood is brought in from Baltimore and the prices are more than reasonable. Even the crab cakes are worthwhile. Nick's is open weekdays from 11:00 A.M. to 2:00 P.M. and 5:00 to 10:00 P.M.; Saturday hours are 5:00 to 10:00 P.M. They're closed on Sunday. (301) 733–8560.

Trivia

The **Beaver Creek School,** *almost next door to the Beaver Creek B&B, is a turn-of-the-century one-room schoolhouse and museum, with a hat shop, music shop, dressmakers' parlor, and tool shed, that's open on Sunday from 2:00 to 5:00 P.M. from June through September. (301) 797–8782.*

For lodgings with a real twist, you'll want to visit ***Maple Tree Campground*** near Gathland State Park. The unusual feature of this campground is that you sleep in a tree house. Did you always want one when you were a kid, but you lived in the city, or the only adults around had sixteen thumbs? This is not quite as rustic as you might remember, but it is as close as most of us will ever get. Your tree house—on stilts about 7 feet off the ground—has a couple of bunks (bring a sleeping bag), a wood stove, a table with benches, and a filled woodbin. A communal bathhouse is nearby, you have twenty-six acres of woods to roam through and explore, and you're not far from the Appalachian Trail. You may bring your tent for "regular" camping.

When Phyllis Sorocko started this campground after retirement, she dreaded the idea of tearing up the land and trees for campsites and dumpsites and was thrilled with this compromise. Pets, on leash at all times, are welcome. Reservations are recommended. The campground is located on Townsend Road, Gapland 21736. Call (301) 432–5585.

Trivia

The **War Correspondents Arch**, *Gathland State Park, built in 1896 by George Alfred Townsend, famous Civil War author and war correspondent, was the first monument in the world erected to the memory of war correspondents. (301) 791–4767.*

The ***Washington County Museum of Fine Art*** in Hagerstown is an outstanding museum overlooking the fifty-acre City Park Lake (home to numerous waterfowl). It was the idea and gift of Mr. and Mrs. William Henry Singer Jr., who had collected many possessions during their European travels and were looking for a beautiful place to house them. The cornerstone was laid on July 15, 1930, by Mrs. Singer's grandniece, Anna Spencer Brugh.

The museum was built of homewood brick with Indiana limestone trim. Two wings were added in 1949: the Memorial Gallery, in honor of Mr. Singer, who died in 1943, and the Concert Gallery, in honor of Mrs. Singer's love of music. Mrs. Singer was eighty-six when she died in Laren, Holland, in 1962.

Among the museum's collection are the works of Mr. Singer, who was a post-impressionist painter of note. Many of his landscapes show the fishing villages, fjords, and snow-covered mountains of Norway, where the Singers lived. Also in the collection are old masters, twentieth-century sculpture and painting, and a variety of decorative arts from around the world. The emphasis, though, is on American art.

In addition to tours, the museum offers art classes (weaving, clay, acrylics, quilting, and more), lectures, films, and music recitals. A bimonthly calendar is available.

The museum, located on City Park Lake, is open Tuesday through Saturday from 10:00 A.M. to 5:00 P.M. and Sunday from 1:00 to 5:00 P.M. There is no admission fee, but a donation is requested. Call (301) 739–5727, (301) 739–5764 (TDD), or visit www.washcomuseum.org.

After you've finished the War explorations, travel between Boonsboro and Sharpsburg to find the ***Red Byrd Restaurant and Motel*** in Keedysville to disprove the statement that not only can airport restaurants be good (see the note about Nick's above), but motel restaurants can provide a tasty repast, as well. Definitely try the pies, and the daily special, and even the crab cakes. Yes, crab cakes in the wilds of western Maryland. 19409 Shepherdstown Pike (Route 34), Keedysville. (301) 791–5915.

Sweet 'lopes

Boonsboro is known for its Civil War museum, but those who really know it know to visit in August and September, when Boonsboro cantaloupes ripen. You can buy them from a roadside stand, particularly on Saturday and Sunday, but it's best to plan an outing and pick your own. Then you'll really enjoy the thin-skinned, "Heart of Gold" variety with all its natural sweetness.

Three ***Hagerstown Post Office murals*** represent different aspects of the railway transportation of mail. The paintings were done by Frank Long of Berea, Kentucky, in 1938 as part of the Section of Fine Arts program—placing appropriate art in federal buildings. The first painting depicts mailbags being loaded onto a train. A central panel depicts a railway post office in operation, with postal clerks sorting letters on a train. The third panel, over the lockboxes, shows figures on the station platform watching an approaching train that will pick up the mail. Frank Long also painted post office murals in Louisville and Berea, Kentucky; Crawfordsville, Indiana; and Drumright, Oklahoma.

The ***Wilson Village Old General Store*** is a classic country store with a post office, loose "penny" candy, yard goods, and much more. You'll also see a one-room schoolhouse. The store is on Old Route 40, and it is open daily. The general store is at 14921 Rufus–Wilson Road, Clear Spring. Call (301) 582–4718 for hours and details.

On your way to Wilson Village from Hagerstown, you may stop by the ***Historic Wilson Bridge*** Picnic Area. It's located along Route 40 West, adjacent to Historic Wilson Bridge, which is the oldest, longest, and most graceful of the twenty-three stone-arch bridges in the county. The five-arch span was built in 1819 as an early extension of the National Pike to the Ohio Valley. The structure was erected by Pennsylvanian Silas Harry at a cost of $12,000. Its style represented a triumph for the justices of the Levy Court (until 1829, the body similar to a Board of

Wilson Village Old General Store

County Commissioners), who insisted on an all-stone structure in the face of army engineers' arguments that a wooden bridge laid over stone piers would suffice.

The bridge is about 200 feet north of the west end of the "new" bridge crossing Conococheague Creek, 5 miles west of Hagerstown on Route 40. This one-acre site offers picnic tables, parking, and canoe access to the Conococheague.

Of particular interest to sports fans is the ***Hagerstown Suns*** baseball team of the South Atlantic League, and an affiliate of the Toronto Blue Jays. This Class-A team draws more than 160,000 fans a year. In previous years, loyalists have seen the likes of Jeff Ballard, Jim Palmer, Bill Ripken, and Craig Worthington, all of whom have gone on to be well known in the baseball world. Palmer was elected to the Baseball Hall of Fame in 1989, his first year of eligibility. For information call the Municipal Stadium at (301) 791–6266.

The Washington County tourism office has a number of interesting brochures, and the personnel there are delighted to help you. Those traveling with children, or those who are young at heart, will like visiting Crystal Grottoes caverns or going on the ghost walk at Fort Frederick at Halloween time.

Seven miles west of Hancock, near the border between Allegany and Washington Counties, is ***Sideling Hill***. A relatively new freeway, officially designated I–68, diverts traffic off a steep, tricky road that twists to a roundhouse curve at the top of Sideling Hill. The 4½-mile section of the road took twenty-eight months to complete and cost about $21 million. Workers blasted an incredible, breathtaking 360-foot-deep cut in the mountain, which revealed millions of years of geological history; all this to achieve a relatively flat roadway. A three-and-a-half-story, handicapped-accessible interpretive center, which is approachable from both sides of the highway, will let you see all those layers and folds of multihued rocks that have been exposed by the cut and will explain their geologic history. This is one of the best rock exposures in the northeast.

If you can make only one side trip in Maryland, only a momentary detour, this is the one to make. A late-fall visit just may bring a surprise of a southern migration of ladybugs. In 1994 and 1995, there were so many millions of these critters that they obscured the windows and just about any other surface on which they could land. They've always migrated this way, but never before in these numbers. The sight is truly amazing.

The center is open daily from 8:30 A.M. to 6:00 P.M. from Memorial Day through Labor Day; from 9:00 A.M. to 5:00 P.M. the rest of the year. For information about Sideling Hill, call Fort Frederick State Park at (301) 842–2155.

For additional tourism information write to the Washington County C&VB, 16 Public Square, Hagerstown 21740; (301) 791–3246 or (800) 228–7829.

Places to Eat in Western Maryland

Cumberland
The Inn at Walnut Bottom,
120 Greene Street,
(301) 777–0003

Frostburg
Au Petit Paris,
86 East Main Street,
(301) 689–8946

Grantsville
Penn Alps Restaurant,
125 Casselman Road,
(301) 895–5985

Hagerstown
Nick's Airport Inn,
18615 Terminal Drive,
(301) 733–8560

Keedysville
Red Byrd Restaurant,
19409 Shepherdstown Pike,
(301) 791–5915

La Vale
Gehauf's/Hennys,
1268 National Highway,
(301) 729–1746

Oakland
Four Seasons Dining Room,
20160 Garrett Highway,
(301) 387–5503, ext. 2201

Trader's Cafe
and Coffeehouse,
21311 Garrett Highway,
(301) 387–9245 (cafe) or
(301) 387–9246
(coffeehouse)

Places to Stay in Western Maryland

Amanda's B&B
Reservation Service,
(800) 899–7533,
(410) 225–0001,
www.amandas-bbrs.com,
or AmandasRS@aol.com
(e-mail)

Boonsboro
Old South Mountain Inn,
6132 Old National Pike,
(301) 432–6155

Cumberland
Inn at Walnut Bottom,
120 Greene Street,
(800) 286–9718 or
(301) 777–0003

Flintstone
Rocky Gap Lodge,
16701 Lake View Road NE,
(800) 724–0828 or
(301) 784–8400

Frostburg
Frostburg Inn,
147 East Main Street,
(301) 689–3831

Hagerstown
Beaver Creek House
Bed and Breakfast,
20432 Beaver Creek Road,
(301) 797–4764

La Vale
Braddock Best Western,
1268 National Highway;
(301) 729–3300,
(800) 296–6006, or
www.bbonline.
com/md/beavercreek

Mt. Savage
The Castle,
15925 Mt. Savage Road,
(301) 759–5946

Oakland
Will O' The Wisp,
20160 Garrett Highway,
(301) 387–5503,
ext. 2206 or www.gcnet.
net/wow

Wisp Resort Hotel,
209 Marsh Hill Road;
(800) 462–9477,
(301) 387–4911, or
www.wisp-resort.com

Other Attractions Worth Seeing in Western Maryland

Albert Powell Trout Hatchery, Hagerstown; (301) 791–4736

Barron's C&O Canal Museum, Sharpsburg; (301) 432–8726 or www.fred.net/kathy/canal.html

Bell Tower Building, Cumberland; (301) 722–2820

Bietscheheof Farm, Grantsville; (301) 895–3742

Boonsborough Museum of History, Boonsboro; (301) 432–6969

C&O Canal Boat Replica, Cumberland; (301) 729–3136

C&O Canal Museum and Visitors Center, Hancock; (301) 578–5463

Clarysville Bridge, Cumberland; (301) 777–5905

Crystal Grottoes Caverns, Boonsboro; (301) 432–6336

Fort Frederick State Park, Big Pool; (301) 842–2155

Friend Family Association Museum and Library, Friendsville; (301) 746–5615

Frostburg Depot (circa 1891), Frostburg; (301) 689–1221

Frostburg Museum, Frostburg; (301) 689–6853

Frostburg State Planetarium, Frostburg; (301) 689–4270

George Washington's Headquarters, Cumberland; (301) 777–8214

Hager House and Museum, Hagerstown; (301) 739–8393

Hagerstown Roundhouse Museum, Hagerstown; (301) 739–4665, (301) 739–1998; ccpl.carr.lib.md.us/~dwhite/roundhouse, or www. trainweb.com/roundhouse/index.htm

Michael Cresap Museum, Oldtown; (301) 478–5154

Miller House, Hagerstown; (301) 797–8782

Muddy Creek Falls, Oakland; (301) 334–9180

Rocky Gap Veterans Cemetery, Flintstone; (301) 777–2185

Rose Hill Cemetery, Hagerstown; (301) 739–3630

Stanton's Mill (1797), Grantsville; (301) 895–5211

Washington County Planetarium, Hagerstown; (301) 766–2898 or (301) 791–4172

Western Maryland Station Center, Cumberland; (301) 724–4398 or (301) 777–5905

Wisp Ski Resort, McHenry; (301) 387–4911, (800) 462–9477, or www. gcnet.net/wisp

Calendar of Annual Events in Western Maryland

January
Kick and Glide Cross-Country Ski Race, Herrington Manor State Park; (301) 334–9180

February
Cabin Fever Weekend, Spruce Forest Artisan Village; (301) 895–3332

April
Easter Egg Hunt, Herrington Manor State Park; (301) 334–9180

Eighteenth Century Market Fair and Rifle Frolic, Fort Frederick State Park; (301) 842–2155

Maryland Archaeology Month, statewide; (410) 514–7661

Muzzleloader Shoot, Fort Frederick State Park; (301) 842–2155

Spring Fling, Hagerstown Junior College; (301) 791-2346

May

C&O Canal Fest, Canal Place Cumberland; (301) 724-3655

French and Indian War Rendezvous, Fort Frederick State Park; (301) 842-2155

Halfway Park Days, Hagerstown; (301) 739-3219

Music at Penn Alps, Grantsville; (301) 895-3332

Sharpsburg's Memorial Day Parade, Town Square; (301) 432-8410

Train Meet, Allegany Fair Grounds; (301) 777-5905

June

George's Creek Days, Lonaconing; (301) 463-2189

Governor's Youth Fishing Derby Against Drugs, Herrington Manor State Park; (301) 334-9180

Grantsville Days, Grantsville Park; (301) 334-1948

Heritage Days, Cumberland; (301) 777-2787

McHenry Highland Festival, Garrett County Fairgrounds; (301) 334-1948

Western Maryland Blues Fest, Hagerstown; (301) 739-8577, ext. 116

YMCA Rocky Gap Triathlon, Rocky Gap State Park; (301) 777-9622

July

Accident's Fourth of July Homecoming, Accident; (301) 746-6346

Allegany County Fair and Agricultural Expo, Allegany County Fairgrounds; (301) 777-0911

Fiddler's Contest, Banjo Contest, Friendsville; (301) 746-8194

Maryland Mountain Cruise, Allegany County Fairgrounds; (814) 767-9521

Maryland Symphony Orchestra Independence Celebration, Sharpsburg; (301) 797-4000

Military Field Days, Fort Frederick State Park; (301) 842-2155

Rocky Gap Country Music Bluegrass Festival, Allegany College; (888) ROCKYGAP

Summerfest and Quilt Show, Grantsville; (301) 895-3332

August

Antique and Custom Auto Show, Frostburg; (301) 689-5431

Augustoberfest, Hagerstown; (301) 739-8577, ext. 116

Garrett County Agriculture Fair, Garrett County Fairgrounds; (301) 334-4715, ext. 321

Jonathan Hager Frontier Craft Days, Hagerstown; (301) 739-8393

Maryland State Chili Championship, Ali Ghan Shrine picnic grounds; (301) 722-5970

September

A Taste of Fall Fest, Allegany County Fairgrounds; (301) 729-3321

Apple Butter Boil, Oakland; (301) 334-9180

Boonesborough Days, Shafer Park; (301) 432-5889

Canal Apple Festival, Hancock; (301) 678-6555

Governor's Invitational Firelock Match, Fort Frederick State Park; (301) 842-2155

Outdoor Concert in the Park, Grantsville; (301) 895-3332

Rails-With-Trails Bike Train, Cumberland; (800) TRAIN-50

Sharpsburg Heritage Festival, Sharpsburg; (800) 228-STAY

Western Maryland Street Rod Round-Up, Allegany County Fairgrounds; (301) 777-3456

October
Alsatia Mummers' Parade, Hagerstown; (301) 733–0033

Autumn Glory Festival, Oakland; (301) 334–1948

Fall Color Hayrides, Herrington Manor State Park; (301) 334–9180

Ghost Walk, Fort Frederick State Park; (301) 842–2155

Greater Gortner Airport Fly-in, Oakland; (301) 334–3541

Hagerstown American Indian Pow-Wow Festival, Hagerstown; (800) 228–STAY

Maryland Railfest, Western Maryland Station; (800) TRAIN–50

November
Muzzleloader Shoot, Fort Frederick State Park; (301) 842–2155

Venice Christmas Arts and Craft Shows, Hagerstown; (301) 739–6860

Victorian Christmas at History House, Cumberland; (301) 777–8678

December
Antietam National Battlefield Memorial Illumination, Sharpsburg; (301) 733–7373

Christmas Faire, Hagerstown; (301) 791–2346

Christmas in the Village, Grantsville; (301) 895–3332

Christmas Model Train Open House, Allegany Fairgrounds; (301) 777–5905

Central Maryland

Perhaps nowhere in the state is there more diversity than in the area referred to as central Maryland. In the rolling foothills and picturesque landscapes of this region are horse farms and vineyards, the commercial center of Baltimore City, huge stone farmhouses and old mills, busy waterways surrounding the Chesapeake Bay and its tributaries, some of the oldest towns in the country, and modern, vibrant cities. This core of six counties and two major cities encompasses it all.

Sixteen million vehicles use the ***William Preston Lane Jr. Bridge*** (Chesapeake Bay Bridge) every year. Only 50,000 people walk across it, though, on Chesapeake Bay Bridge Walk Day. Once Maryland was a leading contender in the number of "kissing" or covered bridges; now there are only a few. See also Frederick and Prince George's Counties in the Greater Washington section for more bridges.

Countless people stop by Annapolis to see its waterfront, Ego Alley (where the expensive boats parade), and the United States Naval Academy. They watch the sailboats in the harbor—even in the winter, when there is a Frostbite series of sailboat races—or the Naval Academy's noon meal formation, when the brigade of midshipmen assembles in front of Bancroft Hall for inspection. I chatted with Robert F. Sumrall, who re-creates scale models of the ships that have plied the bay.

Whenever anyone talks about Chesapeake Bay, blue crabs and oysters are sure to be discussed. I include a German restaurant that can compare with many fine-art galleries, an old inn that is relatively new, and a scenic waterside eatery for sightseeing while you dine.

Trivia

Edwin Booth's first theatrical performance was in the original Harford County Courthouse.

Trying to pick a starting point is tough, for several interstates lead into and out of this area of five counties and Baltimore City, including I–95 going north to Philadelphia and New York and south to Washington, D.C., I–83, going north into Pennsylvania, US 40 and I–70 going into the western part of the state, and I–97, heading south and then east, into Annapolis.

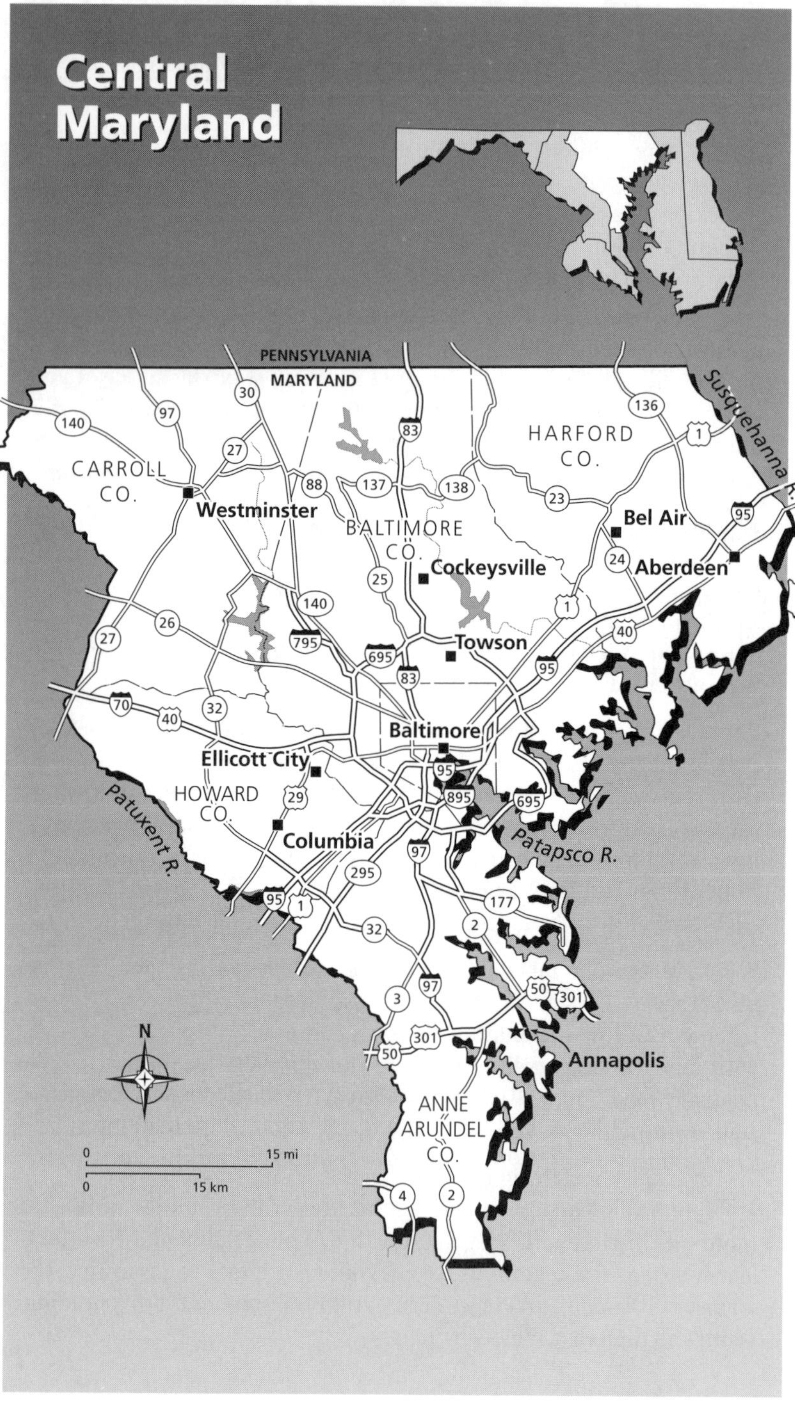
Central Maryland
PENNSYLVANIA
MARYLAND
CARROLL CO.
Westminster
BALTIMORE CO.
Cockeysville
Towson
HARFORD CO.
Bel Air
Aberdeen
Susquehanna R.
Baltimore
Ellicott City
HOWARD CO.
Columbia
Patuxent R.
Patapsco R.
Annapolis
ANNE ARUNDEL CO.
N
0
15 mi
0
15 km
140
97
30
27
88
137
83
138
136
1
23
95
24
25
140
795
695
26
27
40
70
32
29
895
295
177
2
50
301
3
4

Anne Arundel County

Judy's Favorite Attractions in Central Maryland

Cider Mill Farm

Havre de Grace Decoy Museum

Oriole Park at Camden Yards tour

U.S. Naval Academy

Perhaps the best place to start is at BWI, ***Baltimore-Washington International Airport,*** where millions of people pass through either going to or coming home from some place or picking up a passenger. It may be a scandalous thought, but you might actually want to arrive early or even stay a few minutes, for BWI has become a destination in itself. There's a beautiful observation gallery with information about flying and pieces of airplanes on display. The $6.4 million gallery has cutaway airplane sections (great to view if you or someone in your party has never flown or seen the workings of a plane), an interactive weather station (so you can see what a cold front is and how it affects weather, or check for the temperature in your destination city), and a 147-foot-wide observation window to watch airplanes refueling, taxiing, taking off, and landing. Plunk yourself in front of a computer screen, punch in your flight number, and the screen displays just where the plane is, how high, how fast it's flying, and when it's expected to land. Should you be an aviation history buff (or even just one or the other), then the story of Maryland aviation should satisfy your curiosity. A children's play area is in the lower of the two levels and is open twenty-four hours a day. The upper level with the gift shop, cafe, and interactive displays is open from 9:00 A.M. to 9:00 P.M. There is no admission charge.

Trivia

Across the Severn River from the Naval Academy in Annapolis is a memorial to Marylanders who served in **World War II.** *Dedicated on July 23, 1998, the $2.7 million memorial is off Route 450, just below the Gov. Ritchie Overlook, with a commanding view of the Severn River, the Naval Academy, and Annapolis. A four-sided, open-air amphitheater is surrounded by a 100-foot-diameter ring of forty-eight, nine-foot-tall, gray-granite slabs etched with the names of the 6,454 Marylanders killed during the war.*

About 50 shops fill about 56,000 square feet of retail space throughout the airport. Some of the boutiques are a Smithsonian Shop, Starbucks, ASU Bags, Just Plane Crabs, 24-Hour Flower, Altitunes, the Museum Company, Tie Rack, Hudson News, the Body Shop, and more than a dozen eateries. BWI is one of the first major East Coast airports to establish a Web site for services, general information, and regional tourism information, which offers links to airline and other travel-service Web sites. The Web site has a terminal location map and travel tips. The BWI Web site is http://baltwashintlairport.com.

A shuttle bus connects the airport to the nearby Amtrak station, and limousine (van and bus) service provides door-to-door transportation to and from the airport. Walking tours of the airport are provided through the marketing office for groups of twelve to thirty people, with a minimum age of nine. Usually groups include schoolchildren or civic organizations, VIP groups, or special-interest groups, such as firefighters or engineers, who receive a "behind-the-scenes" tour. Individuals who want an airport tour may call to see if a group tour is scheduled that they could join. The normal tour includes visits to and explanations of the baggage claim area, airline ticket counters, restaurants, gift shops, gate departure areas, the National Weather Service, and all the major concourses. Call at least a week to ten days ahead for group tours. Call (301) 261–1000 from the Washington, D.C., area or (410) 859–7026 from elsewhere.

When airport construction was started on May 4, 1947, the airport site was known as Friendship, and many old homes and farms on the 3,200-acre tract were demolished. Only Rezin Howard Hammond's home was left standing, where it remains today at the edge of the airport. Originally known as Cedar Farm because of the cedar trees on the property, it was built in 1820 from bricks made of clay dug on the farm. It is now the ***Benson-Hammond House*** and is used by the Anne Arundel County Historical Society, whose purpose is to encourage

One Fab Crab

Figuratively flying in and out of BWI almost as frequently as planes and passengers has been the **stained-glass crab sculpture.** *As of this writing, it's out. But it may be back in by the time you read this. Or it may not. If you have a first or second edition of* Maryland: Off the Beaten Path, *then you may recall that Jackie and John Douglass of Shady Side, Maryland, created this 400-pound crab in 1986. It's gorgeous. It's almost delectable enough to eat, and it certainly makes one want to go out and steam up a bushel of those savory crustaceans. For various reasons it was displayed, it wasn't, it was, etc. The crab is made of white glass from West Germany and other colors of Blenko glass from West Virginia. It's 5 feet high, 10 feet wide, and 7 feet deep. Then, in 1966, it was stored during the airport's expansion. Newly elected (1998) Anne Arundel County Executive Janet S. Owens says she wants it back again. But it needs a pedestal, and it needs a $14,000 glass enclosure to prevent harm being done to it. It also needs about $5,000 in repairs to stress fractions it suffered when it was moved and stored. Now we're talking about more money than the cost of the original sculpture. Maybe they could suspend it from the ceiling instead of floor-mounting it. Anyway, if you see it upon your arrival/departure at BWI, you'll know what it is. If you don't, you can complete a comment card saying you want it returned.*

appreciation among the general public of "the smaller centers of culture where so much of our heritage lies hidden." Within the house are a collection of dolls, a display of tokens known as picker checks (made of aluminum, fiberboard, and brass stamped into various shapes and used as currency by farmers, each of whom had his own set of checks with his initials), and a miniature replica of Angel's Store in Pasadena. The museum is open for tours on special occasions and Thursday through Saturday from 11:00 A.M. to 3:00 P.M. Tours are $2.00 a person. The Browse and Buy Shoppe is also located at the house; it is open for the same Thursday hours and other times as volunteers are available.

Call the Benson-Hammond House (at Aviation Boulevard and Andover Road) at (410) 768–9518 for tours and additional information.

A second Browse and Buy Shoppe is located at Jones Station, at the corner of Old Annapolis and Jones Station Roads. This late-nineteenth-century building was one of the "step-down transformer" power stations for one of the two railroads serving Annapolis. There are no railroads performing that function these days; reportedly, Annapolis is the only state capital without such service. Hours at the Browse and Buy Shoppe are Tuesday through Saturday, 10:00 A.M. to 3:00 P.M.; call (410) 544–3370.

Now, hop (figuratively, not literally) onto I–97 south, tool into historic Annapolis, and prepare yourself for a treat. Annapolis is full of authentic colonial architecture; Colonial Williamsburg in Virginia had to recreate what is already here. Annapolis is called a "museum without walls" because of the dozens of eighteenth-century buildings in the city, but Annapolitans are quick to point out that it is a living museum, not an artificial one. Annapolis is Old-World charm, the United States Naval Academy, sailboats and powerboats by the hundreds (168,000 boats were registered in Maryland in 1984), antiques shops, taverns, and, most of all, narrow, winding, hilly, and brick-paved streets that invite walking and exploring.

The ***Banneker-Douglass Museum*** is installed in a handsome Victorian–Gothic structure that was the Mount Moriah African Methodist Episcopal Church, the first African Methodist Episcopal Church of Annapolis, serving the community from 1874 until 1971. A storm damaged the building in 1897, so it was rebuilt with its present Gothic-Revival facade, including the splendid stained-glass rose window. The building is listed with the National Register of Historic Places, as a National Historic District, and in the National Register of Historic Districts.

The museum is named for Benjamin Banneker (mathematician, scientist, astronomer, and surveyor) and Frederick Douglass (writer, journalist, civil libertarian, abolitionist, and U.S. minister and consul general to Haiti), both of whom were born and lived in Maryland. Banneker was appointed to serve on a commission that surveyed and laid out the capital. He had such a phenomenal memory that he produced, in detail, Pierre L'Enfant's plans for the District of Columbia when L'Enfant left—with the plans—before the job was finished. There are rotating displays within the Hall of National Greatness, the Gallery of Black Maritime History, the Herbert M. Frisby Hall (Frisby was a Baltimore science educator, war correspondent for African-American newspapers, and explorer who made twenty-one trips to the Arctic region and was the second black explorer to reach the North Pole), and the reference library. The museum features African-American arts and crafts, lectures, and films, all to encourage a better understanding of the contributions of African-Americans to Maryland and the United States. Today's legacy is represented by such prominent African-American artists as Josephine Gross, Gerald Hawkes, Laurence Hurst, and Hughie Lee-Smith, whose works adorn the walls of the gallery.

The Banneker-Douglass Museum is located at 84 Franklin Street, Annapolis. Hours are Tuesday through Friday, 10:00 A.M. to 3:00 P.M., and Saturday, noon to 4:00 P.M. There is no admission charge. Call (410) 974–2893.

The Charles Carroll House and St. Mary's Church gardens, Duke of Gloucester Street, are open to the public periodically during the year (the dates are advertised in the local newspapers), or you can call Jane Jackman at (410) 269–1737 to set an appointment for a tour.

'Dem bones, 'dem bones

In July 1989, some fifteen small, brittle bones, carefully wrapped in yellowed paper, were gently placed in a golden urn and laid to rest in a shady cemetery plot near St. Mary's Church in Annapolis. In mid-1987, the Reverend John Murray of St. Mary's had found these remains of St. Justin, who was beheaded at the age of twenty-six in the second century A.D. According to Murray, it is not unusual for churches in Europe to have special tombs containing the relics of saints or martyrs, but few churches in the United States can claim such items because the country is so young. St. Justin's remains arrived in Baltimore in 1873 so the Reverend Joseph Wissel could protect them while Italy was in the middle of a political upheaval. Reverend Wissel and those who followed him displayed them prominently, but during the 1960s the church was renovated and the remains were placed in a box in a church safe. Call (410) 263–2396 for additional information.

There are many interesting things to see at the ***U.S. Naval Academy***. Start with a visit to the ***Armel-Leftwich Visitors Center*** (just inside and to the right of Gate 1 off King George Street), with a movie (*To Lead and To Serve*) and displays about life as a midshipman. You can then explore on your own or take a one-hour-and-ten-minute guided tour. The hours of operation vary according to the day and the season, but the noon tour departs at 11:45 to see the Noon Meal Formation. The center is open from 9:00 A.M. to 5:00 P.M. from March through November, and 9:00 A.M. to 4:00 P.M. the rest of the year. It is closed Thanksgiving, Christmas, and New Year's days. Call (410) 263–6933 or log onto their Web site for more information (www.nadn.navy.mil/. /homepage.html).

A short walk from the visitors center, along the seawall, is the foremast of the USS *Maine,* still misshapen from the mysterious explosion in Havana Harbor on February 15, 1898. The mast was recovered on October 6, 1910, and erected along the Academy Seawall at Trident Point on May 5, 1913.

At the site of the Noon Meal Formation is the Tecumseh Statue (in front of Bancroft Hall), a bronze replica of the wooden figurehead that graced the USS *Delaware*. It is frequently decorated by midshipmen as a symbol of victory and passed exams. Bancroft Hall Dormitory, by the way, houses the *entire* 4,000-member brigade and (depending on who you consult) is either *the* largest dormitory in the world, or only one of the largest. Take a peek in the building, check out one of the model rooms, and delight in the murals and art works that decorate the public area.

One of the most fascinating exhibits in Annapolis is the display of model ships at the ***U.S. Naval Academy Museum*** on the ground floor of Preble Hall, housed in the Class of 1951 Gallery. My mind is totally boggled every time I visit this exhibit. In the collection are ship models from about the time the pilgrims landed in America to just after the War of 1812. The big (100-gun) ships took one person from four to six years to build, plus another year for the rigging. More likely than one person doing all the work, there would have been a master model maker supervising a crew of workers or apprentices, thus speeding up the process. You'll also want to see Bone Ships, which were crafted by prisoners of war on frigates from meat bones. They are intricate and accurate portrayals of the fighting ships of the times.

Trivia

The lyrics to the "Star-Spangled Banner," as penned by Francis Scott Key in 1814 after watching the Battle of Baltimore, is on display at the Maryland Historical Society in Baltimore. (410) 685–3750.

If you visit during the week, you may see Robert F. Sumrall, curator in charge of repairing and maintaining the fleet of 225 little ships, and others working on the ships in the collection. Due to age, heat, vibrations, and other forces of nature, the ships need periodic attention and repairs. Although patience is a virtue, enjoying what you do is even more important in this field.

The main floor of the museum houses your typical 30,000-item collection of naval history, including class rings of all the graduating classes of the academy, silverware from naval vessels, flags, uniforms, medals, weapons, navigational instruments, documents, and the stories of several naval heros, including John Paul Jones. The Naval Academy Museum provides a valuable and convenient reference source for studying naval history. The good news here is the start of a massive fund-raising drive to modernize the exhibits and the exhibit area.

The museum, in Preble Hall, is open Monday through Saturday from 9:00 A.M. to 4:30 P.M., and Sunday from 11:00 A.M. to 5:00 P.M. It is closed on Thanksgiving, Christmas, and New Year's days. There is no admission charge. Call (410) 293–2108 or log onto www.nadn.navy.mil/museum for details.

Also on the ground floor is the ***U.S. Naval Institute and Bookstore*** for books and other naval-related items. The institute has 100,000 members and advances scientific and literary knowledge of the sea services. It publishes *Proceedings* and *Naval History* magazines, more than 400 books, and has a collection of more than 450,000 historic photographs. The store, at 118 Maryland Avenue, is open Monday through Saturday from 9:00 A.M. to 5:00 P.M., and Sunday from 11:00 A.M. to 5:00 P.M. (410) 268–6110.

The basement of the ***Naval Academy chapel*** is one of those "gee, I didn't know that" spots that I love to take visitors to, because that's where the crypt of Revolutionary War hero John Paul Jones is located. A little history and some personal effects complete this final resting place.

Upstairs the chapel is pretty awesome as well, with Tiffany studio-designed stained-glass windows behind the altar and several others. Built on the highest point of ground at the academy (or "in the Yard"), the chapel cornerstone was laid in 1904 by Admiral Dewey. When you see newly married couples exiting a chapel under raised swords, this is the chapel they're exiting. United States Naval Academy Grounds, (410) 263–6933. Web site: www.nadn. navy.mil/. /homepage.html.

The skipjack is the symbol of the Chesapeake Bay waterman. These boats were developed in the 1890s, and they are the last surviving commercial sailing fleet in the United States. The oyster-dredging boats have become an endangered species, as their number has dwindled from about 1,500 at the turn of the century to about eighty on the water in 1958. There are about three dozen in working condition now.

If hot is so "hot" it's *très chic,* can it really be off the beaten path? Well, yes, if it's some place you might not expect it. So for you cayenne, serrano pepper, and capsaicin lovers, head toward the Market House down at City Dock in Annapolis, at the end of Ego Alley. That's where you'll find ***Chesapeake Heat*** and more than 350 different hot, spicy sauces. Gerry and Gloria Freedenberg and their son, Nathan, run this stand, and for those with stomachs not of cast iron but of cotton candy, they also offer jams and other mild items. The joy here is the tasty bar. To borrow from Brylcreme, a little dab will do you when it comes to Dave's Special Reserve sauce (bottle signed by Dave), China Syndrome pepper sauce, or Jump Into an Open Grave BBQ sauce. To check out this place before you visit Annapolis, hop over to their Web site and browse through their catalog. Then mention their Web page (www.chilepepper.com) and receive a ten percent discount on your purchase when you visit. Or call (888) 98–CHILE or (410) 269–0941.

Ship of State

Some people are just luckier than others, and Robert F. Sumrall has to be among the luckiest of the lucky, for his occupation is playing with model ships. Sumrall is the curator charged with repairing and maintaining the academy's fleet of 225 little ships, some of them more than 300 years old. Sumrall built his first model when he was six and went on to be a naval architect, author, historian, model builder, and one of the most highly regarded authorities on ship models and model construction. Sumrall has built models of significant and famous Maryland ships, including the Dolphin, *the* Pride of Baltimore, *the* J. T. Leonard *(a unique oyster dredger), and the skipjack* Minnie V. *Most of the work Sumrall does for the academy museum is in the realm of repair, maintenance, and restoration. His creative work, such as the commission for a 6-foot-tall model of the skipjack* Stanley Norman *(the original of which still operates on the Chesapeake) for the Occidental Restaurant in Washington, D.C., he does at home. He also has done an interpretive model of the* Arizona *wreck for the National Park Service memorial at Pearl Harbor, and he is doing another of the Japanese flagship* Akagi. *Private collections, which are located in Coronado, Virginia Beach, New York, and a gallery in Old Town Alexandria, hold his battleship* Wisconsin *and several destroyers.*

Annapolis has always been a vital area for commerce and trade, particularly when it comes to importing and exporting goods. But it played one of its most unusual commercial roles in 1862, when it became the major depot in the East for holding exchanged prisoners of war. Prisoners were held here until their back pay (earned during their incarceration) could be given to them. At first they were camped at St. John's College, but the eight small, wooden barracks were inadequate for groups as large as 6,000 men at one time. Two hundred and fifty acres of farmland outside Annapolis were rented from Charles S. and Ann Rebecca Welch for $125 per month, and barracks and other buildings were constructed there. The forty-four barracks and all other buildings were sold at auction some time after 1865, when all the prisoners had been released. All that remains of this mustering place for Union prisoners, called Camp Parole, is the name of the town, Parole, on the western side of Annapolis.

Whether by land or sea, when you're near Annapolis you may as well take a drive over to ***Cantler's,*** noted for Jimmie Cantler, hospitality, crabs all year, and delicious food since the 1970s. The crab-cake and soft-shell crab sandwiches are superb. You can also reach Cantler's from the water. 458 Forest Beach Road, Annapolis. In either case, call (410) 757–1311 for directions.

An unofficial declaration of spring's arrival is the annual ***Chesapeake Bay Bridge Walk Day***, held on the first Sunday in May. The walk was first held in 1975 after a Towson, Maryland, scout leader noticed that one span was closed for construction and suggested one span could be closed for a daylong walk. An estimated 50,000 pedestrians, as well as people in wheelchairs and on crutches, cross the eastbound lanes of the

Trivia

One of my favorite hangouts over the years has been the King of France Tavern in the cellar of the Maryland Inn. Located on Church Circle, the inn was constructed by Thomas Hyde in 1772 and has operated continuously as an inn since the late eighteenth century. This triangular piece of land, called the "drummer's lot," was where the town drummer, or crier, told of the day's news in the early eighteenth century. For me, two centuries later, the King of France Tavern tells the news of today's best entertainers. Ethel Ennis, Charlie Byrd, Tim Eyermann, and others have filled its brick-walled room with delightful sounds and good times. 16 Church Circle, Annapolis 21401, or call (410) 263–2641. The toll-free number is (800) 847–8882.

bridge, and the only automobiles and trucks permitted belong to official vehicles and media trucks. Jogging, running, skateboarding, biking, and pets (except Seeing-Eye dogs) are prohibited; an early-morning race has been established for those who want to speed across the bridge instead of spending about ninety minutes walking and investigating various expansion joints, girder construction, architectural design, and engineering and assembly facets. Pedestrians normally are not allowed on the 4 1/3-mile structure connecting the Annapolis area to the large spit of land known as the Eastern Shore. Blue waters lap innocuously about 185 feet below the twin spans of the bridge, also known as the William Preston Lane Jr. Memorial Bridge. Parking lots in Annapolis, at Anne Arundel Community College, and also on the Eastern Shore start filling up at 8:00 A.M. Buses start taking walkers to the east side at 9:00 A.M. There is no charge for parking, but there is a $1.00 charge for the bus. Call (410) 228–8405 for information.

Trivia

The town of Dublin, in Harford County, is named after Dublin, Ireland. In the eighteenth century it was a Scotch-Irish settlement.

Capt. Salem Avery was a waterman of the 1860s, and to the delight of the members of the Shady Side Rural Heritage Society, his home on the banks of the West River became available to them to use as a museum. The ***Captain Salem Avery House*** opened its doors in mid-September 1989 as a museum to "protect, document, and illustrate the history and traditions" of Shady Side. The society is particularly pleased that they were able to obtain some of the original Avery furniture from the owners of the house. The Captain Salem Avery House is located at 1418 East West Shady Side Road, Shady Side. The house is open by appointment and on Sunday from 1:00 to 4:00 P.M., except during January and February, on Easter Sunday, and around Christmas. There is no admission fee. Call (410) 867–4486 for additional information.

For additional information about Anne Arundel County, write to the Annapolis and Anne Arundel County Conference and Visitors Bureau, 26 West Street, Annapolis 21401. Call (410) 280–0445.

Baltimore City

Now, zip on back to I–97 and head north to Baltimore. It's a slight left zig (off a right-hand ramp) to the beltway (I–695) to the west, and then a hop north onto the Baltimore–Washington Parkway (which becomes Russell Street), and there you are.

As you enter, on your left, you'll see the Lee Electrical building, at 600

West Hamburg Street, near Camden Yards, and on it a Wyland whale painting done in 1993. The mural is of extinct Atlantic gray whales, and it's 260 feet long by 20 feet high. Mayor Kurt L. Schmoke dedicated the mural on August 16. Wyland was born in 1956 in Detroit, and it's said he created his first painting, of dinosaurs, at the age of four. He saw his first whales a decade later, painting his first whales and dolphins in 1972, and his first whale mural in 1981 in Laguna Beach, California.

Trivia

Port Discovery, which opened in Baltimore in late December 1998, is one of the largest children's museums in the country. Aimed toward the six- to twelve-year-old, there's still plenty to keep the young-at-heart occupied. Port Discovery, Baltimore; (410) 727–8120.

Almost across the street is the new Ravens football stadium, and not far away is ***Oriole Park at Camden Yards,*** where the Baltimore Orioles baseball team nests for home games. Sell-out games are commonplace, even if the O's aren't doing that well, and scalpers have been known to ask, and get, ten times face value for tickets, just so one can get into the park. The O's management has tried to solve that problem by having a scalp-free zone where people who have tickets to sell meet with people who want to buy tickets, with the stipulation that the sellers can't charge more than face value. The scalp-free zone is wonderful, and other teams should adopt this practice.

Arrive at the park early; in fact, make a reservation to take the approximately ninety-minute tour of the stadium. They're given just about every day of the year, but it's a very limited schedule on day games. As you take the tour, you'll hear that the warehouse, which houses the Orioles offices, souvenir shop, reception areas, Camden Club, etc., is the longest building east of the Mississippi. Then, depending on which tour guide you get, you'll hear that the warehouse is longer than the Empire State Building is tall. The validity of that statement depends on whether you count antennas. At the very least, this is a long building. Should your guide not tell you, ask about the break-proof windows and how many home-run balls have hit the building on the fly (to give you a clue, none in regulation play). As you walk around the stadium, you'll see the town homes or row houses across the street that were part of an urban revitalization project. It's said they went for $1.00 a piece and were overpriced. The stipulation, of course, was the buyer had to renovate and was obligated to a residency requirement. You'll also see a party room, a sky suite, the press room, some of the 25 miles (length depending on your

Trivia

The Basilica of the Assumption in Baltimore was the first Roman Catholic cathedral built in the United States. It was founded in 1821, and mass is still celebrated there daily.

tour guide) of beer pipe for draft brews (so they don't have to schlep kegs around the stadium, clean up, have refrigeration for the kegs at each refreshment stand, etc.). The tour, as of 1998, cost $5.00 and is well worth it. 333 Camden Street; (410) 685–9800.

Okay, so you've heard about the fantastic Walters Gallery and the incredible Baltimore Museum of Art. You've seen pictures of Harborplace, and you know you're going to go there for some eats and souvenir shopping. Good. There are a few other things you should see.

A spectacular way to start your Baltimore visit is at the ***Top of the World observation deck and museum***. On a clear day you will see an eye-opening, five-sided panoramic view of the city, its harbor, and beyond from the twenty-seventh floor of the tallest pentagonal building in the country, designed by I. M. Pei. Exhibits, films, and audiovisual material will familiarize you with Baltimore's past, present, and future. The World Trade Center is at 401 East Pratt Street. Hours are Monday through Saturday from 10:00 A.M. to 5:00 P.M., and Sunday from noon to 5:00 P.M.; call about extended summer hours. Admission for adults is $3.00; for children 15 and under and seniors, $2.00. (Children are admitted free if they're in strollers or carriages; there's a charge if they're walking.) The phone number is (410) 837–8439.

If you would like an organized or specially designed personal tour, call ***Baltimore Rent-A-Tour***. Ruth Fader started her business in the early 1970s when she realized no one was giving tours of Baltimore. Now her company conducts about 900 tours a year. Baltimore Rent-A-Tour specializes in the distinctive, such as African-American tours with such

15 Minutes of Warhol

The Baltimore Museum of Art has the second largest collection of Andy Warhol's work on permanent display, located in the $10 million wing that opened in October 1994. Included in the display are several pieces that had never been on permanent public exhibit, including Brillo Box, Del Monte Box, *and gold* Jackie. *The New Wing for Modern Art has an unusual design allowing the display of the large Warhol works. Instead of doors in the middle of each exhibit room, the "doors" are located at the corners, normally dead areas in an exhibit space. This also allows visitors a chance to look into the other three connecting galleries. An energy-saving cooling system creates big sheets of ice overnight when energy costs are low, which then are dropped into an underground pool during the day to sustain the seventy-degree temperature desired in the building.*

highlights as the Great Blacks in Wax Museum, the Civil War Museum, and the Eubie Blake Cultural Center. Another favorite tour is the early-bird insomniac tour, which always includes the Edgar Allan Poe grave site at Westminster Church, a poetry reading, and a sherry toast; the Baltimore Streetcar Museum for a ride on a turn-of-the-century trolley; the Enoch Pratt Library for a poke among the books; and a nighttime view of the city from the Top of the World Trade Center. So, if you're in town with a convention, are part of a ski group, or belong to some other organization, check out Baltimore Rent-A-Tour. You can also find them at www.Baltimorerent-a-tour.com. 3414 Philip Drive, Baltimore 21208, or call (410) 653–2998.

On May 28, 1989, the ***Maryland Vietnam Veterans Memorial,*** a circular-shaped version of the national Vietnam memorial, was dedicated to the memory of 1,046 Marylanders who were killed or became missing in action in the Vietnam conflict. The names and inscriptions are readable whether one is standing, in a wheelchair, or at a child's-eye level. The veterans' names are etched into granite, along with this inscription:

> MARYLANDERS, WHILE IN THIS PLACE, PAUSE TO RECALL OUR NATION'S IDEALS, ITS PROMISE, ITS ABUNDANCE, AND OUR CONTINUING RESPONSIBILITIES TOWARD THE SHARED FULFILLMENT OF OUR ASPIRATIONS. REMEMBER, TOO, THOSE WHOSE EXERTIONS AND SACRIFICES UNDERLIE THESE BLESSINGS. REMEMBER, INDEED, THE LIVING AND THE DEAD.

Funds were raised by Maryland veterans who called themselves "The Last Patrol." They marched across the state during sweltering August

Architectural Monument with a View

The Washington Monument and Museum in Baltimore, a 178-foot column, was the nation's first architectural monument (distinguishing it from the monument honoring George Washington that's in Boonsboro in western Maryland). It was designed by Robert Mills, architect of the Washington Monument in Washington, D.C. You reach the top via a 228-step spiral stairway, where you can get a four-window panoramic view of the city. I'm not sure what the difference is in that definition of "architectural monument" compared to the one in Washington State Park, for they both claim they were the first. The marble, a white, crystalline metalimestone, is Cockeysville marble, from a quarry near Texas, about 1½ miles north of Baltimore. This stone was also used for the first 152 feet of the Washington Monument in Washington, D.C. The admission is $1.00. (410) 396–7837.

Maryland Vietnam Veterans Memorial

heat in 1986, from Oakland in western Maryland to Ocean City in the east, and another 200 miles from Point Lookout to Baltimore the next year. Architect Paul Spreiregan designed the monument that stands beside the Patapsco River in Middle Branch Park, off Route 2.

Old Baltimore has long been known for its blocks and blocks of row houses, with their brightly scrubbed white-marble steps. Almost as historic, but not nearly as well known, are the ***painted screens*** for windows and doors that decorate the houses lining the streets of East Baltimore. It is said that William Oktavec painted the first screen on a hot summer day in 1913. A green grocer, his fresh produce was wilting in the heat, so he took it inside and painted groceries on the screens to show his customers what he had available.

When you understand that this area is all cement and brick, with very

Barry Levinson's Baltimore

This city could be known as Barry Levinson's Baltimore, for he's shot such movies as Diner, Tin Men, Avalon, *and* Liberty Heights *in and around the town. His most regular presence is felt, though, through the shooting of the NBC television series,* Homicide: Life on the Street. *Headquartered in Fells Point (you can get there via the watertaxi), everywhere you turn, you're likely to catch a moment from the show, whether it's a building, perhaps a person working as an extra—or you might even see them filming a sequence. And, if not, you're sure to enjoy the many shops, eateries, and the farmers' market on Broadway.*

little greenery, no front yards, and few gardens or trees, you can appreciate the thoughts some had about providing a little colorful decoration. Another advantage of the painted screens is that windows and doors can be left open for the breezes, because the paint allows those who are inside to look out, but outsiders cannot see in.

People started painting on the screens pictures of red-roofed bungalows and ponds with ducks or swans swimming around in them. There are rainbows and religious scenes, but mostly the artwork reflects the memories of the inhabitants' home countries in Europe and scenes of a new life in America. The scenes depicted the single-family, country-cottage homes of the sort everyone dreamed of owning.

For the best screen viewing, start at Haussner's Restaurant (see below) and travel along both sides of Eastern Avenue. The Hatton Senior Center, at the corner of Fait and South Linwood Avenue, has screens in each of its twenty windows. Remember, this generally is a seasonal display, with the screens in place between May and October. Six or seven screen painters remain, but they are in their fifties or older. They still work away at it, saying, "Practice makes perfect, and perfect practice makes art."

You can have a screen painted for about $20 and up, even if you do not live in or visit Baltimore. Write the Painted Screen Society of Baltimore, Box 12122, Baltimore 21281.

Although there are many restaurants of note in Baltimore neighborhoods, including Fell's Point, Little Italy, Charles Street's Restaurant Row, and, of course, Harborplace, there's probably none more famous inside and outside of Baltimore than ***Haussner's***, where the menu has more than one hundred entrees, many of them German specialties.

Trivia

The NBC television series Homicide *is shot primarily in the Fell's Point area of Baltimore, one of the stops on the water-taxi route. Barry Levinson, the show's producer, is a Baltimore native who attended Forest Park High School, and he has set many of his movies, including* Diner, Tin Man, *and* Liberty Heights, *in town and in the suburbs of his younger days. John Waters also is a product of the area and has shot a lot of his films here.* Hairspray *was set here. Divine, the female impersonator who starred in* Pink Flamingos, Mondo Trasho, *and* Polyester *and died on March 7, 1988, grew up at 1824 Edgewood Road in Loch Raven (no, his parents aren't living there anymore). Divine is buried in Prospect Hill Cemetery, York Road, Towson.*

Inspirational desserts are available here or to take home, if you could begin to eat dessert after one of their meals.

Haussner's may be even better known for its extensive collections of original nineteenth-century paintings, etchings, china, and sculptures, one of the most important private collections in the country. People have been coming to this family-owned and -operated restaurant since 1926 to dine and view the artwork created by some of Europe's renowned masters. Here you can enjoy Baltimore's largest privately owned art collection and feast on German-American and seafood delicacies. Imagine dining with Rembrandt, Gainsborough, and Whistler! At Haussner's, you can. Haussner's is located at 3242 Eastern Avenue, Baltimore 21224; call (410) 327–8365. Reservations are accepted for lunch and dinner during the week only. Hours are Tuesday through Saturday from 11:00 A.M. to 10:00 P.M.

Trivia

The first umbrella factory in the United States was established in Baltimore in 1828. The umbrellas carried a very Madison Avenue–type slogan: BORN IN BALTIMORE—RAISED EVERYWHERE.

Now, on to a few fascinating factory tours. The ***General Motors (Truck Group) Baltimore Assembly Plant*** turns out GMC Safaris and Chevrolet Astros at the rate of about forty an hour, sixteen hours a day, five days a week. In a cavernous room split by railroad tracks and boxcars, you can watch a flat piece of stamped sheet metal, instrument panel shells, heater controls, windshields, roofs, carpet (watching water nozzles cut carpet is really interesting), engines, and all the other components come together to form a van. It is a throbbing, pulsating, noisy, smelly operation, but big and little engineers love to watch it. The tour follows a 2½-mile-long assembly line and takes about two hours. Tours are offered weekdays at 9:00 A.M. and 6:30 P.M. They accept a minimum of ten and a maximum of twenty-five people and advise that no cameras are allowed, and puh-lease, no open-toed shoes, sandals, or high heels should be worn. Children must be ten or older, and safety glasses are provided.

Trivia

Johns Hopkins Hospital in Baltimore was the site of the first use of silk sutures and the first use of rubber gloves to reduce the risk of surgical infection.

Reservations with three weeks' notice are requested and can be made by calling Harry Chandler (410–631–2111) or by writing to General Motors Baltimore Assembly Plant, 2122 Broening Highway, Baltimore 21224. The plant is located near Sparrows Point. Take I–95 north to Fort McHenry Tunnel, turn right at Boston Street (the first exit after the tunnel), and right again on Broening Highway.

The ***Calvert Distilling Company, Seagram's America*** lets you follow the preparation of fine whiskey, vodka, and gin from distillation through the bottling process to quality control. The tour includes a view of the warehouses filled with the finished product and a sampling of one of the products. The ninety-minute tours are offered only from Memorial Day through Labor Day, only on Friday, and about 1:00 P.M. Wear sturdy shoes please. You should be twenty-one years of age or older, and a maximum of ten people are allowed on the tour. Reservations are required, for they call in retirees to guide the tour. Call (410) 247–6019.

Public transportation around Baltimore City has become pretty convenient in the last few years. The trolley system is good and inexpensive. The subway system is also fine. There's also ***Ed Kane's Water Taxi,*** which goes to almost every popular waterfront attraction, including Harborplace, the Maryland Science Center, the National Aquarium in Baltimore, the Baltimore Museum of Industry, Fell's Point, and Little Italy. Thus, you can park for the day and take the water taxi around to various spots you want to visit, not having to worry about finding parking places, having correct change, or fighting traffic. The blue-and-white water taxis, or water buses, run about every eight to eighteen minutes from April through October and about every forty-five minutes the rest of the year. Operating hours are 11:00 A.M. to 11:00 P.M., Monday through Friday, and 10:00 A.M. to 11:00 P.M. on Saturday and Sunday, but call for seasonal hours. Adult fare is $3.50; the fare for children ten and under accompanied by an adult is $2.25. These prices cover unlimited use on the day of purchase. Call (800) 658–8947 or (410) 563–3901.

Another option is the ***light-rail system,*** taking you from the suburbs to Oriole Park at Camden Yards and back again for less expense and aggravation than driving into the city and parking. It runs from Glen Burnie to Hunt Valley Mall, with stops in downtown Baltimore, including Camden Yards, and there are spurs to BWI Airport and Penn Station. It operates about every fifteen minutes from 6:00 A.M. to 11:00 P.M. Monday through Friday, every fifteen minutes from 8:00 A.M. to 11:00 P.M. on Saturday, and every thirty minutes from 11:00 A.M. to 7:00 P.M. on Sunday. Hours are extended or modified during the baseball season. Free parking is available at designated light-rail stops, and all light-rail trains are handicapped accessible. The cost is $1.35 per trip, $2.70 for a round-trip, or $3.00 for an all-day pass that's good on the subway, the bus system, and the light-rail. Call (410) 539–5000. For additional Baltimore information, write the Baltimore Area Visitors Center, Pier One, Constellation Dock, Baltimore 21202, call (800) 282–6632 or (410) 837–4636, or log onto www.baltimore.org.

Baltimore County

Baltimore City is surrounded on the east, north, and northwest by Baltimore County, and the easiest way (barring rush-hour accidents) out of the city is to the north along I–83.

One of the things I like to do is check out ***post office murals***. No, they're not murals of post offices, but located in them, painted and installed in the late 1930s and early 1940s. Heading north and then a little to the east brings you to Towson and a set of murals at the Towson Post Office that caused a real ruckus.

Nicolai Cikovsky, a Russian-born, naturalized citizen, was an artist who lived in Washington, D.C. In 1939 he gave the postmaster, at the postal official's request, a series of panels depicting "Milestones in American Transportation." The populace took one look and cried foul. They declared the subject of the paintings was trite, derivative, and clichéd. They also were upset by inaccuracies, such as a wagon pulled by horses without reins, smokestack smoke going the wrong direction (ahead of the train), a train looking like a model railroad engine rather than a real locomotive, and a gun holster worn backward. This was the work of a painter who had studied at several distinguished schools in Russia, taught in the United States at the Corcoran Gallery, and sold paintings to the Chicago Art Institute, the Whitney Museum of American Art, and numerous other celebrated galleries across the country. The residents thought the paintings looked like bad "B" movie posters, at best. They wanted murals that reflected the life and history of Towson, and they wanted the artist to visit the area; often artists only went to see the location where their paintings would hang. The upshot is that the errors were corrected, and the murals stayed. They can still be

Oops

Many of the WPA murals that supposedly depicted area activities were more figments of imagination or expressions of scenes from other parts of the country or world than a reflection of local reality. One mural in Barre, Vermont, shows men working in the quarries on stone that has never been found in Vermont and with tools that were never used in Vermont. The Prince George's County mural in Upper Marlboro, Maryland, is another example, for it shows tobacco that's not grown in Maryland, but in North Carolina. And it's shown being harvested the way it's done in North Carolina, not the way it's done in Maryland.

found at 101 West Chesapeake Avenue, Towson—no longer the main post office, but the finance office.

At Towson State University, in the Fine Arts Center, is the ***Asian Arts Center*** at the Roberts Gallery. The gallery is named in honor of Frank Roberts, who donated a large number of Asian artifacts and artworks to start this collection. Changing and permanent displays of Asian, African, and pre-Columbian works are featured. Concerts, films, lectures, and workshops are sponsored throughout the school year. The Asian Arts Center is open Monday through Friday 10:00 A.M. to 4:00 P.M. No admission is charged. Groups are welcome by appointment. Call (410) 830–2807.

Southerners have known the joys of ***Krispy Kreme doughnuts*** for more than sixty-one years. A few years ago, sophisticated New Yorkers became devout fans. Then, on November 3, 1998, KK came to Baltimore, disrupting traffic and not meeting the demand for donuts, even though the 3,000-square-foot store is capable of making 270 dozen doughnuts per hour, or 6,480 dozen doughnuts per day. By far, the company's most famous and best-selling product is the glazed, yeast-raised doughnut known for generations as the "Krispy Kreme Original Glazed." If you've never seen a doughnut being made, then you should definitely pop on over to KK to watch the old-fashioned doughnut machine. Nine more locations are planned in Maryland over the next four years. When the glowing, red-hot HOT DOUGHNUTS NOW light is on, the doughnuts are literally coming out hot *now,* and that's when you should eat them. About 1 mile north of the Beltway, on Route 1, at 8010 Belair Road, exit 32B, KK is open from 5:30 A.M. to midnight, Monday through Friday; 5:30 A.M. to 1:00 A.M. on Saturday; and 5:30 A.M. to 11:00 P.M. on Sunday. By the time you read this book, their drive-through window should be open twenty-four hours a day. (410) 377–8660.

One of the remaining covered bridges in Maryland connects Harford and Baltimore Counties and crosses over Gunpowder Falls. The ***Jericho Covered Bridge*** was constructed in 1864 and measures 88 feet, with a 14$^{2}/_{3}$-foot roadway. Steel beams, steel stringers, steel crosstie rods, and bottom chord were installed later for reinforcement, and today it remains in good condition. To reach the bridge, take Route 152 from exit 74 off I–95, turn left onto Jerusalem Road, and proceed to Jericho Road.

Ashland Furnace is one of the six relatively easy-to-reach furnaces in Maryland (the others are Catoctin Furnace, Lonaconing Iron Furnace, Antietam, Principio in Cecil County, and Nassawango in Worcester County). Said to have been named for the Kentucky home of Henry

Clay, Ashland's three furnaces, engine room, and casting house were kept functioning from around 1844 to 1893. Originally there were also large storage buildings for raw materials and a village with a school, church, store, and about five dozen houses. The ore was mined in Phoenix, Glencoe, Riderwood, Texas, Oregon Ridge, and other parts of what is now north-central Baltimore County.

Now the area is mined by a developer, and the Strutt Group has incorporated about a dozen of the old village's buildings. The office and mid-nineteenth century store, the school, several houses, and a group of dwellings called Stone Row have been renovated and assimilated into the industrial site. The old Ashland Presbyterian Church, near the gates of the new community, is still an active place of worship. Ashland Furnace is east on Paper Mill Road from York Road, just north of Cockeysville.

Still a little farther north of Baltimore is the ***Oregon Ridge Park and Nature Center,*** a great place to take a break after hours of driving and seeing regular tourist attractions. Within its 836 acres are a number of marked trails of varying length and difficulty, downhill and cross-country skiing areas, a greenhouse, an archaeological research site, an outdoor stage, and a launching site for hang gliders. Starting in the nature center, you can see how a honeybee hive works, look at local flowers and plants in the greenhouse, or check on such live animals as fish, frogs, mice, salamanders, snakes, and Stubby, the pet opossum, all native to the park.

A huge tree exhibit reveals the various parts of the forest ecosystem, from the worms and moles living among the roots and underbrush to the owls and hawks perching in its highest limbs. The area's history is depicted by artifacts retrieved from archaeological digs in the park. These items were reclaimed from the digs by students in the Baltimore County public school system. Students also constructed a full-scale replica of an 1850s storage shed, set on its original foundation outside the nature center. The nature trails crisscross the park, so a hiker sees the natural interactions of birds, fields, ponds, streams, swamps, wildlife, and woods.

For those who like nature on the cultured side, summer concerts are presented here by the Baltimore Symphony. Oregon Ridge Park and Nature

Trivia

The Glenn L. Martin Aviation Museum, in Middle River, was the first museum dedicated to Maryland's aviation history. Opened on June 11, 1993, the museum is named in honor of the aviation pioneer and the tremendous contribution he made to Maryland's aviation history. Among the exhibits are a restored Martin RB-57A jet bomber, "the Intruder," modeled after the British Canberra. For more information about the museum, located at Martin State Airport, northeast of Baltimore, call (410) 682–6122.

Center, Beaver Dam Road, is reached by the Shawan Road exit 20-B off I–83; go west 1 mile, turn left on Beaver Dam Road, bear right at the fork, and follow the signs. Call (410) 887–1815 for more information.

Northwest of Baltimore City is Owings Mills, and there you'll discover ***Wild Acres Trail,*** a mile-long wildlife habitat demonstration trail that was opened in late 1989. It's part of the seventy-two-acre Gwynnbrook Wildlife Management Area, and the trail features twenty-three ways gardeners and wildlife watchers can help invite birds, butterflies, and other animals to their property. Trail maps are available for the self-guided tour, and the trail is open from dawn to dusk daily except on Wednesday. No pets are allowed. Included along the trail are a backyard pond and rock garden; a bee, butterfly, and hummingbird garden; nesting structures for birds and squirrels; bird feeders; and a variety of garden plants that produce fruit eaten by all sorts of animals. Other examples are shown for owners of large properties. More than 120 kinds of birds live in or visit the Gwynnbrook area, making bird-watching a marvelous recreational attraction. Photo opportunities are wondrous because of the wildflowers that bloom in the spring and fall.

Southwest of Baltimore, in Catonsville, are ***post office murals*** done by Avery Johnson in 1942. Johnson painted five scenes of historic note, entitled *Incidents of History of Catonsville.* The murals start with Native Americans, go on to farmers rolling tobacco in hogsheads to market, and then depict the romance of Richard Caton and Mary "Holly" Carroll. Holly, the daughter of Declaration of Independence signer Charles Carroll, was only sixteen when Caton proposed. Her father refused because he said Caton had a reputation for not paying his debts. Caton prevailed, and they were married in 1788. Charles Carroll built a house for them, Castle Thunder, on Frederick Road, where the library is now; then he built a newer home in Green Spring Valley (that home still stands). The last panel shows Caton, Holly, and Charles Carroll with his plans for the town of Catonsville.

Several years ago the post office roof began to leak, and that did not bode well for the plaster walls or the paintings. The late Thomas Cockey, whose family also goes back to the eighteenth century, decided the murals should be repaired. Federal officials balked at the $35,000 repair bill, but Cockey (as in the town of Cockeysville, also in Baltimore County) and the Historical Society prevailed. A plaque documenting the story depicted in the panels has been installed by the society. For additional tourism information write to Office of Promotion and Tourism, 23 West Chesapeake Avenue, Towson 21204, or call (410) 887–8040.

Carroll County

West of Baltimore County, out US Route 30 or 140, you're getting into horse country with some beautiful scenery to go along with your history. The county was named for Charles Carroll, an American Revolutionary War leader and Maryland signer of the Declaration of Independence.

Near Westminster, the county seat, is the ***Carroll County Farm Museum***. This complex has a general store that's reminiscent of the 1800s and sells items handcrafted by Farm Museum artisans, souvenirs, nickel candies, and much more. Among the activities scheduled on the grounds are a Civil War encampment (19th Georgia Regiment), a day honoring Older Americans Month, a fiddlers' convention, a day devoted to antique farm machinery, and a day to celebrate Maryland wines.

General admission is $3.00 for adults, $2.00 for those twelve to eighteen and sixty and over, and free for those under twelve. Group tours and rates are available. The museum is open weekends May through October from noon to 5:00 P.M. and Tuesday through Friday in July and August from 10:00 A.M. to 4:00 P.M. Call (800) 654–4645 or (410) 876–2667.

Carroll County's streams, valleys, farms, woodlands, and villages provide an ideal backdrop for exploring off the highway, and an ideal way to do that is by bicycle. Bicycle tours have been designed by resident cyclists outlining ten of their favorite routes, ranging from short to long and easy to challenging. Each route is on a separate map with its own description of the tour. Brochures are available at the visitors center in Westminster.

For example, the Taneytown route, northwest of Westminster, is nearly 14 miles long with a moderately hilly ride. It starts at Taneytown Memorial Park, "where a public pool and picnic grounds offer warm-weather possibilities. Your tour heads toward Littlestown, Pennsylvania, and winds through rustic areas where deer and pheasants abound. Pick out an early Christmas tree at one of the tree farms, or stop and listen to the ripplings of Pipe Creek. Wind back through the alleys of Taneytown and by the beautiful Fish and Game Club pond."

The New Windsor tour, west of Westminster, has rolling hills and is 8 miles long. "Wind through the beautiful Wakefield Valley on your way past Robert Strawbridge's Home (birthplace of American Methodism). This ride offers splendid country scenery, picturesque eighteenth- and nineteenth-century homes, and an opportunity to stop at the New Windsor Service Center and visit its unique International Gift Shop."

According to local legend, you and I are not the only visitors to Carroll County. Several apparitions also frequent the countryside, and you may even meet a friendly one. The first of the ghosts of Carroll County is at the Shellman House, 210 East Main Street, Westminster. A little girl in white, they say, delights at having visitors stop by the visitors center, located at the Historical Society of Carroll County. Spirits, in addition to the liquid kind, are said to reside at Cockey's Tavern, 216 East Main Street; since the early 1800s this tavern has been the site of political rallies for Andrew Jackson, antitax meetings, fancy balls, and all-night debauchery. At Main and Court Streets, the ghosts of slaves supposedly return to the Carroll County auction block, where slave trading was done in pre–Revolutionary War times. Other specters have been reported at Ascension churchyard, the courthouse, the old Westminster jail, Western Maryland College (Levine Hall has a musical ghost), and Avondale—the home of Legh Master, the most celebrated of Carroll's ghosts—on Stone Chapel Road in Wakefield Valley. It is said that Master was a tyrant, a miser, a lecher, and a cad.

Two Confederate ghosts reportedly visit the last remaining building of Irving College on Grafton Street, and during a full moon, an Indian walks along a ridge in the tiny town of Lineboro. For those of you who choose to pursue these nocturnal visitors, talk with the Historical Society in general (through the Office of Promotion and Tourism) and Amos Davidson, a local historian, in particular. Additional tourism information is available from the Carroll County Office of Tourism. Write to them at 125 North Court Street, Westminster 21157, or call (800) 876–2085.

Harford County

Head northeast of Baltimore City and east of Baltimore County, and you're probably taking I–95 to or from the Northeast corridor. Known as the Gateway to the Chesapeake Bay, take a few minutes off that interstate highway and you'll find that Harford County goes from covered bridge to lighthouse.

Havre de Grace (pronounced as it is spelled, not with a French pronunciation) is the home of the ***Concord Point Light,*** constructed in 1827. Following its decommissioning in 1975, it was vandalized and then, thank goodness, restored, and it is now in tip-top shape. You can climb the twenty-eight steps plus six steps on a ladder and see an impressive view of the Susquehanna River and Chesapeake Bay. The lighthouse is open on Saturday and Sunday afternoons from 1:00 to 5:00 P.M. May through October, or by appointment. It is located at the foot of Lafayette Street in Havre de Grace. The phone numbers are (410) 939–1340 and 939–2016. From the lighthouse you can walk the ½ mile to Tydings Park via a promenade (boardwalk) along the shore of the Chesapeake Bay.

Another interesting attraction is the ***Susquehanna Museum of Havre de Grace,*** where you can learn just about everything you need to know about the southern terminus of the Susquehanna and Tidewater Canal. There's a restored lockhouse and a pivot bridge. There's no admission fee. The museum's address is P.O. Box 253, Havre de Grace 21078; the phone number is (410) 939–5780.

Concord Point Light

A self-guided tour brochure is available from Harford County Tourism in Bel Air; it highlights a sample of the 800 structures that contribute to the ***Havre de Grace Historic District***. The buildings range in period from the 1780s through the Canal era (1830–1850) and the Victorian era (1880–1910) to the contemporary.

Havre de Grace is the self-proclaimed decoy capital of the world, and the ***Havre de Grace Decoy Museum*** has complete collections of decoys by Madison Mitchell and Paul Gibson. An annual Decoy Festival is held about the first weekend of May at the museum and at the Havre de Grace Middle and High Schools. The Decoy Museum is open Tuesday through Sunday, from 1:00 to 5:00 P.M., except major holidays. The address is R. Madison Mitchell Place, P.O. Box A, Havre de Grace 21078. Call (410) 939–3739.

About 10 blocks up the road, at Franklin Street and North Union Avenue, is the ***Susquehanna Trading Company***. Owner Duane Henry has more than 2,500 old and new Chesapeake Bay decoys on display and locally handcrafted decoys for sale, starting at $9.95. He also features a large selection of waterfowl decorations, including miniature decoys; wildlife-decorated personal, household, and office accessories; limited-edition prints; and decoy lamps.

The Susquehanna Trading Company is open seven days a week from 10:00 A.M. to 5:00 P.M. at 322 North Union Avenue; (410) 939–4252.

Crossing the Susquehanna River north of Harve de Grace via Route 40 is the ***Thomas J. Hatem Memorial Bridge***, between Harford and Cecil Counties (nice to know about when the bridge on I–95 is backed up). It opened in 1940 as the Susquehanna River Bridge and was renamed in 1986 to honor Hatem, a prominent Harford County resident who devoted his life to public and civic service. The bridge is 1½ miles long and rises 89 feet above the river, connecting the communities of Havre de Grace and Perryville. More than seven million vehicles use the bridge each year. The toll is $2.00 (northbound only) for passenger cars.

South of Havre de Grace is Aberdeen, once known primarily for its military base, the Aberdeen Proving Grounds. Driving through the grounds is like the reverse of a military parade, for here you drive past tanks and artillery, and combat vehicles and more, rather than them parading past you. It's a parade that's open every day of the year, not just on May 1, Veterans Day, or Memorial Day.

On the grounds of the base is the ***U.S. Army Ordnance Museum,*** with a comprehensive collection of small arms and just about everything else military you'd want to see that would be too small to fit in a parade or would not be suitable for exterior display.

The museum is open daily from 10:00 A.M. to 4:45 P.M. except major holidays, except it is open on Memorial Day, July 4, and Veterans Day/Armed Forces Day. There is no admission charge. Call (410) 279–3602 for additional information.

The other big gun from Aberdeen is Cal Ripken Jr., the Iron Man, the one who broke Gehrig's record of 2,130 consecutive games played. So, if you can't get to Camden Yards, or if it's not baseball season, or for when the day comes that Cal hangs up the cleats for the last time (except old timers' games), then head over to the ***Ripken Museum***. Hailed as a "repository of baseball and other Ripken family memorabilia," its mission is to "interpret and preserve the traditional values of Cal Ripken and to portray Cal's life and career as a symbol of American family values and the multifaceted meanings of pride, discipline and leadership." It also honors Cal Sr. and Billy. The museum is located at 8 Ripken Plaza.

The Ripken Museum opened on December 6, 1996, and in its first year of operation the museum welcomed more than 14,000 visitors. Charter membership, at $300, entitles one to an exclusive collectible charter club lapel pin, lifetime personal entry into the museum, subscription to the museum newsletter, and an invitation to special museum events. Oh, and your name will be included on the Charter Club plaque, permanently displayed in the museum.

The Ripken Museum is located in what was the former public meeting room of the Aberdeen City Hall building. It took over a year and many hundreds of thousands of dollars to renovate this room into the showpiece it is today. In March 1998 the museum took another bold step in its future by purchasing City Hall from the city of Aberdeen. Architectural plans for the museum's expansion are underway, and it is anticipated that renovations to this area of the building should be completed by mid-2000. To accomplish the expansion project, the Ripken Museum Inc. is going forward with a $2.5 million capital campaign. There are some great opportunities for corporate partnerships with the museum as it expands.

Museum hours vary seasonally, with summer (Memorial Day Monday through Labor Day) hours from noon to 3:00 P.M., Monday through Friday; 11:00 A.M. to 4:00 P.M. on Saturday; and noon to 3:30 P.M. on Sunday. In the fall it's open Thursday through Monday, noon to 3:00 P.M. It's closed on major holidays. Call for winter hours. Admission is $3.00 for adults, $2.00 for seniors (sixty-two and above), and $1.00 for students (six to eighteen). (410) 273–2525.

Trivia

Ellicott Mills, in Howard County, was started in 1772 by three Ellicott brothers from Bucks County, Pennsylvania. By 1774, it was said to be the greatest gristmill in Colonial America, with seven mills in operation at its peak. Besides producing animal feed, flour, iron nails, oil, lumber, paper, wagons, and wool, the first commercial electricity in the county was produced in 1891 in a mill on Tiber Alley.

Northwest of Aberdeen is Bel Air, the Harford county seat, and there you'll enjoy the pleasures of ***Liriodendron,*** a Palladian-style mansion with Greek columns, French doors, marble walls in the kitchen and bathroom, and thirteen fireplaces. Built as a palatial summer home in 1898 for Dr. Howard A. Kelly, one of the "Big Four" founders of Baltimore's Johns Hopkins Hospital and Medical School, the "Kelly Mansion" is now on the National Register of Historic Places. This historic house museum features changing exhibits and art displays as well as a permanent exhibit of memorabilia from the Kelly Collection.

It also serves as a cultural center for Harford County, with superb facilities for exhibitions, lectures, and concerts. Tours are available on Sunday from the first Sunday in March through the second Sunday in December, from 1:00 to 4:00 P.M. except on national holidays. Call

(410) 838–3942 or 879–4424. The address is Liriodendron, 502 West Gordon Street, Bel Air 21014.

For additional tourism information on Harford County, write to Discover Harford County Tourism Council Inc., P.O. Box 635, Bel Air 21014.

Howard County

South and west of Baltimore City, out I–70 or down I–95, is Howard County, a place offering tremendous contrasts in lifestyles: from Ellicott City, a former mill town, with its original stone buildings, antiques and specialty shops, historic sites, and B&O (Baltimore and Ohio) Railroad Station Museum; to Columbia, the planned village, with its Merriweather Post Pavilion, huge mall, and Columbia Information Center. As usual, I will cover some of the less-visited and more countrified places.

If you travel from Baltimore County to Howard County, just off Route 1, you can spot a bridge of note that is for trains rather than cars, known as the ***Thomas Viaduct*** (1833). Crossing the Patapsco River, eight elliptical arches support a 60-foot-high granite block structure, which allowed tall ships to pass under. Just as the Ellicott City Railroad Station has endured as a landmark to the growth of railroading in Maryland, so does the viaduct. When B&O Railroad officials began looking to expand the railroad south to Washington, D.C., they faced a monumental problem: how to cross the Patapsco River. They solved it with a monumental structure, Thomas Viaduct. Named for Philip Thomas, the first president of the B&O Railroad, it was designed by Baltimorean Benjamin Latrobe, and it was the first curved, stone-arched bridge in America. Construction began July 4, 1832, and it was completed exactly three years later at a cost of a little over $142,000. It still carries passenger and freight trains. The viaduct is off Levering Avenue in Elkridge. Picnic areas are in nearby Patapsco State Park.

Another bridge of interest, at Savage, is the ***Bollman Truss Bridge*** (1869). The red cast-iron, open railroad bridge is the only one of its type in the world. It is said to be the first bridge constructed of iron, as opposed to wood or stone. Restoration of the bridge took place in 1974, near Savage Mill (which is now filled with antiques shops and artists' studios), and there is a nice little park and hiking trails around the bridge. You can find the bridge off Route 1, at Savage, near Savage Mill.

Away from bridges and on to a few farms that are open for pick-your-own fruits and vegetables and lots of family fun.

Historic ***Cider Mill Farm*** (1916) has organic produce, herbs, pies, honey, and other country goods from mid-September through November and mid-April through mid-May. During the apple season they offer guided tours of the cider-making process, including antique hand- and electric-press demonstrations in which children can participate and receive free cider samples. Tom Owens, the owner, says you can bring your own jug for fresh cider if you like. Weekend activities include face painting, marble and yo-yo presentations, apple butter making, scarecrow making, storytelling, pumpkin carving (bring your own tools and a blanket), and a teddy bear contest (bring your own bear). Remember to bring your camera. A schedule of contests and activities is available.

Trivia

In 1820 Amos Williams and his three brothers borrowed $20,000 from friend John Savage to start a textile-weaving business on the banks of the Little Patuxent River. With water flowing over a huge 30-foot water wheel, Savage Mill, named after their friend, was in use from 1822 through 1947. It is now a complex filled with artisans and antiques dealers. (301) 498–5751 or (410) 792–2820.

Cider Mill Farm is open 10:00 A.M. to 6:00 P.M. It is located at 5012 Landing Road (off Montgomery Road, Route 103) Elkridge 21227; call (410) 788–9595 or 788–9596 or visit the farm's Web site: farmmd.com.

Larriland Farms has a pick-your-own season starting in late May or early June with strawberries and ending with a cut-your-own season for Christmas trees in December. In addition, the farm has succulent and delicious fruits and vegetables and beautiful flowers. The market is in a 125-year-old post-and-beam barn. Larriland Farms, owned and operated by the Moore family, also offers hayrides, evening campfires, and other programs that let city folk enjoy the pleasures of rural life. The farm is open May through August, Monday through Friday 8:00 A.M. to 8:00 P.M. and September through October, Monday through Friday 9:00 A.M. to 5:00 P.M. Weekend hours are Saturday 9:00 A.M. to 5:00 P.M. and Sunday 10:00 A.M. to 5:00 P.M. In December it's closed on Monday. The address is 2415 Woodbine Road, Woodbine 21797. Larriland Farms is 3 miles south of I–70 (exit 73) on Route 94, near Lisbon. The phone number is (410) 489–7034; in season you can call (410) 442–2605 or (301) 854–6110 for a recording of what fruits and vegetables are available. Their Web site is www.pickyourown.com.

Toby's the Dinner Theatre of Columbia celebrates the creative genius of Toby Orenstein and her dedication to fine theatrical productions. All the time she is working to entertain you, she is working to teach her "kids" the hows and whys of show business so they can go on to professional careers in entertainment if they wish.

The most interesting aspect of Toby's is the theater, which has performances in the round, for the theater was built to be just that, not adapted from some other use. You are never far from the action.

The productions may be an outstanding Broadway show from years gone by, such as *Funny Girl* or *Singin' in the Rain* or an entirely new attraction, such as a musical version of *It's a Wonderful Life,* which was created at Toby's and offered during the 1989 holiday season. Other selections have included *The Pirates of Penzance, Sunday in the Park with George,* and *Ain't Misbehavin'.* In other words, it's good family entertainment.

Dinner at Toby's is an all-you-can-eat buffet that features prime roast beef, steamed shrimp, fresh salad and vegetables, and a dessert table.

Toby's is at South Entrance Road, 1/2 block east of Little Patuxent Parkway, Columbia. The phone numbers are (410) 730–8311; (301) 596–6161 (in Washington); (410) 995–1969 (in Baltimore); and (800) 88–TOBYS (in Maryland and surrounding states).

For additional information on Howard County, write to Karen Justice, Executive Director, Howard County Tourism Council, P.O. Box 9, Ellicott City 21041, or call (800) 288–TRIP (8747) or (410) 313–1900.

PLACES TO EAT IN CENTRAL MARYLAND

ANNAPOLIS

Buddy's Crabs and Ribs,
100 Main Street,
(410) 261–2500

Cantler's,
458 Forest Beach Road,
(410) 757–1311

Carrol's Creek Cafe,
410 Severn Avenue,
(410) 263–8102

Corinthian,
126 West Street,
(410) 263–7777

Pusser's Landing,
80 Compromise Street,
(410) 268–7555

Riordan's,
26 Market Street,
(410) 263–5449

Treaty of Paris,
16 Church Circle,
(410) 263–2641

BALTIMORE

Admiral's Cup,
1645 Thames Street,
(410) 522–6731

Attman's Delicatessen,
1019 Lombard Street,
(401) 463–2666

Burke's Cafe,
36 Light Street,
(401) 752–4189

Chick and Ruth's Delly,
165 Main Street,
(410) 269–6737

Donna's Coffee Bar,
2 West Madison,
(410) 385–0180

Hampton's Restaurant,
Harbor Court Hotel,
550 Light Street,
(410) 234–0550

Haussner's,
3242 Eastern Avenue,
(410) 327–8365

Nate and Leon's,
300 West Pratt Street,
(410) 234–8100

Obrycki's Crab House,
1727 East Pratt Street,
(410) 732–6399

Phillips Harborplace,
Light Street Pavilion,
(410) 685–6600

Ruth's Chris Steak House,
600 Water Street,
(410) 783–0033

Sabatino's,
901 Fawn Street,
(410) 727–9414

Vaccarro's,
222 Albemarle Street,
(410) 685–4905

COLUMBIA
King's Contrivance,
10150 Minstrel Way,
(410) 995–0500

Toby's Dinner Theatre of Columbia,
South Entrance Road,
(410) 730–8311,
(301) 596–6161,
or (800) 88–TOBYS

ELLICOTT CITY
The Trolly Stop,
6 Oella Avenue,
(410) 465–8646

LOTHIAN
G&M,
804 North Hammonds Ferry Road,
(410) 636–1777

NORTH EAST
Woody's Crab House,
29 South Main Street,
(410) 287–3541

PLACES TO STAY IN CENTRAL MARYLAND

ANNAPOLIS
Amanda's B&B Reservation Service,
1428 Park Avenue,
(800) 899–7533,
(410) 225–0001,
www.amandas-bbrs. com,
or AmandasRS@aol.com (e-mail)

Annapolis Marriott,
80 Compromise Street,
(410) 268–7555

Gibson's Lodgings,
110 Prince George Street,
(410) 268–5555

Loews Annapolis Hotel,
126 West Street,
(410) 263–7777

Maryland Inn,
16 Church Circle,
(410) 263–2641

BALTIMORE
Admiral Fell Inn,
888 South Broadway,
(410) 522–7377 or
(800) 292–INNS

Harbor Court Hotel,
550 Light Street,
(410) 234–0550

Marriott Inner Harbor,
110 South Eutaw Street,
(410) 962–0202

Mr. Mole Bed and Breakfast,
1601 Bolton Street,
(410) 728–1179

COLUMBIA
Columbia Hilton Inn,
5485 Twin Knolls Road,
(800) 235–0653 or
(410) 997–1060

ELLICOTT CITY
Turf Valley Resort,
2700 Turf Valley Road,
(410) 465–1500

FRIENDSHIP
Herrington Harbour Marina Resort,
7161 Lake Shore Drive,
(410) 741–5100

TOWSON
M Gettier's Orchard Inn,
1528 Joppa Road,
(410) 823–0364

OTHER ATTRACTIONS WORTH SEEING IN CENTRAL MARYLAND

African Art Museum of Maryland, Columbia;
(410) 730–7105

American Visionary Art Museum, Baltimore;
(410) 244–1900

B&O Railroad Museum, Baltimore; (410) 752–2490

Babe Ruth Birthplace and Orioles Museum, Baltimore; (410) 777–1539 or (800) 435–BABE

Baltimore American Indian Center/Museum, Baltimore;
(410) 675–3535

Baltimore City Hall, Baltimore; (410) 837–5424

Baltimore Equitable Insurance Fire Museum, Baltimore; (410) 727–1794

Baltimore International College, Baltimore; (410) 752–4710

Baltimore Museum of Industry, Baltimore; (410) 727–4808

Baltimore Streetcar Museum, Baltimore; (410) 547–0264

Baltimore Zoo, Baltimore; (410) 396–7102

Barge House Museum, Eastport (Annapolis); (410) 268–1802

Cab Calloway Jazz Institute, Baltimore; (410) 383–5522

Charles Carroll House of Annapolis, Annapolis; (410) 269–1737

Chase-Lloyd House, Annapolis; (410) 263–2723

City Fire Museum, Baltimore; (410) 727–2414

Cylburn Arboretum, Baltimore; (410) 367–2217

Edgar Allan Poe House, Baltimore; (410) 396–7932

Eubie Blake National Museum and Cultural Center, Baltimore; (410) 625–3113

Fire Museum of Maryland, Lutherville; (410) 321–7500

Ft. George G. Meade Museum, Fort Meade; (301) 677–6966

Fort McHenry, Baltimore; (410) 962–4290

Great Blacks in Wax Museum, Baltimore; (410) 563–3404

Hammond-Harwood House, Annapolis; (410) 263–4683

Helen Avalynne Tawes Garden, Annapolis; (410) 974–3717

Historic Annapolis Foundation Museum Store, Annapolis; (410) 268–5576

Historic Oakland, Columbia; (410) 730–0075

Historical Electronics Museum, Linthicum; (410) 765–2345

Irvine Natural Science Center, Stevenson; (410) 484–2413

Jewish Museum of Maryland, Baltimore; (410) 732–6400

Kunte Kinte Plaque, Annapolis; (410) 263–7940

Lacrosse Hall of Fame Museum, Baltimore; (410) 235–6882

Ladew Topiary Gardens, Jarrettsville; (410) 557–9466

Lexington Market, Baltimore; (410) 685–6169

London Town House and Gardens, Edgewater; (410) 222–1919

Maryland Science Center, Baltimore; (410) 586–5225 or www.mdsci.org

Maryland State House, Annapolis; (410) 974–3400

Maryland State Police Museum, Pikesville; (410) 486–3101

Merriweather Post Pavilion, Columbia; (301) 596–0660 or (410) 730–2424

Mother Seton House, Baltimore; (410) 523–3443

Mount Clair Mansion, Baltimore; (410) 837–3262

National Aquarium in Baltimore, Baltimore; (410) 576–3800

National Cryptologic Museum, Fort Meade; (301) 688–5849

National Museum of Dentistry, Baltimore; (410) 706–0600

1901 Falls Road, Baltimore; (410) 547–0264

Oella–Benjamin Banneker Site, Oella (no phone)

Old Treasury Building, Annapolis; (410) 267–8149

Patapsco Female Institute, Ellicott City; (410) 465–8500

Pride of Baltimore II, Baltimore; (410) 539–1151

Quiet Waters Park, Annapolis; (410) 222–1777

Rash Field Ice Rink, Baltimore; (410) 752–8632

St. Anne's Episcopal Church, Annapolis; (410) 267–9333

Shiplap House Museum, Annapolis; (410) 267–7619

Shot Tower, Baltimore; (410) 837–5424

Star-Spangled Banner Flag House and 1812 Museum, Baltimore; (410) 837–1793

Thomas Point Lighthouse, Annapolis (no phone)

Union Mills Homestead and Gristmill, Westminster; (410) 848–2288

Walters Art Gallery, Baltimore; (410) 547–9000

William Paca House and Garden, Annapolis; (410) 263–5553

Calendar of Annual Events in Central Maryland

January

Baltimore on Ice Winterfest, Baltimore; (410) 837–4636 or (800) 282–6632

February

Chinese Lunar New Year Festival, Baltimore; (410) 377–8143

March

Jewish Cultural Festival, Baltimore; (410) 685–3750

Marlborough Hunt Races, Davidsonville; (410) 798–5040

Maryland Day Convocation, Baltimore; (410) 617–5025

St. Patrick's Day Bash, Baltimore; (410) 685–3750

St. Patrick's Parade, Baltimore; (410) 837–0685

April

Carroll Carvers Annual Festival of Carving, Westminster; (410) 854–0067

Celebration of Asian Culture, Towson; (410) 830–2807

Decoy, Wildlife Art, and Sportsman Festival, Havre de Grace; (410) 939–3739

Harborplace Street Performers' Auditions, Baltimore; (800) HARBOR–1

Maryland Archaeology Month, statewide; (410) 514–7661

Maryland Hunt Cup Celebration, Worthington Valley; (410) 685–3750

Maryland Hunt Cup Race, Glyndon; (410) 833–4188

Maryland Orchid Society's Orchid Show, Owings Mills; (410) 256–5503

My Lady's Manor Steeplechase Races, Monkton; (410) 557–9466

Rites of Spring, Timonium; (410) 554–2662

Savage Mill Woodworking Show, Savage; (301) 490–0187

Spring Fair, West Friendship; (301) 791–2346

Springtime at the Mill, Ellicott City; (410) 661–5633

Symposium on Archaeology, Crownsville; (410) 514–7661

Taste of Southern Maryland, Rose Haven; (410) 741–5101

Towson Gardens Day, Towson; (410) 825–2211

Upper Bay Skipjack Invitational Races and Earth Day Festival, Havre de Grace; (800) 406–0766

Welcome the Skipjacks Bull and Oyster Road, Havre de Grace; (800) 406–0766

May

A Cappella Singing Festival, Towson; (410) 488–6824

Annapolis Waterfront Arts Festival, Annapolis; (410) 268–8828

Annual Flower and Plant Market, Union Mills; (410) 848–2288

Art Blooms in Maryland, Annapolis; (410) 974–3531

Blue Angels Demonstration, Annapolis; (410) 268–7600

Chesapeake Bay Bridge Walk, Annapolis; (410) 228–8405

Civil War Encampment at Steppingstone Museum, Havre de Grace; (410) 939–2299

Cylburn Market Day, Baltimore; (410) 367–2217

Dublin Country Fair, Dublin; (410) 457–4275

Flower and Jazz Festival, Westminster; (800) 272–1933

Herb Festival, Sykesville; (410) 795–3274

Howard County Jewish Festival, Columbia; (410) 730–4976

International Children's Spring Festival, Lutherville; (410) 321–8555

Ladew Plant Sale, Monkton; (410) 557–9466

Living American Flag Program, Baltimore; (410) 563–3524 or www.ubalt.edu/flagday

Memorial Day, Timonium; (410) 666–0490

Preakness Celebration, Baltimore; (410) 542–9400 or (410) 837–3030

Preakness Celebration Parade, Baltimore; (800) 282–6632

Preakness Crab Derby, Baltimore; (410) 685–6169

Springfest, Baltimore; (410) 727–3939

The Preakness, Baltimore; (410) 542–9400

Towsontown Spring Festival, Towson; (410) 825–1144

June

Annapolis Jazzfest, Annapolis; (410) 349–1111

CitySand, Baltimore; (800) HARBOR–1

Cylburn Solstice Celebration, Baltimore; (410) 367–2217

Darlington Herb Festival and Garden Party, Darlington; (410) 836–7764

Father's Day Party Music Crab Feast, Baltimore; (410) 484–5600

Gay, Lesbian, Bisexual and Transgender Pride Festival, Baltimore; (410) 837–5445

Latino Festival, Baltimore City; (410) 783–5404

Maritime Festival of the Havre de Grace Maritime Museum, Havre de Grace; (410) 734–6357

Maryland Rose Society Show, Owings Mills; (410) 252–2845

National Pause for the Pledge of Allegiance, Baltimore; (410) 453–3524 or www.ubalt.edu/flagday

North Bay Deer Creek Fiddlers' Convention, Westminster; (410) 876–2667

St. Nicholas Greek Folk Festival, Baltimore; (410) 633–7700

Scottish Festival, Havre de Grace; (410) 939–2299

South County Festival, Tracy's Landing; (410) 867–3129

Strawberry Festival, Sykesville; (410) 795–0494

Summer Fair, West Friendship; (301) 791–2346

USNA Flag Day, Annapolis; (410) 263–6933

July

Baltimore's Fourth of July Celebration, Baltimore; (410) 837–4636

Baltimore Symphony Orchestra Fourth of July Celebration, Hunt Valley; (410) 783–8000

Catonsville's July Fourth Celebration, Catonsville; (410) 744–7042

Fourth of July Fireworks Cruise, Annapolis; (410) 268–7600

Gumbo Jam, Annapolis; (202) 861–6825

Harborplace's Birthday Celebration, Baltimore; (800) HARBOR–1

Havre de Grace Independence Celebration, Havre de Grace; (410) 939–4362

Heritage Fair, Dundalk; (410) 284–4022

Howard County Pow-Wow, West Friendship; (919) 257–5383

Ice Cream Festival, Baltimore; (410) 688–6169

John Paul Jones Day, Annapolis; (410) 263–6933

Old-Fashioned July Fourth, Westminster; (410) 876–2667

World's Greatest Crab Feast, Music Festival and Fireworks, Baltimore; (410) 484–5600

August

Celebrate Taneytown Festival, Taneytown; (410) 751–1100

Howard County Fair, West Friendship; (410) 442–1022

Kunta Kinte Heritage Festival, Annapolis; (410) 349–0338

Maritime Maryland, Annapolis; (410) 263–6933

Maryland Renaissance Festival, Annapolis; (410) 266–7304

Maryland State Fair, Timonium; (410) 252–0200, ext. 226

September

Anne Arundel County Fair, Crownsville; (410) 923–3400

Bel Air Festival for the Arts, Bel Air; (410) 836–2395

Big M All Ford and Mustang Fall Show, Bel Air; (410) 357–5615

Chesapeake Airshow, Middle River; (410) 686–2233

Children's Day at Ladew Topiary Gardens, Monkton; (410) 557–9466

Duck Fair, Havre de Grace; (410) 939–3739

Fall Harvest Day, Marriottsville; (410) 922–3044

Honey Harvest Festival, Westminster; (410) 848–9040

Lake Elkhorn Festival, Columbia; (410) 381–0202

Maryland Wine Festival, Westminster; (410) 876–2667

Navy Way Days, Annapolis; (410) 263–6933

Parkville Towne Centre Fair, Parkville; (410) 665–0100

Patapsco Valley Barbershop Show, Woodlawn; (410) 795–2175

Reister's Towne Festival, Reisterstown; (410) 356–0688

Septemberfest, Havre de Grace; (410) 939–3303

Smallwood Festival, Westminster; (410) 848–8254

The A-Maize-ing Place: A Mammoth Maze and Harvest Happening, Columbia; (410) 313–7275

Westminster Fallfest, Westminster; (800) 272–1933

October

Blacksmith Days, Westminster; (410) 876–2667

Blessing of Baltimore's Work Boats, Baltimore; (800) HARBOR–1

Chocolate Festival, Baltimore; (410) 685–6169

Darlington Apple Festival, Darlington; (410) 457–4189

Fall Harvest Days, Westminster; (410) 876–2667

Fell's Point Fun Festival, Baltimore City; (410) 675–6756

Mount Airy Fall Festival, Mount Airy; (301) 829–2112

Old Bay Crab Soup Stakes, Baltimore; (800) HARBOR–1

Ship of Ghouls, Baltimore; (800) HARBOR–1

United States Powerboat Show, Annapolis; (410) 268–8828

United States Sailboat Show, Annapolis; (410) 268–8828

November
Annapolis by Candlelight, Annapolis; (410) 267–7619

Art Festival, Annapolis; (410) 268–0474

Baltimore's Thanksgiving Day Parade, Baltimore; (410) 837–4636

Holiday Train Garden, Towson; (410) 321–1909

Lights on the Bay, Annapolis; (410) 260–3161

Potters Guild of Baltimore Show, Baltimore; (410) 235–4884

Savage Mill Open House Weekend, Savage; (800) 788–MILL

December
Annual Lighted Boat Parade, Baltimore; (800) HARBOR–1

Candlelight Pub Crawl, Annapolis; (410) 263–5401

Eastport Yacht Club's Lights Parade, Annapolis; (410) 885–2415

First Night Annapolis, Annapolis; (410) 280–0700

Frosty Follies, Annapolis; (410) 956–0512

Governor's Holiday Open House, Annapolis; (410) 974–3531

Holiday Tour, Westminster; (410) 876–2667

Merry Tuba Christmas, Baltimore; (800) HARBOR–1

State House by Candlelight, Annapolis; (410) 974–3400

Street Cars of Desire, Timonium; (410) 461–0687

Greater Washington

Prince George's, Montgomery, and Frederick Counties make up the Greater Washington area. Washington, D.C., is at the center of a huge suburban megalopolis formed by the blending of these three counties. Although there are areas of dense population, and seemingly miles upon miles of row or town houses, there are also miles and miles of parkland, green spaces, and open spaces. Because so many people who live here come from other places, such as places where it never snows, traffic seems to get jammed as soon as the TV and radio weather forecasters think about snow. Forget about what happens when it actually does snow. If you should be here when it snows, or it's thinking about snowing, tune into a radio or TV station, and go for public transportation. Or find a nice fireplace and cuddle up with a good book.

As a native of this area, I have received a steady stream of visitors over the years who want to tour Washington. I take them to the subway station, and the Metro Rail takes them downtown to the many Smithsonian buildings, galleries, the zoo, or anything else they want to see. The Washington Metro is as clean and safe as any subway system around and at last count was the second or third busiest subway in the country.

There are three lines running in Prince George's County: the Green, the Orange, and the Blue. Green Line stations are located at Greenbelt, College Park, Prince George's Plaza, and West Hyattsville; Orange Line stations are at New Carrollton, Landover, and Cheverly; and Blue Line stations are at Addison Road and Capitol Heights.

There's one line with two branches running in Montgomery County: the Red Line, with stations at Shady Grove, Rockville, Twinbrook, White Flint, Grosvenor, Medical Center, and Bethesda going in toward Washington on the northwestern branch, and Takoma Park, Silver Spring, Forest Glen, Wheaton, and Glenmont coming out the more northerly route.

Trains run 5:30 A.M. to midnight on weekdays, 8:00 A.M. to midnight on Saturday, and 10:00 A.M. to midnight on Sunday. Trains run about every five to fifteen minutes, depending on the time of day. Fares are based on

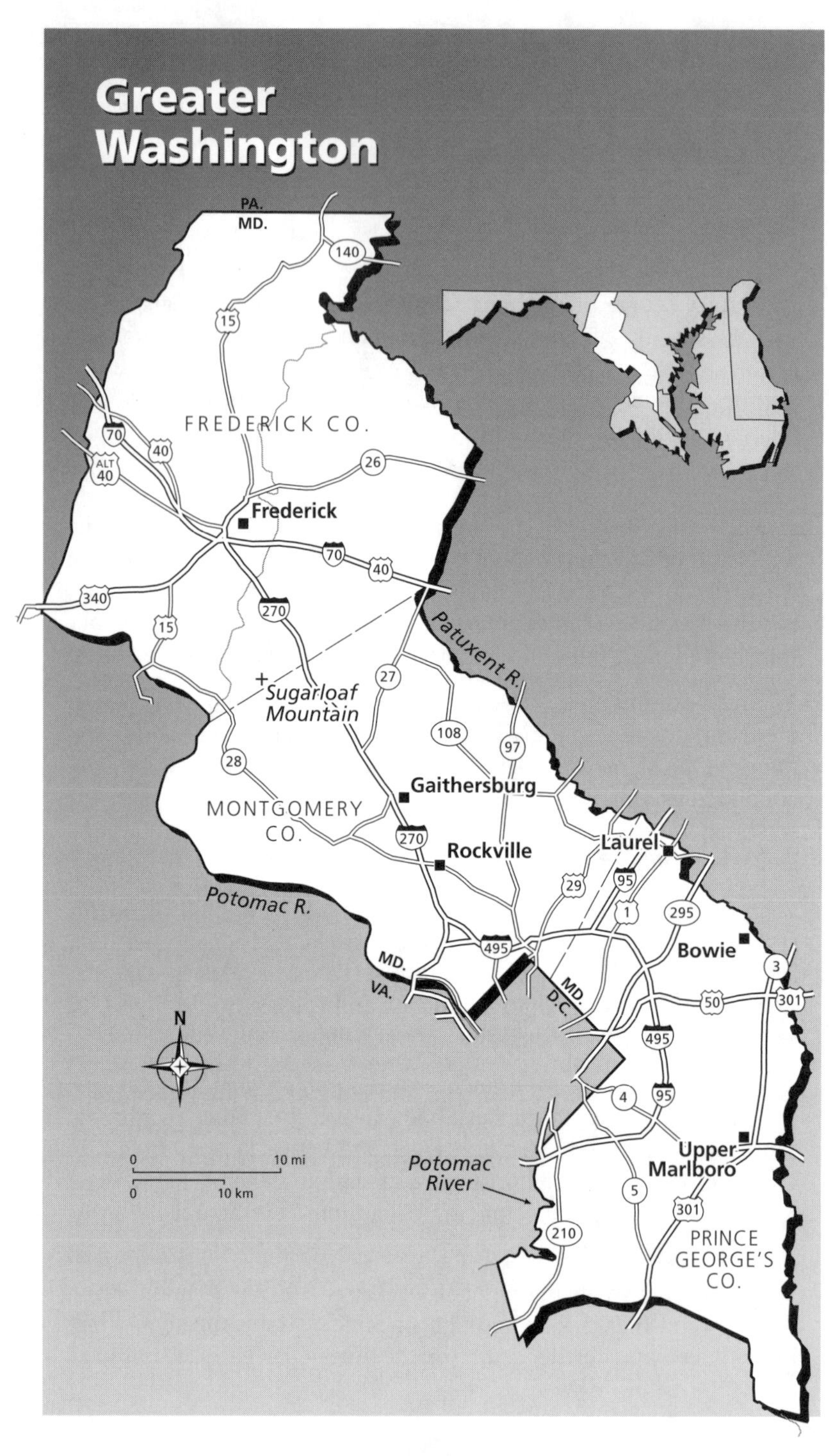
Greater Washington
PA.
MD.
140
15
FREDERICK CO.
70
40
ALT 40
26
Frederick
70
40
340
270
15
Patuxent R.
27
Sugarloaf Mountain
108
97
28
Gaithersburg
MONTGOMERY CO.
270
Rockville
Laurel
95
29
Potomac R.
1
295
Bowie
495
MD.
VA.
MD.
D.C.
3
50
301
N
495
4
95
Upper Marlboro
0
10 mi
0
10 km
Potomac River
5
301
210
PRINCE GEORGE'S CO.

time and distance, with rush hour (5:30 to 9:30 A.M. and 3:00 to 7:00 P.M., weekdays) costing more than off-peak times. For a bicycle permit, call (202) 962–1116. For general information about Metro Rail and Metro Bus (such as how to get from your door to your destination), call (202) 637–7000. This number is operational from 6:00 A.M. to 11:30 P.M. daily.

Of course, this book is designed for people who are interested in seeing sights other than those along the subway routes. In the Greater Washington area you will find orchards, covered bridges, historic cemeteries, campgrounds, murals, a ferry, places to eat and to be entertained, old farm tools, and a museum dedicated to poultry, among other things.

JUDY'S FAVORITE ATTRACTIONS IN GREATER WASHINGTON

College Park Airport Museum

Mount Olivet Cemetery

Patuxent Wildlife Research Center

Roddy Road Covered Bridge

U.S. Department of Agriculture Research Center

White's Ferry

Prince George's County

People hear more about Prince George's County in the news than they realize. A marriage is performed on the old wooden roller coaster at the Six Flags (formerly Adventure World) theme park outside Kettering; space flight information is reported from the Goddard Space Flight Center (and Museum) in Greenbelt, the hub of all NASA tracking activities; or the President or visiting dignitary arrives at Andrews Air Force Base, the home base for Air Force One.

Of course, Prince George's County is rarely mentioned, but all of this commerce and history is taking place here on a day-to-day basis. Prince George's County is a place of "firsts" and "lasts."

Upper Marlboro is the county seat for Prince George's, and it's a good place to start. Understanding that Prince George's County was and still is a very agrarian county, you will appreciate the work of W. Henry DuVall. A lifelong Prince Georgean, DuVall had the foresight to save tools from the nineteenth century, whether it was a scythe, can opener, carpenter's plane, or foot-operated dental drill. This was the beginning of the ***DuVall Tool Collection***. There is even a white building block that is blackened on one side, which apparently was obtained during a nineteenth-century architectural revision of the White House. The dark stains are said to be soot from the burning of the building during the War of 1812. The Maryland–National Capital Park and Planning Commission had the foresight to buy the agglomeration so that it would not be lost to the twentieth or twenty-first century. DuVall's collection, which he started in the 1930s, had more than 1,200 items by the time he died in 1979. More tools are accepted, so if you have something tucked away in your attic or out in the garage someplace—particularly if it is unique to southern Maryland history—donate it here instead of to the dump.

You can return to yesteryear by viewing the DuVall Tool Collection, located in the Patuxent River Park, Sunday from 1:00 to 4:00 P.M. and by appointment. The address is 16000 Croom Airport Road, Upper Marlboro 20772. Call (301) 672–6074.

Just south of Upper Marlboro is the old-turned-to-new Prince George's Equestrian Center and the newer ***Show Place Arena***. Once a functional horse racetrack, it was closed and converted to fringe parking for county employees before it was reborn as an architectural masterpiece and the home of the annual county fair, concerts, the Chesapeake Icebreakers ice-hockey team and their mascot Frostbite (a six-foot cuddly polar bear) of the East Coast Hockey League (making ice hockey an affordable and accessible spectator sport), and other special events. There are even a few days of horse racing now and then. You'll find the center and arena at 14955 Pennsylvania Avenue, at the intersection of Routes 301 and 4. Call (301) 952–4720.

To the west of Upper Marlboro is Largo, the home of the former USAirways Arena (née Capital Centre, née USAir Arena, and if McDonald's had

The City of Brotherly Love—in Suitland

Few of us can claim to be natives around this area, for people come and go with military assignments or as the "ins" of the government change, sometimes every two years. Although we may ask "where you from?" because we're fairly certain it isn't from here, we don't have a third-generation or more litmus test before accepting you. One of the reasons is all the great things you bring from wherever it was you were before. Such is the case with **LiLeons** *(pronounced Lillian's)* **Philadelphia Steaks and Hoagies.** *Those of you who really pine for a South Philly cheese steak, or those who've never had one, will be thrilled that the genuine article can be found in this Suitland eatery. And, just so you won't miss the City of Brotherly Love too much, or maybe it will make your absence that much more severe, are banners for the '76ers, Flyers, and Eagles. LiLeons is at 3674 St. Barnabas Road, Suitland. It's open from 11:00 A.M. to 11:00 P.M. Monday through Saturday. (301) 899–8233.*

bought it, would it be the McArena?). And now the home of the Cookie, or the Jack Kent Cooke Stadium, where the Washington Redskins play.

Nearby you'll find the flagship restaurant ***BET Soundstage***, from BET Holdings Inc., the first and only cable network for the African-American community. This restaurant features a dynamic sensory experience through taped performances and a state-of-the-art multimedia display of video and music. Music celebrities, sports figures, artists, and business professionals provide a mix of the famous and the familiar among its clientele. A gift shop, filled with the latest BET-branded merchandise, including T-shirts, jackets, and caps, is on the premises. BET Soundstage is located at 9640 Lottsford Court, Largo, near Lottsford Road and Route 202. (301) 883–9500.

Trivia

The original events upon which the movie The Exorcist *was based took place in Mount Rainier, starting on January 18, 1949, when weird noises were heard from the home at 3210 Bunker Hill Road. Father Albert Hughes came from nearby St. James Catholic Church to perform the exorcism, but four months later he still had not been successful. Okay, so Hollywood changed a few things, and the movie was set in the Georgetown area of Washington, D.C. The original home has been demolished.*

Heading west of there is Bladensburg and the ***Bladensburg Dueling Grounds,*** a small, wooden glen in the northeastern corner of Fort Lincoln Cemetery, adjacent to Colmar Manor. It was a court of last resort for nearly fifty years for offended gentlemen and politicians, who faced each other at ten paces with pistols and muskets. As noted on the historical marker placed by the Maryland–National Capital Park and Planning Commission: One of the most famous was that between Commodores Stephen Decatur and James Barron, which was settled here on March 22, 1820. Commodore Decatur, who had

Ten-Story Roar

The **Six Flags** *park east of Upper Marlboro has had more names and themes than you can shake a stick at, for it started life as an animal park, converted to water park, then a more general amusement park, and in 1998 it came under the stewardship of the Six Flags company. Its latest addition, installed while it was still Adventure World and part of Premier Parks Inc., is a $10 million wooden roller coaster called Roar. It has 3,200 feet of track, is taller than a ten-story building at its highest point, and has twelve curves, twelve drops, and six reversals as it crisscrosses itself twenty times. This is the second wooden coaster at the park. Roar was designed by Michael Boodley, co-owner of Great Coasters International Inc. of Pennsylvania. Boodley is a mechanical engineer who has helped design forty rides.*

gained fame as the conqueror of the Barbary pirates, was fatally wounded by his antagonist.

Although Congress passed an anti-dueling law in 1839, duels continued here until just before the Civil War. The dueling grounds are in Anacostia River Park and near the intersection of Bladensburg Road and Thirty-eighth Avenue in Bladensburg. Also at Anacostia River Park is the Maryland–National Capital Park and Planning Commission Interpretive Center at the site of the old Bladensburg Marina.

Trivia

On June 17, 1784, the first documented unmanned balloon flight in the United States took place in a field near the town of Bladensburg. Peter Carnes, the balloon owner, sent the manned balloon aloft a week later in Baltimore.

At the junction of the Beltway (I–95, I–495) and John Hanson Highway (US 50) is the New Carrollton Metro station, a MARC and AMTRAK railroad station, a first in intermodel transportation stops.

Several years ago the arts organizations of Prince George's and Montgomery Counties in Maryland, northern Virginia, and Washington, D.C., agreed to promote a ***MetroArts*** contest for public art to be displayed in subway stations throughout the system. It was very successful, and a number of artists had works displayed at several metro stations, such as New Carrollton, for a year. A second contest, this one with prize money totaling $100,000, has been held.

A 1998 installation at the New Carrollton station will be permanent. *Dawn and Dusk* was created by architect Ben Van Dusen and Kensington artist Heidi Lippman, and the Italian glass mosaic covers more than 2,000 square feet of the four stairway and elevator towers of the parking garage and the clock tower. Besides decorating these surfaces, the installation should save taxpayers money because it should protect the concrete surface from weather erosion.

Head north, around the Beltway, and you'll come to College Park, home of the University of Maryland and near there, the ***College Park Airport,*** where the first military training in a military-owned airplane took place in October 1909. The plane was designed by Orville and Wilbur Wright. College Park claims to be the "world's oldest continually operated airport," and today it is the only operating airport within the Capital Beltway. Pilots say they get a kick out of flying from the same airfield that the Wright Brothers used eighty-some years ago.

Budding aviators are sure to enjoy the 26,000-square-foot ***College Park Airport Museum,*** which opened in early 1998. Tours, movies, and special events are scheduled throughout the year, including an annual AirFair in September.

The museum is at 1909 Corporal Frank Scott Drive (named for the first civilian killed in an air accident). It's free and is open from 11:00 A.M. to 3:00 P.M. Wednesday through Friday and 11:00 A.M. to 5:00 P.M. Saturday and Sunday. Call (301) 864–1530.

To Fly is to Sing

Mrs. Ralph H. Van Deman said, "Now I know why birds sing," after becoming the first woman in America to fly as a passenger in an airplane when she went aloft with Wilbur Wright in College Park on October 27, 1909.

Just minutes from College Park is a planned city whose history starts in the 1930s. If you think planned cities are something new, then visit ***Greenbelt***. From its inception, Greenbelt had a sense of history about it. It has been chronicled, cataloged, dissected, scrutinized, and studied many times over in thorough detail. Although the town is now surrounded by townhouse communities for Washington commuters, you still can see the core of the town, its Art Deco architecture, and its attempts to retain its identity.

Greenbelt is one of three planned greenbelt towns that were to be satellite towns on the edge of larger urban cores (the other two are Greenhills, Ohio, and Greendale, Wisconsin, outside of Cincinnati and Milwaukee, respectively). The town was built around an inner core, allowing residents to walk everywhere they had to go on pedestrian paths so that people on foot would not have to intermingle with cars. The town was superorganized and highly democratic, and residents met to discuss everything. (In fact, at one point they met to declare a moratorium on meetings.)

For a more thorough explanation and visual interpretation, stop by the ***Greenbelt Museum*** on Sunday between 1:00 and 5:00 P.M. There's no admission charge. The museum is located at 10 B Crescent Road. Call (301) 474–1936. Greenbelt is at the northwest corner of the intersection of the Baltimore-Washington Parkway (I–295) and the Capital Beltway (I–495).

Head north up Baltimore-Washington Parkway (I–295) and you'll come to the outskirts of ***Laurel,*** the Montpelier Arts Center, and the Montpelier Mansion.

The ***Montpelier Arts Center*** is noted for its visual arts, serving as a home for eighteen professional resident artists. A rather full curriculum of visual arts classes is offered. (301) 953–1993 or (301) 490–2329.

Next door is the ***Montpelier Mansion***, built in 1783 by Maj. Thomas Snowden, a significant landowner in Prince George's County. At one point the Montpelier site was about 10,000 acres of gently rolling parkland. Among the famed guests who stopped here were George and Martha Washington and Abigail Adams.

William Breckinridge Long, Undersecretary of State in the Franklin Roosevelt administration, and U.S. Ambassador to Italy from 1933–36, was the twentieth-century owner, and his guests also were notable, including Presidents Roosevelt and Wilson. Long's daughter, Christine Long Wilcox, donated the house in the late 1950s to the Maryland–National Capital Park and Planning Commission. The mansion and other buildings sit on about seventy-five acres of the original estate.

Many original Snowden pieces are still in the mansion, and other furnishings are period antiques. You may take a tour through almost a dozen rooms of the historic mansion most Sunday afternoons, between the hours of noon and 4:00 P.M. ($3.00 for adults, $2.00 for seniors fifty-five and older, and $1.00 for children five to fifteen).

And, if you wish, enjoy a lovely afternoon tea at the mansion, with a choice of teas and some delicious nibbles, usually on the second and fourth Friday of the month, at 2:00 or 4:00 P.M., for $15. Reservations and prepayment required. Call (301) 498–8486 for reservations.

That phone number will get you to the Little Teapot at Montpelier, a gift shop that's open during the summer season from 10:00 A.M. to 6:00 P.M., Tuesday through Saturday, and from noon to 4:00 P.M. on Sunday. Call for winter hours.

Reading is Fun-damental

Special library collections abound in Prince George's County. The Greenbelt Library has the Tugwell Room. As the Belair Estate in Bowie claimed to be the "Cradle of American Racing," it seems entirely appropriate that the Bowie Library has the Selima Room, with its extensive collection of horse-racing records and materials. Selima was one of the original mares who started the bloodline that flows in almost every racehorse in this country. Other special collections in the Prince George's County library system include the Sojourner Truth Room in the Oxon Hill branch, the Kerlan Room children's collection in the Hyattsville branch, and the Documents Library in the County Administration Building in Upper Marlboro, which appears to have every document pertaining to Prince George's County that was ever printed or penned.

Montpelier Mansion is located at 12826 Laurel Bowie Road. (301) 953–1993 or (301) 490–2329.

If you like murals as much as I do, you will be curious about Prince George's County's post office murals. The ***Laurel Post Office Mural*** of the *Mail Coach at Laurel,* painted by Mitchell Jamieson in 1939, reportedly was taken down during a General Services Administration restoration of the building and has not been returned.

The Chesapeake Bay area is noted for its seafood, and one of the better places to enjoy it—on the half shell, in crab cakes, or as part of a seafood platter—is at the ***Bay 'n Surf*** restaurant. This has been an institution of fine food since Roxanne and Patrick Edelmann opened it in 1965. The community has grown up and changed around it, but Bay 'n Surf retains that friendly "Cheers" atmosphere. Of course, there are non-seafood options. Bay 'n Surf is located at 14411 Baltimore Avenue (US Route 1), Laurel. Call (301) 776–7021.

East of Laurel is Beltsville and the home of the ***U.S. Department of Agriculture Research Center,*** with a visitors center in the Log Lodge. Built by the Civilian Conservation Crops during the 1930s, it contains a Hall of Fame of Agriculture scientists.

Approximately half of the 125 pounds of potatoes you eat each year are found in processed foods, a lot of which are instant potato flakes, developed in 1954 to use up a surplus of potatoes. Approximately 400 million pounds of potato flakes are produced each year in the United States. John F. Sullivan is honored for that invention and other works.

He's one of 44 scientists honored for their contributions to our agricultural well-being. Herbert J. Dutton is enshrined for pioneering research leading to the establishment of soybean oil as the predominant edible vegetable oil in the world. And James H. Tumlinson III is celebrated for his research leading to the eradication of the boll weevil from the southeastern United States.

The visitors center, in Building 186 (East), is open weekdays from 8:00 A.M. to 4:30 P.M. Guided tours are available by appointment. Call (301) 504–9403 or log onto www.ars.usda.gov.

The mailing address is United States Department of Agriculture, National Agriculture Library, Second Floor, 10301 Baltimore-Washington Boulevard, Beltsville 20705. There is no admission charge.

Traveling east still, there is other wildlife occupying the minds of specialists in Prince George's County. Situated on 4,700 acres, the ***Patuxent***

On Booth's Trail

In the spring and the fall, the Mary Surratt Society sponsors a "Booth's Trail" tour that follows the path of John Wilkes Booth from Ford's Theatre in Washington, D.C., to Dr. Mudd's home, to the Garrett Farm in northern Virginia. These fascinating tours fill up very quickly, and reservations are essential. Call (301) 868–1121 for tour dates and information.

Wildlife Research Center specializes in research on endangered species, migratory birds, and environmental contaminants. Established in 1839 as America's first national wildlife experiment station, the center is charged with protecting and conserving the nation's wildlife and natural habitats through research and critical debate. Throughout the years, the center has been involved in history-making discoveries, including the detrimental effects of DDT. Rachel Carson did most of her research here for her book *Silent Spring.* Currently the center is working to save the endangered whooping crane, California condor, Mississippi sandhill crane, and masked bobwhite. It has successfully completed a program of repopulating America's proud symbol, the bald eagle.

Scientists from more than fifteen countries conduct research at the center on a regular basis. Patuxent is the largest wildlife research center in the world, and it is an exciting place to learn about global concerns, be a field researcher and travel through the five full-scale habitat areas, view acres of natural wildlife habitat, and see dramatic dioramas of wildlife. Tram tours (small fee) of the surrounding woods and lakes to learn about wildlife management are offered during the summer at 10:30 and 11:30 A.M. and 12:30 and 1:30 P.M. Groups may schedule tram tours. A gift shop offers a variety of environmental books, gifts, and educational materials. If you have a really excellent memory, you may recall that the Center and the National Fund for the Patuxent Wildlife Research Center were featured on a December 1989 *CBS Sunday Morning* with Charles Kuralt.

The fund is a special committee of the Prince George's County Parks and Recreation Foundation Inc., which facilitates a public/private

Hoofbeats Heard Under the Bridge

The newest **covered bridge** *in Maryland is in Bowie. Nothing historic about this bridge, as far as its age goes, for it was built in 1988, but its use could be unique. It's located at the Bowie Race Course, which is now an equestrian center rather than a racetrack. The bridge is used for horses to move from the stables to the track for their workouts, not for people or cars.*

partnership to raise funds on a national basis for the multimillion-dollar National Wildlife Visitor Center. The visitors center's mission is to "educate the public, especially students, about wildlife conservation from a global perspective." The research center is located off Powder Mill Road, 2 miles east of the Baltimore/Washington Parkway. The mailing address is 10901 Scarlet Tanager Loop, Laurel 20708-4027. Call Nell Baldachinno (301–479–5760 or 479–0300) at least several days in advance to arrange a tour.

Travel down US 1 into Hyattsville and you'll discover Eugene Kingman, a noted muralist, painter, and museum director who created the five panels in the ***Hyattsville Post Office*** in 1938, jointly entitled *Hyattsville Countryside.* He was born in 1909, attended Yale University College of Fine Arts, and received an honorary Ph.D. from Creighton University. His work is in the Library of Congress collection and at the Philbrook in Tulsa, Oklahoma, among many other places. He also created murals in Wyoming, Rhode Island, and in the lobby of the New York Times Building in New York City.

The Hyattsville post-office murals depict the working man in heroic proportions. They reflect the remains of the agricultural and pastoral quality of the Hyattsville lifestyle that still existed in 1937, when Kingman used such muralist techniques as stylized horses, foreshortening, and a decorative cornstalk border.

The Hyattsville Post Office is at 4325 Gallatin Street, Hyattsville 20781. Call (301) 669–8905.

For additional information about Prince George's County, from events to lodgings, contact Matt Neitzey and his staff at the Prince George's County Conference and Visitors Bureau, 9475 Lottsford Road, Suite 130, Landover 20785. Call (301) 925–8300.

Montgomery County

West of Prince George's County and north and west of Washington, D.C., Montgomery County goes from really high-density suburbia at the south end to gorgeous open country with huge landed estates and farms in the middle and then into a mixture of townhouse developments set in the rolling countryside that are the approaches to the foothills of the Appalachian Mountains.

Start at the D.C./Maryland border, where the unincorporated area known as Silver Spring is about to see a long-promised redevelopment.

Silver Spring Acorn

(I remember when the first department store opened out there and when the bus cost five cents, but you could never stand at a bus stop long enough to catch a bus, because a neighbor would drive by and give you a ride into town.)

Just blocks from the D.C./ Maryland line, just off Georgia Avenue, is the ***Silver Spring Acorn***. It is easy to spot this little park, located near the spring from which the area received its name, with its gazebo shaped by pillars and a "hat" with the configuration of an acorn. Benches are provided for a lunch break or a moment of rest. Francis Preston Blair—a wealthy and prominent eighteenth-century landowner, power broker, newspaper owner, and member of President Jackson's Kitchen Cabinet—and his daughter were out riding one day when they found this spring. The sunlight reflecting off the sand or mica in the bottom made the minerals look like silver, and thus was born the name of his estate and the area, Silver Spring. In 1942 the park was acquired by a local citizens group, and it was restored in 1955. The Silver Spring Acorn is on Newell Road at the intersection of East-West Highway and Blair Mill Road, 1 block south of Georgia Avenue (across the street from the Canada Dry bottling plant).

Not far from the acorn is a ***Post Office Mural*** painted in 1937 by Nicolai Cikovsky (of the Towson transportation mural incident); it's called *The Old Tavern,* reflecting life in the area during and after the antebellum period. The Old Post Office Building is at 8412 Georgia Avenue, Silver Spring 20901.

Trivia

Incidentally, the area, which is not incorporated, is called Silver Spring, not "springs," as in the Florida town.

Continuing out Georgia Avenue, which parallels the railroad and subway tracks, you'll come to the intersection of Georgia and Colesville Road, and the Silver Spring subway station. A mural, 100 feet long and 8 feet high, was installed as part of the MetroArt I arts project (see also Prince

George's County). Created by Sally Callmer of Bethesda, who previously was a miniaturist, the ***Penguin Rush Hour Mural*** was meant as a temporary installation but has become such an integral part of the community that the Montgomery County Department of Transportation has purchased the twenty-five panels as a permanent fixture.

If you head north of Silver Spring, on Route 29, you'll come to Burtonsville, and there, after a day of sightseeing, you can stop by the ***Burn Brae Dinner Theatre,*** the first dinner theater in the Washington area (opened in 1968). It has continued to provide outstanding entertainment. At times it presents a full-blown production with a huge cast, such as *Joseph and the Amazing Technicolor Dreamcoat* or *Evita*, and at other times it shows small, intimate plays such as *I Do! I Do!* There may even be a preshow tabletop magician or a weekly children's magic show. With each show there is a menu change, but a typical buffet might consist of seventeen items, including salad, fish, roast beef, honey-basted Virginia ham, pasta primavera, chicken, meatballs, hot vegetables, homemade bread and muffins, and desserts.

Trivia

The **Forest Glen metro station,** *which is nearly 200 feet below ground level, is the deepest in the system and maybe in the world.*

When Burn Brae opened in an unused dressing room of a community pool in 1968, little did Bernie Levin and John Kinnamon realize they were starting a terrific tradition. At one time the Washington area was the home of the largest number of dinner theaters in the country. Because there were so many of them, they fostered a group of performers who knew they would receive excellent training as well as be seen by the many talent scouts who came through this area.

MBHS Alums

The humongous building behind the noise-barrier walls along the outer loop of the Beltway (I–495) between the Colesville Road and University Boulevard exits is Montgomery Blair High School, home to approximately 2,500 students. It has all the bells and whistles one would like in a high school that saw its first students in September 1998. Its predecessor stands at Dale Drive and Wayne Avenue near downtown Silver Spring, maybe a mile away as the crow flies. That school opened in 1935, and I was graduated from there a few years later (quite a few, thank you). Among the other students attending Blair (go Blazers!) a few years before, after, and during my time there were Goldie Hawn, Ben Stein, Carl Bernstein, Sylvester Stallone, and Steve Barber.

Burn Brae Dinner Theatre is at 15029 Blackburn Road, Burtonsville 20866; call (301) 384–5800.

Head west out of Silver Spring and longtime area residents (anyone who's been here for more than fifteen years) can tell you about the awkward, sprawling image of the ***Bethesda Triangle*** intersection of Wisconsin Avenue, Old Georgetown Road, and East-West Highway. Personally, I remember it from when we used to hang out at the Hot Shoppes restaurant on Saturday after high school football games between archrivals Montgomery Blair (go, Blazers!) and Bethesda Chevy Chase.

Known as the ***Bethesda Urban District,*** this area has more than 170 restaurants, from traditional to trendy, from down-home to deluxe. One of these is the Benihana in the Airrights Building, which is one of the oldest restaurants in the district and, when it opened in 1974, was only the sixteenth in the Benihana chain.

The presence at this intersection of the ***Pioneer Lady statue***, or Madonna of the Trail, symbolizes the importance of these roads even in their early days. Harry Truman dedicated the statue on April 19, 1949, in honor of the pioneer spirit and the National Pike, which connected the country from this spot on the East Coast to the town of Upland, California, on the West Coast. This was the twelfth of twelve statues to be installed. The other statues were erected (chronologically) in Springfield, Ohio; Wheeling, West Virginia; Council Grove, Kansas; Lexington, Missouri; Lamar, Colorado; Albuquerque, New Mexico; Springerville, Arizona; Vandalia, Illinois; Richmond, Indiana; Washington, Pennsylvania; and Upland, California. The memorial (which faces east, whereas most of the other statues face west) is dedicated to the pioneer mothers of the covered-wagon days.

The engraving reads: OVER THIS HIGHWAY MARCHED THE ARMY OF MAJOR GENERAL EDWARD BRADDOCK, APRIL 14, 1755, ON ITS WAY TO FORT DUQUESNE, AND [THIS IS] THE FIRST MILITARY ROAD IN AMERICA, BEGINNING AT ROCK CREEK AND POTOMAC RIVER, GEORGETOWN, MARYLAND, LEADING OUR PIONEERS ACROSS THE CONTINENT TO THE PACIFIC.

The Pioneer Lady statue is located between the post office and the Hyatt Regency Hotel at the corner of Wisconsin Avenue, East-West Highway, and Old Georgetown Road in Bethesda. When the statue was installed in 1986, after years in storage due to subway and hotel construction, it was the first in a collection of perhaps twenty-five commissioned works by visual artists to be installed along Bethesda's streets.

A few blocks from the Pioneer Lady statue is the ***Montgomery Farm Woman's Cooperative Market,*** which is open on Wednesday and Saturday throughout the year. This market was started during the Depression, with its first sale date set for February 4, 1932. A second sale was held on April 20, and it became so popular that they began a traditional Wednesday and Saturday selling date.

You can stop by the market and find all manner of foods—including Pennsylvania Dutch double-baked ham and baked goods—and even some rocking chairs and other craft items, particularly during the winter. My favorite stall is the Marquez Farm Stand in the back left-hand corner as you walk in from Wisconsin Avenue, where Rick and Chun II Marquez, and sometimes their daughter, sell the most delectable pies, cakes, scones, Baltimore cheese breads, quiches, tarts, muffins, all-beef summer sausage, bratwurst, German salami, nitrite-free bacon, and the list goes on.

You can reach the Marquez family at (301) 530–9098. The Montgomery Farm Woman's Market, at 7155 Wisconsin Avenue, Bethesda 20814, is open Wednesday and Saturday 7:00 A.M. to 2:00 P.M.

Another view of the market is in the ***Bethesda Post Office mural*** painted

Montgomery Farm Woman's Cooperative Market

by Robert Gates in 1939. This definitely represents a Montgomery County tradition, unlike the transportation scene painted in the Towson Post Office. The Bethesda mural was restored in 1967 with funds provided by the Montgomery Farm Woman's Cooperative Market. The post office is at 7400 Wisconsin Avenue, Bethesda 20814.

Take Old Georgetown Road west out of Bethesda, just outside the beltway, and you can stop by the ***Dennis and Phillip Ratner Museum.*** The Ratners are cousins; Phillip a multimedia artist (sculpture, painting, etched glass, tapestry, drawing, and graphic arts) and native Washingtonian; his work is in the permanent collections of the Smithsonian Institution, the U.S. Supreme Court, the Library of Congress, the White House, and many other places. Dennis is the founder and chairman of the Hair Cuttery, the nation's largest privately owned salon chain with more than 600 locations in fifteen states. His civic involvement includes raising funds for the Leukemia Society of America, the National Zoo, the Whiteman-Walker Clinic, the Institute for Advancement in Immunology and Aging, the United Jewish Appeal of Greater Washington, and other organizations.

The Ratner Museum has three buildings. The original historic house serves as a resource center with a library; conference space; computer room; guest room; chapel with an ark, Eternal Light, Menorah, and Torah; and a small kosher kitchen. A second and larger structure serves as the museum, devoted to exhibition space on two levels with a central atrium. There are also outdoor exhibition areas. The third building is Phillip Ratner's studio, a classroom, and temporary exhibition space. The collection includes examples of Phillip's sculptures, drawings, paintings, and graphics, and exhibits of the works of professional and student artists, both from various institutions and seminars in the museum. This facility is open to groups by appointment, with no admission fee charged. The Ratner Museum is located at 10001 Old Georgetown Road. Call (301) 897–1518.

Move westward and one comes to Rockville. One of the delights there, particularly if you like nature or have children who have excess energy to burn (and how many children fit into that category?), is the ***Cabin John Regional Park,*** part of the Maryland–National Capital Park and Planning Commission park system. (There's also Wheaton Regional, in Wheaton; Watkins Regional, in Kettering; and Cosca Regional, in Clinton.)

Cabin John covers more than 500 acres, with an ice skating rink (with Monday night curling, at least as of this writing), hiking trails, sports fields, indoor and outdoor tennis courts, picnic tables and pavilions, a nature center, and most important for the moment, an Action Playground. Designed by Heidi Sussman, this playground is an elaborate obstacle course covering more than a half acre of ground. There's a section for toddlers, one for preschoolers, one for older children, and places for parents to sit. Among the challenges are a 40-foot net tunnel, a 30-foot tire bridge, and a 50-foot tunnel slide. What's really nice about these parks is if you can lose your inhibitions for a few moments, you can enjoy the swings, slides, and challenges, too. Well, at least some of them. Sussman also designed the play area for Wheaton Regional Park. Cabin John is at 7400 Tuckerman Lane, Rockville 20854; (301) 299–4555.

The ***Rockville Post Office Mural*** was done by New York artist Judson Smith in 1940 and is of *Sugar Loaf Mountain.* Supposedly, it was painted from the porch of an estate called Inverness, which was built in 1818 by Benjamin White. The view includes fields and farm buildings, and the mural hangs over the wall where the lock boxes used to be located. Rockville Post Office is at 2 West Montgomery Avenue, Rockville 20850.

Northeast of Rockville is the little town with the theater that has the big reputation. The ***Olney Theatre*** opened in 1942 as a stop on the summer "straw hat" circuit, closed because of the war, and then reopened in 1946 with Helen Hayes starring in *Good Housekeeping.* Other luminaries who have graced its stage include Tallulah Bankhead, Gloria Swanson, and Bea Lillie. The late Reverend Gilbert Hartke, head of Catholic University's drama department, took over the management in 1953, providing exposure for his students as well as Carol Channing, John McGiver, and Frances Sternhagen. Bill Graham is now managing director, and James D. Waring is artistic director.

Trivia

F. Scott and Zelda Fitzgerald, once residents of the area, are buried in the St. Mary's Church cemetery in Rockville, located at the corner of Viers Mill Road and Route 355 (Rockville Pike).

Also known as the State Summer Theatre of Maryland, Olney Theatre started a new tradition in 1989 with the annual production of *The Butterfingers Angel, Mary & Joseph, Herod the Nut,* and *The Slaughter of 12 Hit Carols in a Pear Tree*, a Christmas entertainment by noted playwright William Gibson. The theater also is known for the elected officials it attracts, particularly on opening night, both to see the outstanding presentations and to be seen. The Victorian farmhouse (circa 1880) next door is the Actors' Residence, where housing is provided for the cast in season. Actually, two casts stay there at one time, one for the show in production and one for the show in rehearsal. On opening night post-performance festivities take place here.

The mailing address for Olney Theatre is P.O. Box 550, 2001 Route 108, Olney 20832; (301) 924–3400 or www.olneytheatre.org.

Northwest of Rockville is Gaithersburg, and when you tell someone you're going to ***Roy's Place,*** they think you're talking about that old cowboy movie star. But this Roy's Place is in Gaithersburg, and it is far from fast food and fast eating. In fact, the menu tells you that if you are in a hurry, go someplace else. No, it is not fine dining. It is just sandwiches and more sandwiches—some of the weirdest sandwiches you've ever imagined. How would you like a sandwich with roast beef, fried oysters, and a side serving of tartar sauce? Would you prefer provolone cheese, anchovies, blue-cheese dressing, onions, and lettuce? Or would you like something else?

The menu features more than one hundred different sandwiches, or you can start at the front page with a salad selection and skip to the back page for a simple hamburger, if you do not feel like reading the equivalent of a novella before you eat. Roy's has been open since 1971, and several local and national celebrities have had sandwiches named after them. The decor is just as interesting and offbeat as the menu, with posters, old advertisements, and a sign by the skylight that says THIS WAY OUT.

Roy's Place is at 2 East Diamond Avenue, Gaithersburg (301–948–5548). Hours are Monday through Thursday 11:00 A.M. to 11:00 P.M., Friday and Saturday 11:00 A.M. to midnight, and Sunday noon to 11:00 P.M. Reservations are not accepted.

Speaking of the White family, ***White's Ferry,*** well west of the Beltway, is the only remaining ferry system on the Potomac River, connecting White's Ferry, Maryland, to Leesburg, Virginia. It probably is more important these days than when it began operation in 1828, for it is the only river crossing between the American Legion Bridge on the Washington (or Capital) Beltway to the south and east, and the Point of Rocks bridge to the north and west. Regular commuters and tourists can easily tell when there is a major backup on the Beltway because these back-country roads become filled with drivers escaping the jam. The ferry *General Jubal Early* (named for a Confederate leader) runs the 1,000-foot crossing on a cable propelled by a diesel tug in about three minutes. It can hold fifteen cars and operates all year, weather and river conditions permitting, on a demand basis. A country store selling sundries and souvenirs is open on the Maryland side from spring through fall. The ferry is off Route 107. Call (301) 394–5200 for information.

Just up the ramp from White's Ferry landing is the ditch that was once the ***Chesapeake & Ohio Canal*** and is now the longest and thinnest National Historical Park in the country, narrowing to less than 50 feet at one point. There was a time when there were twenty trading posts along the 185-mile canal, which ran from Cumberland to Washington, D.C., roughly paralleling the Potomac River. In 1988 conservationists spent three months clearing away foliage and found the 150-foot foundation of a nineteenth-century depot and granary. From the Civil War until 1924, canal boats headed down to Washington, D.C., where they would tie up to a three-story wooden storage building called the Granary to load up with grain from area farms. In the sixty years since the canal closed, the Granary and canal have been neglected and overgrown by trees and shrubbery.

For additional tourism information, write to the Visitors Center Manager, Conference and Visitors Bureau of Montgomery County, MD Inc., 12900 Middlebrook Road, Suite 1400, Germantown 20874, or call (301) 428–9702 or (800) 925–0880.

Frederick County

Abutting the northwest border of Montgomery County and going north to the Pennsylvania state line, with the Potomac River on its southern border, Frederick County is renowned in certain circles for the antiques shops in New Market and the city of Frederick. Steeped in history, the county also is hope to the restored train depot and museum at Brunswick; the Barbara Fritchie and Roger B. Taney homes; wineries and orchards; the Catoctin Mountains (where Camp David, the presidential retreat, is located); the Grotto of Lourdes and the St. Elizabeth Ann Seton Shrine; the Lily Pons Water Gardens; Gov. Thomas Johnson's Rose Hill Manor and Schifferstadt; many churches and steeples; and, of course, that picturesque stopping point, Sugar Loaf Mountain.

A word about ***churches in Frederick***. There are ten of note and one synagogue, and their histories and architectural styles date from the colonial, revolutionary, and Civil War eras. Tours are available during the year, and a brochure is available from the Frederick Tourism Council that details the history of each house of worship. A special time for all the houses of worship is the Candlelight Tour held in December, when each is decorated for the holiday and hosts are on hand to greet visitors and answer questions. Special music and presentations are provided at various churches throughout the evening, and free parking is available. Hospitality rooms are located at a number of places, and the one at Trunk Hall in the Evangelical Lutheran Church is handicapped accessible.

Many prominent Marylanders now reside in ***Mount Olivet Cemetery***, including Francis Scott Key, Barbara Fritchie, and Gov. Thomas Johnson, along with veterans of the American Revolution, the Civil War (more than 800 Confederate soldiers), and World War II, as well as more than 25,000 other people. A statue of Key stands over 9 feet tall on a monument that is 16 feet high and 45 feet around; you can't miss the statue because it welcomes you at the main entrance. The United States flag standing by him flies twenty-four hours a day in honor of his writing the words to "The Star-Spangled Banner." Much of the money collected for the $25,000 monument was donated in dimes and dollars by people all over the country.

Little green-and-white signs direct you to the graves of Governor Johnson and Barbara Fritchie, who are across the road from each other. Johnson was a Revolutionary War patriot, born in Frederick County in 1732 (the same year as George Washington), and was a prominent member of the Continental Congress. He was the first governor of the state of Maryland and associate justice of the United States Supreme Court. Fritchie was made immortal by John Greenleaf Whittier's poem about her bravery against Gen. Stonewall Jackson, when she flew the Union flag and dared soldiers to "Shoot if you must, this old gray head, but spare your country's flag." A monument of Maryland granite with the Whittier poem on a bronze tablet was unveiled on September 9, 1914. The cemetery is considered one of the most beautiful and distinguished in this part of the country. The address is Mount Olivet Cemetery, South Broadway, Frederick 21701.

The ***Frederick News Post*** offers day and night tours through the newspaper office for adults and children as young as four or five. The tour lasts about forty-five minutes and goes through the editorial, advertising, circulation, and press rooms, and it provides an explanation about how a paper is written and printed. At night Ed Waters gives the tours; during the day it is Mike Powell and Karen James who do the honors. They like to have about two weeks' notice before tours and prefer no more than twenty to a group.

You might think that the building does not seem to connect properly in the middle, and you would be right. Stand back from the front facade and notice that the front door has been filled in; this used to be a trolley barn, and the trolleys would go through the middle of the buildings on either side of this central portion. You can tell from the way the floor goes up and down with almost no rhyme or reason that it was put together after the fact. Sorry, but the trolley tracks have been removed.

For tour reservations or information, contact the *Frederick News Post*, 200 East Patrick Street, Frederick 21701, (301–662–1177).

Between Frederick and Thurmont is the old ***Catoctin Furnace***. For 125 years this was a prosperous iron-making community. Started by a group of men that included the future first governor of Maryland, Thomas Johnson, the stack went into blast in 1776 to produce pig iron, tools, and household items, including the popular ten-plate stove. Bombshells for 10-inch mortars were produced toward the end of the Revolutionary War. By the mid-eighteenth century, the owner of the furnace had eighty houses for his workers, a sawmill, gristmill, company store, farms, ore railroad, three furnace stacks (including an anthracite coal stack), and more than 11,000 acres of land. By 1903 the furnace ceased to operate, although ore was taken out of this area until 1912.

What is left on the northern side of this "company town" is the furnace and an early nineteenth-century double log house, which is preserved by the Catoctin Furnace Historical Society and used as a museum and interpretive center. For additional information write to the Catoctin Furnace Historical Society, Thurmont 21788, or call Cunningham Falls State Park, (301) 271–7574. The furnace, remaining houses in Catoctin Village, and Harriet Chapel can be seen along Route 806, on the east side of Route 15, about 12 miles north of Frederick.

There's just enough winter in Frederick County that covered bridges were desirable to assure safe passage over waterways. Bridges otherwise would have become frozen, slick, and impassible.

There are three covered bridges in Frederick County. The first is ***Loy's Station***. This 90-foot-long bridge, built in 1850, crosses Owens Creek and is surrounded by a five-and-a-half-acre park. It's located on Old Frederick Road, off Route 77, about 3 miles from Thurmont.

Roddy Road Covered Bridge (1856), near Thurmont, is considered the best looking of the state's remaining bridges by covered-bridge fans. It is a single span, about 40 feet long, with a 13⅔-foot roadway. It is a fine example of basic king-post truss design, though steel stringers were installed later. Surrounding the bridge, which crosses Owens Creek, is a seventy-acre natural area for picnicking and gentle afternoon outings.

The ***Utica Covered Bridge***, at 101 feet, is the largest of the three. Built in 1850, it was moved in 1889 and has been structurally reinforced with concrete piers and steel-beam supports. The bridge crossed the Monocacy River until a summer flood in 1889 lifted the span from its abutments and placed it down on the river several yards away. Instead of replacing the still-intact bridge on its supports, it was dismantled, moved, and reassembled over Fishing Creek at Utica Mills. The bridge is located on Utica Road off Old Frederick Road, which is off Route 15.

Fertile ground attracted many settlers, and you can still see and enjoy the fruits of many hard workers at a number of orchards.

Catoctin Mountain Orchard is known for its diversity and quality of all types of berries, soft fruits, apples, and vegetables. Cortland, Red and Golden Delicious, Stayman, York, and Ida Red apples are available in autumn. On weekends, however, the supply is not always sufficient for the demand; they suggest you call early in the day to reserve your fruit. You can pick your own blackberries, black raspberries, sour and sweet cherries, and strawberries, but call ahead for picking days and hours. Catoctin Mountain Orchard also offers preserved fruit and jam, packed in appealing, reusable containers.

The orchard is open daily July l through January, and Friday, Saturday, and Sunday from January through April. It is closed May 1 through mid-July. The orchard is on Route 15, North Franklinville Road, and the mailing address is 15307 Kelbaugh Road, Thurmont 21788. Call (301) 271–2737.

Bell Hill Farm Market and Orchard is a hundred-acre farm, and the family-run fruit stand sits by a pre–Civil War home and stone springhouse. The McKissick family orchard features the traditional Red and

Right Off the Vine, Branch, or Bush

You can buy fresh fruits and vegetables or pick your own at some sixty or seventy farms and orchards in fourteen counties across the state, from Anne Arundel to Washington. Write to Marketing Resource and Development Group, Maryland Department of Agriculture, Annapolis 21401, for a copy of the current Pick Your Own and Direct Farm Markets in Maryland *brochure. Or stop by a library or county extension office to pick up a copy.*

Yellow Delicious and Stayman apples, as well as some older varieties, including Grimes Golden, York, Jonathan, and Winesap. In season you can buy peaches, plums, pears, nectarines, watermelons, cantaloupes, raspberries, corn, beans, cucumbers, potatoes, and other produce.

Bell Hill Farm is 1½ miles north of Thurmont on Route 15 and is open daily from 9:00 A.M. to 5:00 P.M. Call (301) 271–7264.

Trivia

Thurmont originally was called Mechanicstown because Jacob Weller, a mechanic of German descent, settled here with his family in 1751.

Pryor's Orchard has a modern storage facility housed in a rustic barn-type market, complete with racks of antlers and an antique cider press. Pryor's seventy-three-acre orchard is one of the oldest in the Thurmont area and a favorite of local canning enthusiasts. Pryor's is noted for its many varieties of peaches, summer and fall apples, and pears. You can pick your own blueberries and sour and sweet cherries.

The orchard is closed in the winter. It is ½ mile west of Thurmont on Pryor's Road (take a left off Route 77). Call (301) 271–2693.

Scenic View Orchard has a fine selection of produce, including peaches, plums, nectarines, pears, apples (and cider), melons, sweet corn, green beans, and other vegetables. It is open daily 10:00 A.M. to 6:00 P.M. July 15 through November 1.

It's located 5 miles north of Thurmont on Route 550 at 16239 Sabillasville Road, Sabillasville 21780; (301) 271–2149.

Thurmont is not only the gateway to the mountains but also the gateway to ***Camp David,*** which was originally called High Catoctin and was one of three camps built by the Civilian Conservation Corps during the Depression. The other two camps, still in existence, are Misty Mount, used for group camping, and Greentop, used by the Baltimore League of the Handicapped since 1937. The camp buildings were constructed from local timber. High Catoctin was renamed Shangri La by Franklin Delano Roosevelt and then renamed Camp David by Dwight D. Eisenhower. You cannot visit Camp David, but you may be able to drive by Misty Mount or Greentop to see the basic architectural style of Camp David before its presidential changes occurred.

There are numerous campgrounds where you can spend a night or two, and Frederick is close enough to Washington and Baltimore to be used as a base, if you wish. One of the better-known private campgrounds is ***Crow's Nest Lodge Campground,*** owned and operated by Ned and Renna Haynes. It has 110 campsites located along Big Hunting Creek, a mountain trout stream that flows through the Catoctin Mountains. Each spacious campsite is designed to accommodate a large tent, tent trailer, or travel trailer. Most of the sites are shaded, and many have water and electricity. At the campground you can enjoy a spring-fed, freshwater pond for swimming and wading; 10 miles of scenic foot trails that wind through the Catoctin Mountain Park; fishing; nature study; and a half-dozen action sports. Pets are welcome, as long as they are on a leash at all times.

The address is Crow's Nest Lodge Campground, P.O. Box 145, Thurmont 21788. Call (301) 271–7632.

Old Mink Farm campground offers summer and winter escapes. You can rent a log cabin with fireplace, with either one or two bedrooms and equipped kitchens, or log cabinettes with kitchenettes, or stay in the Coffee Hollow Lodge for extended family or management retreats. Reservations are required. Call (301) 271–7012 for additional information.

For additional tourism information, write to the Executive Director, Tourism Council of Frederick County, 19 East Church Street, Frederick 21701, or call (301) 663–8687 or (800) 999–3613.

PLACES TO EAT IN GREATER WASHINGTON

BETHESDA
There are more than 140 restaurants in and around the Bethesda Triangle (at the intersection of Old Georgetown Road, Wisconsin Avenue, and East-West Highway), catering to just about every taste you can imagine. Because of this competition, it's easy to find an excellent place to eat within your budget, from inexpensive to extremely pricey. Here are a few suggestions:

Bean Bag,
10400 Old Georgetown Road,
(301) 530–8090

Benihana,
7315 Wisconsin Avenue,
(301) 652–5391

O'Donnells,
8301 Wisconsin Avenue,
(301) 656–6200

Tastee Diner of Bethesda,
7731 Woodmont Avenue,
(301) 652–3970

Uncle Jed's,
7525 Old Georgetown Road,
(301) 913–0026

BURTONSVILLE
Burn Brae Dinner Theatre,
15029 Blackburn Road,
(301) 384–5800

CLINTON
Wayfarer Restaurant,
7401 Surratts Road,
(301) 856–3343

COLLEGE PARK
94th Aero Squadron,
5240 Paint Branch Parkway,
(301) 699–9400

COMUS
Comus Inn Restaurant,
23900 Old Hundred Road,
(301) 428–8593

EMMITSBURG
Carriage House Inn,
200 North Seton Avenue,
(301) 447–2366 or www.amerimall.com/carriagehouseinn

FREDERICK
Di Francesco's,
26 North Market Street,
(301) 695–5499

Red Horse Restaurant,
996 West Patrick Street,
(301) 663–3030

GAITHERSBURG
Roy's Place,
2 East Diamond Avenue,
(301) 948–5548

LARGO
BET Soundstage,
9640 Lottsford Court,
(301) 883–9500

LAUREL
Bay 'n Surf,
14411 Baltimore Avenue,
(301) 776–7021

POTOMAC
Old Anglers Inn,
10801 MacArthur Boulevard,
(301) 365–2425

SUITLAND
LiLeons,
3674 St. Barnabas Road,
(301) 899–8233

THURMONT
Cozy Country Inn Restaurant and Village,
103 Frederick Road,
(301) 271–7373

PLACES TO STAY IN GREATER WASHINGTON

Most all hotels and motels in the Greater Washington area belong to the major hotel chains, including Best Western, Days Inn, Doubletree, Econo Lodge, Holiday Inn, Marriott, Ramada Inn, Red Roof Inn, and Susse Chalet Inn. If, for some strange reason, you're bypassing all the wonderful things you can do and see in Maryland and you're headed toward the attractions of Washington, you'll probably be staying in Prince George's or Montgomery Counties, and you'll want one that's either on or near a subway line, or that provides shuttle service to a subway.

Amanda's B&B Reservation Service, (800) 899–7533, (410) 225–0001, www.amandas-bbrs.com, or AmandasRS.aol.com (e-mail)

BETHESDA
American Inn of Bethesda,
8130 Wisconsin Avenue,
(301) 656–9300,
(800) 323–7081, or
www.american-inn.com

Bethesda Court Hotel,
7740 Wisconsin Avenue,
(301) 656–2100 or
(800) 874–0050

Hyatt Regency Bethesda,
Wisconsin Avenue and Old Georgetown Road,
(301) 657–1234

FREDERICK
Holiday Inn
(Francis Scott Key Mall),
5400 Holiday Drive,
(301) 694–7500 or
(800) HOLIDAY

LARGO
Club Hotel by Doubletree,
9100 Basil Court,
(301) 773–0700 or
(800) 444–CLUB

NEW CARROLLTON
Ramada Conference and Exhibition Center,
8500 Annapolis Road,
(301) 459–6700 or
(800) 436–0614

ROCKVILLE
Park Inn International,
11410 Rockville Pike,
(301) 881–5200 or
(800) 752–3800

Sleep Inn,
2 Research Court,
(301) 948–7406

THURMONT
Cozy Country Inn Restaurant and Village,
103 Frederick Road,
(301) 271–4301

OTHER ATTRACTIONS WORTH SEEING IN GREATER WASHINGTON

Airmen Memorial Museum, Suitland;
(301) 899–8386

Andrews Air Force Base, Camp Springs;
(301) 981–4424

Antique Carousel, Watkins Regional Park, Kettering;
(301) 390–9224

Baker Park, Frederick;
(301) 694–1440

Barbara Fritchie House and Museum, Frederick;
(301) 698–0630

Beal-Dawson House, Rockville; (301) 762–1492

Belair Mansion and Stable Museums, Bowie; (301) 262–6200 or www.cityofbowie.org/parks.html

Bowie Railroad Station and Huntington Museum, Bowie; (301) 809–3088

Brookside Gardens, Wheaton Regional Park, Wheaton; (301) 949–8230

Brunswick Railroad Museum, Brunswick; (301) 834–7100

C&O Canal National Historic Park, Potomac; (301) 299–3613 or www.fred. net/kathy/canal. html

Catoctin Wildlife Preserve, Thurmont; (301) 271–4922 or (301) 271–3180

Clara Barton National Historic Site, Glen Echo; (301) 492–6245 or www.nps.gov/clba/

Darnall's Chance, Upper Marlboro; (301) 952–8010

George Meany Memorial Archives, Silver Spring; (301) 431–5451

Glen Echo Park, Glen Echo, (301) 492–6282 or www. nps.gov/glec/

His Lordship's Kindness, Clinton; (301) 856–0358

Huntington Railroad Museum, Bowie; (301) 805–4616 or (301) 262–6200

John Poole House, Poolesville; (301) 972–8588

Jug Bridge Monument, Frederick

Laurel Museum, Laurel; (301) 725–0400

Lilypons Water Gardens, Buckeystown; (301) 874–5133

Marietta, Glenn Dale; (301) 464–5291

McCrillis Garden and Gallery, Bethesda; (301) 949–8230

Merkle Wildlife Sanctuary/Visitors Center, Upper Marlboro; (301) 888–1410

Monocacy Battlefield, Frederick; (301) 662–3515 or www.nps.gov/mono/

Mormon Temple Visitors Center, Kensington; (301) 587–0144

NASA/Goddard Visitors Center and Museum, Greenbelt; (301) 286–8981

National Colonial Farm, Accokeek; (301) 283–2113

National Museum of Civil War Medicine, Frederick; (301) 695–1864

National Shrine Grotto of Lourdes, Emmitsburg; (301) 447–5318

National Shrine–St. Elizabeth Ann Seton, Emmitsburg; (301) 447–6606

Olde Bowie Antiques Row, Bowie; (301) 464–1122

Oxon Hill Manor, Oxon Hill; (301) 839–7782

Paul E. Garber Facility, Suitland; (202) 357–1400 or (202) 357–1505 (TDD)

Prince Georges County Trap and Skeet Center, Glenn Dale; (301) 577–7178

R. Brooke Taney and F. Scott Key Museum, Frederick; (301) 663–8687

Riversdale (Calvert Mansion), Riverdale; (301) 864–0420 or (301) 864–3521

Rose Hill Manor Museum, Frederick; (301) 694–1648

Schifferstadt (c. 1756), Frederick; (301) 663–6225

Seneca Schoolhouse Museum, Poolesville; (301) 972–7298

Six Flags (formerly Adventure World), Largo; (301) 249–1500

Stonestreet Medical Museum, Rockville; (301) 762–1492

Strathmore Hall Arts Center, North Bethesda; (301) 530–0540

Sugarloaf's Mountain Works, Gaithersburg; (301) 990–1400

(Mary) Surratt House Museum, Clinton; (301) 868–1121, www.glue.umd.edu/~clwspoon/surratt. html

War Correspondents Memorial, Burkittsville; (301) 791–4767

Calendar of Annual Events in Greater Washington

January
Winter/Spring Display "Spring has Sprung," Wheaton; (301) 949–8230

February
East Coast Jazz Festival, Bethesda and Rockville; (301) 933–1822

March
Fruhlings Fest, Frederick; (301) 663–8687

Hearthside Sampler, Frederick; (301) 663–8687

Maple Syrup Demonstration and Mountain Heritage Festival, Thurmont; (301) 271–7574

April
Farm and Family Festival, Frederick; (301) 694–1650

John Wilkes Booth Escape-Route Tour, Clinton; (301) 868–1121

Marching Through Time, Glenn Dale; (301) 464–5291

Maryland Archaeology Month, statewide; (410) 514–7661

Surratt Open House, Clinton; (301) 868–1121

May
Andrews Air Force Base Open House, Camp Springs; (301) 568–5995

Bowie Heritage Day, Bowie; (301) 805–5029

Grand Exposition, Frederick; (301) 694–1100

Landon Azalea Garden Festival, Bethesda; (301) 320–3200

Laurel Main Street Festival, Laurel (301) 483–0838

Marlboro Day Festival, Upper Marlboro; (301) 627–2828

Montpelier Spring Festival, Laurel; (301) 776–2805

Rose Hill Days Festival, Frederick; (301) 694–1648

Sculpture Show, Wheaton; (301) 949–8230

Spring Festival, Derwood; (301) 924–4141

Springfest, Brandywine; (410) 535–0312

Summer Display, Wheaton; (301) 949–8230

Taste of Wheaton, Wheaton; (301) 217–8122

June
American Indian Inter-Tribal Pow Wow, Frederick; (301) 869–9381

Bowiefest, Bowie; (301) 262–6200, ext. 3068

Frederick Festival of the Arts, Frederick; (301) 694–9632 or www.frederickarts.org

Garlic Festival, Gaithersburg; (301) 417–6698 or www.garliclovers.com

Sandy Spring Museum Strawberry Festival, Brookeville; (301) 774–0022

Strawberry Festival, Thurmont; (301) 271–7373

July
Bowie Fourth of July Celebration, Bowie; (301) 262–6200, ext. 3068

Frederick's Fourth of July, Frederick; (800) 999–3613 or (301) 694–2489

Rockville Independence Day Celebration, Rockville; (301) 309–3330

August
Balloon Fest, Frederick; (301) 694–1100

Butler's Orchard Peach Festival, Germantown; (301) 972–3299

Montgomery County Agricultural Fair, Gaithersburg; (301) 926–3100

Peach Festival, Thurmont; (301) 271–7373

Wings of Fancy Butterfly Show, Wheaton; (301) 949–8230

September
Brunswick Railroad Days, Frederick; (301) 834–7100

Catoctin Colorfest, Thurmont; (301) 271–4432

Fall Festival, Frederick; (301) 694–1650

Germantown Oktoberfest, Germantown; (301) 217–6798

Grand Parade, Frederick; (301) 694–1100

Great Frederick Fair, Frederick; (301) 663–5895

Greeting of the Geese, Upper Marlboro; (301) 888–1410

Harvest Festival, Derwood; (301) 924–4141

In the Street, Frederick; (800) 999–3613 or (301) 694–2489

John Wilkes Booth Escape-Route Tour, Clinton; (301) 868–1121

Olde Towne Gaithersburg Day, Gaithersburg; (301) 258–6310

Pumpkin Festival, Germantown; (301) 972–3299

Riverfest, Laurel; (301) 483–0838

Taste of Bethesda, Bethesda; (301) 961–1112

October
German Fest, Thurmont; (301) 271–7373

Hastings Fair, Glenn Dale; (301) 464–5291

Oktoberfest at Schifferstadt, Frederick; (301) 663–3885

Trolley Museum Fall Open House, Wheaton; (301) 384–6088

Victorian Mums Show Fall Display, Wheaton; (301) 949–8230

December
Festival of Lights, Kensington; (301) 587–0144

Garden of Lights, Wheaton; (301) 949–8230

Surratt Open House, Clinton; (301) 868–1121

Winter Lights, Gaithersburg; (301) 258–6310

Southern Maryland

Although civilization (or at least suburban sprawl) has entered southern Maryland, parts of Charles, Calvert (pronounced "Cawlvert" or "Calvit" by the locals), and St. Mary's Counties, they probably have changed more because of avulsion and accretion than because of developmental encroachment since the first English colonists settled here in the mid-1600s.

As you drive down these roads, you will see signs of early settlements when brave men and women came seeking new lives, religious freedom, and adventure. Dozens of churches, some dating from the early eighteenth century, dot the historic landscape.

Water has made its influence felt, of course; there are many waterside communities, places to buy and eat fresh seafood, and aquatic research centers. In southern Maryland I looked for markets that keep a community alive, and I found several community craft centers and talented artisans. I hope you will take the time to enjoy the maritime influence and the fine and unusual dining surrounding, or perhaps surrounded by, this rich coastal area.

Quick Trips

A few years ago Fran Severn handled public and press relations for Maryland Tourism, and her duties included escorting visiting media around the state. She's still escorting people and introducing them to the wonders of this area, but now it is through her company, Quick Trip Tours. The company offers day-long and overnight trips to a figuratively undiscovered southern Maryland. Cruise aboard a skipjack, Maryland's state boat; a visit to historic Sotterley Plantation; a session of ghost stories that haunt Point Lookout State Park; a feast on a fist-sized crab cake at a waterfront restaurant; and a history lesson about the region's settlers by touring their churches. All tours are accompanied by a professional step-on guide. Quick Trips Tour, (410) 836–0297, (410) 836–7409 (fax), or Quicktrips@aol.com (e-mail).

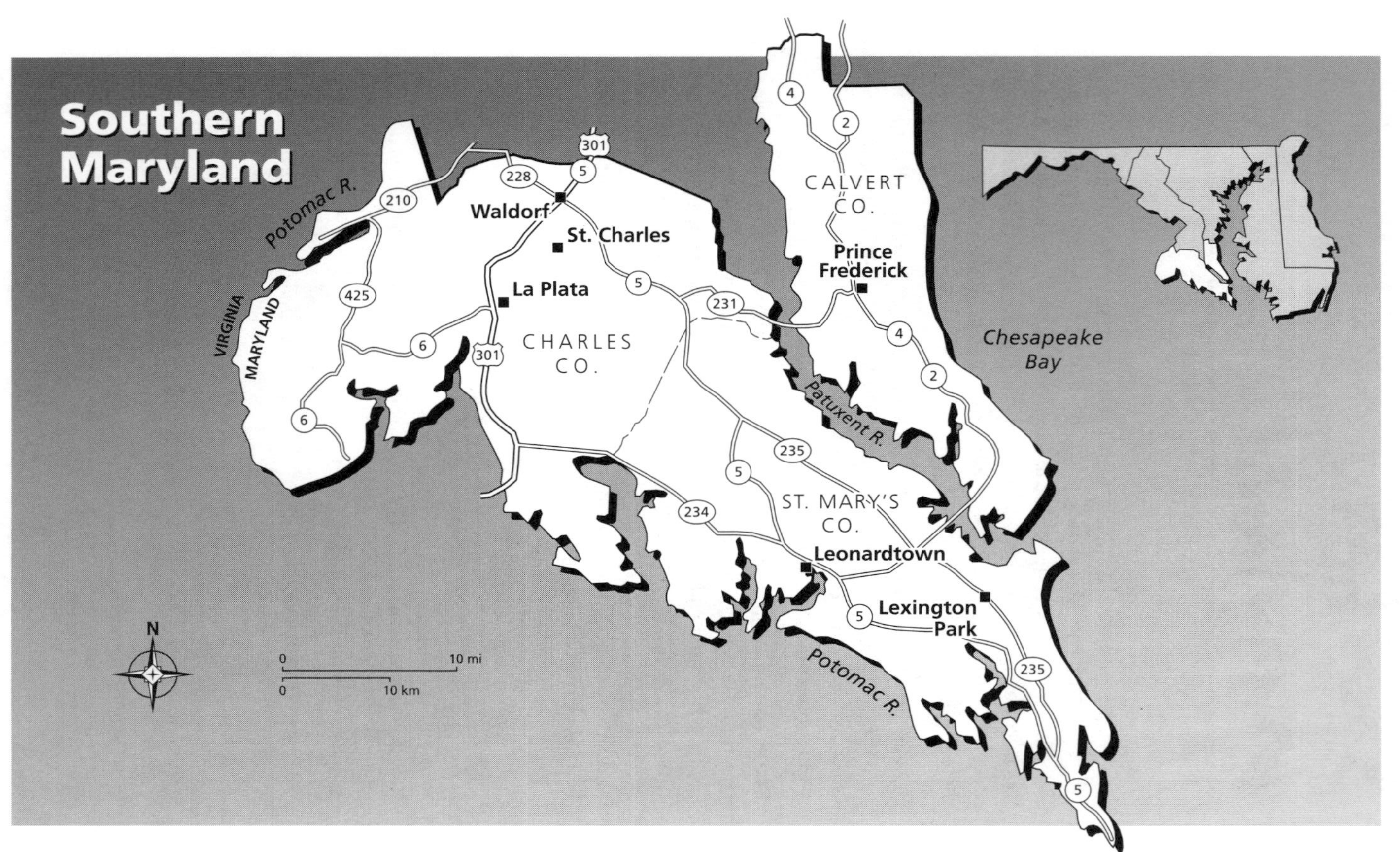
Southern Maryland
Potomac R.
VIRGINIA
MARYLAND
Waldorf
St. Charles
La Plata
CHARLES CO.
CALVERT CO.
Prince Frederick
Chesapeake Bay
Patuxent R.
ST. MARY'S CO.
Leonardtown
Lexington Park
Potomac R.
N
0
10 mi
0
10 km
301
5
228
210
425
6
6
301
5
231
4
2
4
2
235
5
234
5
235
5

Judy's Favorite Attractions in Southern Maryland

Battle Creek Cypress Swamp Sanctuary

Calvert Marine Museum

Flag Ponds Nature Park

Historic St. Mary's City

Calvert County

If you like country crafts, you'll find them in Calvert County; for this is country.

Nearly two dozen local crafters show their work at the ***Country Peddler*** of Calvert County, a showcase for local talent including Janet Richardson, whose "Paws for Thought" collection includes stuffed animals; Nan Reid's crochet and knit items; Mary Rasmussen's counted cross-stitch needlework and silhouettes; Owen Myers' canvas bags; Margaret Clark Smith's ceramics; Madie Winike's stained-glass pieces; and Virgie Finley's needlepoint.

Also sold here are potpourri, homegrown loofahs, and handmade brooms from the Calvert Homestead. The Country Peddler is behind Bowens Grocery, where you can buy hand-cut meats, and across the street from the Bowens Garage Antique Center.

The shop is open 10:00 A.M. to 5:00 P.M. Thursday, Friday, and Saturday; it is located parallel to Routes 2–4, on Old Town Road, Route 524, Huntingtown 20639. Call (410) 257–3105.

Works from nationally recognized crafters can be found at ***The Wright Touch,*** owned and operated by sisters Sue Hill and Eve Wright. Tom Clark Woodspirits may be the biggest-selling items here, and Clark even stops by to talk with his fans. You can find handcrafted gifts, handwoven throws, country pine furniture, collectibles, decorating accessories, Christmas decorations, and Christmas curtains.

The Wright Touch is at 3150 Solomons Island Road, Route 4 southbound (turn at Gardner's Citgo station), Huntingtown 20639. Call (410) 535–5588. The shop is open Tuesday through Thursday 11:00 A.M. to 6:00 P.M., Friday and Saturday 10:00 A.M. to 6:00 P.M., and Sunday noon to 5:00 P.M. Inquire about winter holiday hours and the Christmas antiques festival.

While in the neighborhood you can visit Barbara Burnett at her small ***Calvert Homestead*** barn, the "Home of the R&B Brand," which was featured on one of the home shopping networks, furthering her renown. Travel south on Route 2-4 to Sixes Road (Route 506) and drive in about 3 miles. It will be on your right at 4555 Sixes Road, Prince Frederick. Call (410) 535–3786 for hours and information.

If you want to hobnob and brush shoulders with the movers and shakers of Calvert County, you probably should find your way to

Stoney's Seafood House at the Fox Run Shopping Center in Prince Frederick. Then, sit down for a crab cake or oyster sandwich (you might hear that pronounced "arester," but no matter how you say it, they'll understand you). There's room for 225 people in three areas, including an infamous, somewhat private back room used frequently for deal-making. This is the second restaurant former custom-home builder Phillip Stone has opened; the first is a smaller seasonal variety located on Broomes Island. For more information and opening dates of the Broomes Island restaurant, call (410) 535–1888.

On the way there, you will pass the ***Battle Creek Cypress Swamp Sanctuary***. This is one of the northernmost stands of bald cypress trees in the country, and the only one on Maryland's western shore. Forget the images of cypress tress and the Old South, for there is neither Spanish moss hanging from these boughs nor Southern belles in hoop skirts. The cypress in this swamp are thought to be descendants of trees growing here some 5,000 to 15,000 years ago, shortly (relatively speaking) after the glaciers started receding. Some of the trees reach more than 100 feet in height and are 4 feet in diameter.

Within this one-hundred-acre nature sanctuary is an interpretive center and a great place for nature photography in the spring (when violets, May-apples, and pink lady's slipper orchids are in bloom) and early summer when the blooms are most profuse. Bring fast film and a tripod, because the light is heavily filtered through the canopy. With its rich wetlands, look for such species as sweet gum, ash, southern arrowwood, and spicebush. You'll also see tulip tree, mountain laurel, and Virginia pine.

Just take the 1,700-foot boardwalk through the swamp to get real close to nature. However, you don't want to get too close to some of it. Those thick, fuzzy vines climbing the trees along the boardwalk through the swamp are poison ivy, and they are just as dangerous as their cousin with the three shiny leaves if you are allergic to it.

The sanctuary, the first Nature Conservancy preserve in Maryland, is on Grays Road off Sixes Road (Route 506). Call (410) 535–5327. It's open Tuesday through Saturday from 10:00 A.M. to 5:00 P.M. and Sunday from 1:00 to 5:00 P.M. April through September. It closes at 4:30 P.M. the rest of the year. It is closed on Monday, Thanksgiving, Christmas, and New Year's Day.

Contained within the 327-acre park known as ***Flag Ponds Nature Park*** are wooded uplands, ponds, swamps, freshwater marshes, sandy beaches, and part of Chesapeake Bay. Here you can clearly see the difference between the uplands and the wetlands, between the Cliffs of Calvert and Chesapeake Bay. Wildlife abounds, including fox, muskrat, otter, turkey, whitetail deer, and pileated woodpecker. Special facilities include 3 miles of gentle hiking trails, rare plants such as the blue flag iris (from which the park derives its name), pond observation decks, picnic sites, a beach, a fishing pier, and a visitors center with wildlife exhibits.

One building remains from what was once a thriving "pound net" fishery that supplied trout, croaker, and herring to the bustling Baltimore markets during the first half of this century. From April 1 through October 1 there is a daily vehicle charge of $4.00 for residents and $6.00 for nonresidents, or a seasonal pass for $15.00 and $20.00, respectively. From November through March the charge is $3.00 for both residents and nonresidents.

Flag Ponds is open from 9:00 A.M. to 6:00 P.M. daily and 9:00 A.M. to 8:00 P.M. on weekends during the summer. From Labor Day through Memorial Day the park is open from 9:00 A.M. to 6:00 P.M. on weekends and closed during the week. Call (410) 586–1477 for additional information.

For more information write to Calvert County Department of Economic Development and Tourism, Courthouse, Prince Frederick 20678, or call (800) 331–9771, (410) 535–4583, or (410) 535–6355 (TDD). You can also contact them at their Internet address at www.co.cal.md.us.

There are places called Hollywood and California in Maryland (both in St. Mary's County), and major motion pictures have been made in the state, but nothing equals ***Vera's White Sands*** restaurant. A summer pastime that should not be missed, Vera Freeman's restaurant is decorated with souvenirs from her worldwide travels. Imagine you are Lauren Bacall, Humphrey Bogart, or Peter Lorre, or even Bob Hope, Bing Crosby, or Hedy Lamarr on the road to someplace; you would feel right at home here. What are your decorative tastes? Would you like banana trees framing the flamingo-pink structure? How do you like beaded room dividers, carved elephants inlaid with ivory, giant clamshells, and leopard-skin bar stools to provide the atmosphere? Steam up the scene with a little romantic intrigue, and you do not have to travel far to find the wondrous.

Vera's seafood specialty (bouillabaisse with shrimp, scallops, filet of fish, crab, clams, and mussels) is served in a tomato-and-wine sauce. My personal favorite is Mary's crab cakes, light and gently broiled (you may have them fried), and pure lump meat. Mary's been there for forty years and, as Vera says, is the keeper of the keys. In June, July, and

August, you may have your cocktails poolside. About 6:30 P.M. on Friday, Saturday, and Sunday evenings, you'll be diverted by live entertainment, and around 7:30 P.M. the J. Arthur Rank–style gong (from Hong Kong) will be sounded as Vera makes her entrance. Vera's is a place you will long remember.

The sunset view from the appropriately described picture windows and the piano overlooks historic John's Creek, off the Patuxent River. The creek is wide, and the channel depth is 14 feet. The marina has docking facilities for eighty-four boats (water depth at dock is 12 feet), and a dockmaster is on the premises twenty-four hours a day, year-round. (410) 586–1182.

Trivia

"Pepper" Langley is one of the prime treasures at the Calvert Marine Museum. Although he no longer spends a lot of time there on a daily basis, you can see him once in a while working on a model boat (or see his son, which is almost as good). "Pepper" received his name a very long time ago because of the fastball he used to pitch.

Vera's White Sands is in Lusby on White Sands Drive. The restaurant is open from May 1 through Columbus Day, Tuesday through Saturday 5:00 to 9:00 P.M. and Sunday 1:00 to 9:00 P.M. Reservations are suggested.

Continuing south or southeast on Route 2-4, you will come to Solomons, which has a visitors center that is open from spring through late fall. Across the street is the ***Calvert Marine Museum*** and ***Drum Point Lighthouse***, and parking is behind the administration building.

The Calvert Marine Museum is proof that a museum can be fun, fascinating, and fact filled. This museum has grown from a seed planted by LeRoy "Pepper" Langley in 1970, and it is certainly worth a visit for a number of reasons. The first reason is the Children's Discovery Room, where there is a pile of earth with fossils from Calvert Cliffs that you can dig in. It can be difficult and time-consuming to search for fossils at outdoor sites, but not here. One shark's tooth per person, please. This room is more fun than a bushel of crabs that has just been dusted with seasoning.

Yet there is more, and you are on your own to enjoy, to be entertained, and to be educated. Even the more conventional exhibits about boating, the paleontology of Calvert Cliffs, and the estuarine biology of the Patuxent River and Chesapeake Bay are well handled.

The museum's second treasure is the Drum Point Lighthouse, one of the old screw-pile, cottage-style lighthouses that used to protect the adventuresome watermen of the bay. The two-story, hexagon-shaped structure was built in 1883 to mark the entrance of the Patuxent River from the Chesapeake Bay. A crane and barge moved the stilted cottage to its current location in 1975.

Take a few minutes to walk through the lighthouse (watch your head when going up and down the steps) and mentally transport yourself to the time when people lived here and tended the light. It is romantic to think of the "good old days" when there were lightkeepers, but most don't think this remote lifestyle is very attractive these days.

The third treasure is an old bugeye, the *William B. Tennison,* which takes people on cruises around the bay. This bugeye is a Chesapeake Bay sailing craft built in 1888 at Crabb Island by B. P. and R. L. Miles. Her hull is "chunk built," or made of nine logs, rather than by a plank-and-frame method of construction. Originally rigged for sailing, she was converted to power in 1907, and a new, larger cabin was added aft.

You can cruise on the *Tennison* and see the Governor Johnson Bridge, the Solomons Island and Chesapeake Biological Laboratory, and the U.S. Naval Recreation Center at Point Patience. This is seeing the inner harbor and Patuxent River as you can never see them from land. Capt. Rudy Bennett runs the one-hour cruise at 2:00 P.M. Wednesday through Sunday (minimum of ten people required) between May 1 and October 1, or you can charter the boat for your own event. Fares range from $3.50 per adult, $2.50 per child (five to twelve), or $12.00 per family (regardless of size) to $125 per hour for the charter. Call (410) 326–2042 for additional information.

Drum Point Lighthouse

The Calvert Marine Museum is open daily 10:00 A.M. to 5:00 P.M. except New Year's, Thanksgiving, and Christmas days. A wheelchair is available, but the lighthouse is not handicapped accessible.

Admission is $5.00 for adults, $2.00 for children two to five, and $4.00 for seniors fifty-five and older. You can contact the Calvert Marine Museum at P.O. Box 97, Solomons 20688, or call (410) 326–2042.

Charles County

Most of the usual tourist attractions in Charles County are centered in La Plata and Port Tobacco (one of the oldest communities on the East Coast). On the eastern and western "ends" of the county, however, are two interesting views of early Charles County.

On the northeastern-most tip of Charles County is the town of Benedict, named for Benedict Leonard Calvert, the fourth Lord Baltimore. It was a flourishing town at least three times. The first was a period between 1817 and 1937, when steamboats carrying freight and passengers stopped here on their way to and from Baltimore and ports on the Rappahannock and Potomac Rivers. The second time was when slot machines were legal in the county and people came to gamble from as far north as New Jersey and New York. The third time was in 1988, when the Governor Thomas Johnson Bridge from Solomons Island to St. Mary's was temporarily closed. Ferries were put in service, but many people detoured to Benedict and used the Patuxent River Bridge.

Today this waterside town, the farthest inland port on the Patuxent River, has a post office (Dolores Buick is the postmaster) that is also a paperback lending library, a restaurant or two, and some "boatels" for storing boats.

Sue and Maurice Roach own ***Benedict Pier Restaurant and Marina,***

Trivia

Benedict is also notable as the landing site for 4,500 British troops in August 1814. Local historians say it is the only small town on United States soil that has been invaded by foreign troops, for these were the troops who marched on to the nation's capital. The British troops returned to Benedict with their wounded, and two of their soldiers were buried at Old Fields Chapel cemetery in Hughesville. During the Civil War, Camp Stanton was established here for recruiting and training African-American infantrymen to serve in the Union Army.

and ***Chappelear's*** is owned by Francis and Katherine Chappelear (an old Benedict family), who harvest some of the oysters they serve and buy "peeler" crabs for their delectable soft shells.

Veer off to the right of Route 231, just before the bridge, if you are looking for dockside atmosphere.

Mount Carmel Monastery was the first convent for religious women in colonial America, founded on October 15, 1790. It was started by four Carmelite nuns, three of whom—Ann, Ann Theresa, and Susan Mathews—along with the Reverend Charles Neale were natives of Charles County. The group set up temporary quarters at Chandler's Hope, then owned by the Neale family.

Father Neale donated 860 acres to the Carmelites to build their monastery. Two of the original convent buildings have been restored and are open to visitors during the summer season. The other buildings are still used as an active convent.

If you are driving in from Route 301 on Mitchell Road, Mount Carmel Monastery is on the left about 1/2 mile past Charles County Community College at 4035A Mount Carmel Road, La Plata. The monastery is open in the summer from 8:00 A.M. to 4:00 P.M. Mass is said daily at 7:15 A.M. and on Sunday at 8:00 A.M. Call (301) 934–1654.

Across from the monastery on Mitchell Road, on the Community College property, is ***Friendship House***, one of the oldest homes in the county. This four-room, hall-and-parlor-style house was built by William Dent in 1680 on Nanjemoy Creek. In 1968 it was dismantled by the Historical Society of Charles County and moved to its current location. Openings have been left in the structure so visitors can view the seventeenth-century construction techniques.

Friendship is open for tours and a ten- to fifteen-minute slide presentation from noon to 4:00 P.M. on Saturday and Sunday, May through September. Tours by appointment are available at other times. Call (410) 934–2251, extension 610, for information on Friendship House from the Southern Maryland Studies Center at Charles County Community College.

In your travels through the county, you may see evidence of tobacco, an important (and maybe the most important) crop in this area for 300 years. It takes 250 man-hours to produce one acre of tobacco (less labor-intensive crops may take as little as four man-hours), and Maryland tobacco is air-dried in a "stick" of tobacco made up of individually harvested leaves. In contrast, Virginia tobacco is flue-cured by heat in three days, and the entire plant is cut at one time. During the three- to six-month drying or curing process, each stick of tobacco will lose more than one-and-a-half gallons of water. Tobacco auctions are held every spring at Hughesville, Waldorf, and La Plata, and visitors are welcome to attend the auctions and tour the warehouses.

However, as tobacco is replaced with less labor-intensive crops and as urbanization encroaches into Charles County, fewer farmers are planting tobacco and the auctions have been reduced in number. If you will be here between mid-March and early May, you can get auction schedules and directions by calling the Farmer's Warehouse (410–274–3124), Hughesville Warehouse (410–274–3101), or Edelen Brothers Warehouse (410–934–2601).

Trivia

On January 1, 1873, the first trains started running on the Pope's Creek Line of the Baltimore and Potomac Railroad. Although created so goods could be transported from Charles and Prince George's Counties to Baltimore and used today to transport coal to the power plant on the Potomac, the line also allowed a "spur" to be run from Bowie to Washington, D.C., something that would otherwise have been prohibited because this new line provided competition to the Baltimore & Ohio line between the two cities.

Pope's Creek is the best place to go for crabs and a view of the Potomac River. The 3-mile drive off Route 301 down Pope's Creek Road is also a little history lesson, for it was along this route that John Wilkes Booth found refuge after assassinating Abraham Lincoln. Two historical markers designate where he stopped along Pope's Creek Road for three days and where he crossed the Potomac into Virginia. ***Dr. Samuel A. Mudd***'s house, where Booth was treated, is farther north in the county on Route 232, south of Route 382. It is open for tours from March to November, with a $2.00 admission charge for adults; call (301) 934–8464.

Down at Pope's Creek are the shells of oysters eaten over the centuries, first by Charles County Indians, then by settlers, and today by travelers. These shells cover some thirty acres to a depth of 15 feet in some places.

If you prefer eating crabs and oysters to looking at old shells, stop by Robertson's, Captain Billy's, or Pier 3 for some crabs served in a traditional style. The tables are covered with paper and piles of those tasty crabs; a pitcher of beer accompanies the feast. Here you can learn why Maryland is called the Land of Pleasant Living.

The old building on your right as you drive to the water is an old Rural Electrification Administration powerhouse with lovely arched windows reminiscent of the Palladian style.

The bridge across the Potomac, 3 miles downriver, is the Governor Harry W. Nice Bridge. It opened in 1940, replacing Laidlow's Ferry, and was the first crossing of the Potomac River south of the nation's capital. The 1938 groundbreaking was presided over by President Franklin D. Roosevelt. The bridge is 1⅔ miles long, rises 135 feet above the water, and carries nearly four million vehicles yearly. Passenger cars pay a 75-cent toll in either direction.

For additional tourism information write to Tourism Office, Charles County, P.O. Box B, La Plata 20646, or call (410) 934–0107.

St. Mary's County

There are some counties in Maryland that are off the beaten path even when you are on their most-traveled roads. St. Mary's is one of them. The county offers many different attractions that draw thousands of people each year, yet it remains primarily historic and underdeveloped. From the ***Naval Air Test and Evaluation Museum*** (connected with the Naval Air Station, Patuxent River), to the Old Jail Museum, to Point Lookout State Park with its terrific camping area and beaches, to the crafts at Cecil's Mill and Christmas Country Store, you can spend a good deal of time down here.

Historic St. Mary's City was the first proprietary colony in America and the first capital of Maryland. There are still numerous traces of colonial times in and around this area, including ***Sotterley Plantation***, an eighteenth-century working plantation overlooking the Patuxent River.

The Sotterley tale is one of inspiration, for it has gone from America's most endangered historic site to its most promising. This plantation, the only remaining Tidewater plantation in Maryland open to the public with a number of visitor and educational programs, is older than Mount Vernon and Monticello. Over the years the property had decayed, and it was feared it would have to be shut down. However, John Hanson Briscoe, great-grandson of a Sotterley slaveholder, and Agnes Kane Callum, great-granddaughter of a Sotterley slave, spearheaded the campaign for funds and restoration, and with the help of people across the country and the foundation's trustees, Sotterley is returning to its former impressive self.

Sotterley's grounds are open Tuesday through Sunday from 10:00 A.M. to 4:00 P.M. The manor house, off Route 245 in Hollywood, is closed from October 31 to May 1, although special tours may be arranged. Admission is $2.00 per person Monday through Friday, and $7.00 per adult and $5.00 for children six through sixteen to tour on Saturday and Sunday. (301) 373–2280, (800) 681–0850, or www.eaglenet.com/sotterley.

At the ***St. Clements Island Potomac River Museum*** you can discover the landing site of Maryland's first European settlers. Historic churches abound. St. Mary's City is actually a small town—just St. Mary's College, a post office, Trinity Episcopal Church, and Historic St. Mary's City, an outdoor living-history museum. Scant development and modernization has meant that St. Mary's is the only early permanent English settlement that has remained largely undisturbed; thus it is a favorite of archaeologists, who have uncovered millions of artifacts in a relatively short time.

While visiting Historic St. Mary's City, you can see the replica of the square-rigged ***Maryland Dove***, one of the two ships that brought the first settlers and supplies from England; the reconstructed State House of 1676; the Godiah Spray Tobacco Plantation; archaeological excavations; Farthing's Ordinary (a seventeenth-century inn exhibit and modern restaurant); the Margaret Brent Memorial Garden; and a visitors center with an archaeology exhibit hall, guided walking tours, and museum gift shop. It's difficult to believe you're barely an hour from Washington, D.C. (well, depends on the traffic), while walking through this seventeenth-century capital. The 800 acres of unspoiled tidewater landscape whispers tranquillity.

The exhibits are open from March 24 through the last weekend in November, Wednesday through Sunday 10:00 A.M. to 5:00 P.M. (301) 862–0960, (800) SMC–1634, or www.webgraphic.com/hsmc.

Be My Loveville Valentine

In 1989 Eva C. Hall decided the postmark from her zip code, 20656, should be red and have a cherubic arrow-shooter aiming toward a heart, particularly around the first half of February. It's understandable; 20656 is Loveville, named after Kingsley Love, the town's first postmaster. Hall has worked at the post office for thirty years, and she receives mail from around the world so special mail will have a special stamp for Valentine's Day. About 30,000 cards and letters will be handstamped at this post office, which normally sees about 400 pieces of mail a day. Most come from visitors from nearby Washington, Virginia, Pennsylvania, and, of course, Maryland. But other letters have come from as far away as Japan.

With more miles of shoreline than square miles of land and a college campus full of students, you know this has to be a good party town (the college shudders at that reputation). One can study only so long. St. Mary's College was St. Mary's Female Seminary, and it is considered one of the best buys in education, with an excellent teacher-student ratio and a small enrollment of about 1,300 students. Of course, as a student or parent of a student, that is the reputation that should interest you.

Trivia

The old sailor's rhyme was "Point Lookout, Point Lookin, Point no Point, Point Again." I've seen the first three on a map, but not the fourth. Perhaps it was just rhyme or had some deeper, older meaning I never learned.

The **Freedom of Conscience Statue** at the entrance to the college was erected by the counties of Maryland and symbolizes the religious freedom on which the state was founded. In 1649, at the request of town officials from St. Mary's City, a guarantee of freedom of conscience to all Christians (freedom of other religions came later) was enacted by the state legislature.

The Potomac and Patuxent Rivers, the creeks, the streams, and the Chesapeake Bay are ideal for biology and marine-science studies. But the bay also makes this area ideal for sailing, so it is frequently invaded by sailors seeking a home port.

The annual Governor's Cup Regatta is considered one of the ten best sailing parties of the year by national sailors. The water is also perfect for those interested in sailboarding. With St. Mary's mild winters, students can enjoy boating about six months of the school year.

All is not water, water, everywhere, in St. Mary's County; some of the area is devoted to produce farms. One of the major enticements of the county is the ***Charlotte Hall Farmers Market,*** with its Amish goods, produce, antiques, and curios. As with most farmer's markets, the earlier you arrive, the better the selection.

Buzzy's Country Store

As you head toward Point Lookout, at the very southern tip of St. Mary's, you're likely to find Buzzy's Country Store and its proprietor, Clarence "Buzzy" Ridgell. This is the place to find beer, souvenirs, pennants, bait, wine, and other "stuff." You'll also see, plastered, after a fashion, on the ceiling his collection of more than 400 hats, from as far away as Australia and Russia. If you have a cap you want to donate, feel free to do so. (301) 872–5430.

Freedom of Conscience Statue

The market, open year-round on Wednesday and Saturday from 8:00 A.M. to 5:00 P.M., is on Route 5 in Charlotte Hall. Call (301) 884–3108.

The ***Captain Tyler passenger ferryboat*** runs between Point Lookout State Park and Smith Island, with the one-hundred-minute ride departing at 10:00 A.M. and returning at 4:00 P.M. It operates daily from Memorial Day through Labor Day, other times on Saturday and Sunday, and can carry 150 passengers. The cost is $20 for adults and $10 for children; bicycles are permitted and are included in the fare. For more information call Tyler's Cruises, Rhodes Point 21858 (410–425–2771).

For a picturesque view, you'll want to stop at Point Lookout at the confluence of the Potomac River and the Chesapeake Bay. The light is unique and was the first permanent light built on the Potomac River. It's the only accessible lighthouse in its original location in southern Maryland. This is a great spot for picnicking, fishing, and enjoying the nearby campground (if you're really crazy about mosquitos). The ***Piney Point Lighthouse Museum*** is where you can see exhibits describing the construction and operation of the lighthouse (which was in use from 1836 through 1964) and the role of the United States Coast Guard. The lighthouse is on Lighthouse Road, Piney Point. (301) 769–2222.

The **Black Panther** is a U-1105 German submarine from World War II days that featured a rubber coating that made it "invisible" to the detection devices of the day. The sub was captured at the end of the war, and after going over it with a fine-toothed comb, the United States Navy sank it off the coast of Piney Point. Now it's Maryland's first Historic Shipwreck Diving Preserve and a National Historic Landmark.

Trivia

The Piney Point Lighthouse was known as the Lighthouse of Presidents because starting with James Madison, presidents and other notables spent their summers at Piney Point.

There is a six-acre park surrounding the lighthouse and the museum, which are open seven days a week from sunrise to sunset. The museum and gift shop are open weekends from noon to 5:00 P.M. May through October. Call (301) 769–2222 for weekday hours.

For additional tourism information write to St. Mary's County Division of Tourism, P.O. Box 653, Leonardtown 20650. Call (800) 327–9023.

PLACES TO EAT IN SOUTHERN MARYLAND

BENEDICT
Benedict Pier Restaurant,
Benedict Pier,
(301) 274–4429

Chappelear's,
7350 Benedict Place,
(301) 274–9828

CHESAPEAKE BEACH
Abner's Seaside
Crab House,
3748 Harbor Road,
(410) 257–3689 or
(301) 855–6705

Rod-N-Reel,
Route 261 and
Mears Avenue,
(410) 257–2735 or
(301) 855–8351

Sea Breeze,
8132 Bayside Road,
(410) 257–6126

Smokey Joe's,
Route 261 and
Mears Avenue,
(410) 257–2427

Wesley Stinnett's,
8617 Bayside Road,
(410) 257–6100

COBB ISLAND
Captain John's Crab House,
16215 Cobb Island Road,
(301) 259–2315

LA PLATA
Casey Jones Restaurant,
417 East Charles Street,
(301) 932–6226

LEXINGTON PARK
Emily's Oriental Express,
432 Great Mills Road,
(301) 737–5232

LUSBY
Vera's White Sands,
Route 4,
(410) 586–1182

NORTH BEACH
Neptune's Seafood Pub,
8800 Chesapeake Avenue
at First Street,
(410) 257–7899

POPE'S CREEK
Captain Billy's Crab House,
Pope's Creek Road,
(301) 932–4323

Robertson's Crab House,
Pope's Creek Road,
(301) 934–9236

PRINCE FREDERICK
Adam's, the Place For Ribs,
2200 Solomons Island
Road North,
(410) 586–0001

Stoney's Seafood House,
Fox Run Shopping Center,
(410) 535–1888

RIDGE
Spinnakers,
Point Lookout Marina,
(301) 872–4340

SOLOMONS
C. D. Cafe,
14310 Main Street,
Route 2,
(410) 326–3877

Dry Dock Restaurant,
C Street and Back Creek,
(410) 326–4817

Lighthouse Inn,
14640 Solomons Island
Road South,
(410) 326–2444

Solomons Pier Restaurant
and Lounge,
Solomons Island Road
South,
(410) 326–2424

Places to Stay in Southern Maryland

Amanda's B&B Reservation Service, (800) 899–7533, (410) 225–0001, www.amandas-bbrs.com, or AmandasRS@aol.com (e-mail)

Bel Alton
Bel Alton Motel, Route 301 South, (301) 934–9505

Lexington Park
The Patuxent Inn, Route 235, (301) 862–4100

Solomons
Back Creek Inn, Alexander and Calvert Streets, (410) 326–2022

Solomons Holiday Inn, 155 Holiday Drive, (800) 356–2009 or (410) 326–6311

Solomons Victorian Inn, 125 Charles Street, (410) 326–4811

Waldorf
Holiday Inn Waldorf Hotel, 1 St. Patrick's Drive, (800) HOLIDAY or (301) 645–8200

Other Attractions Worth Seeing in Southern Maryland

Cecil's Old Mill, Great Mills; (301) 994–1510

Chesapeake Beach Railway Museum, Chesapeake Beach; (410) 257–3892

Chesapeake Beach Water Park, Chesapeake Beach; (410) 257–1404 or (301) 855–3803

Joseph C. Lore and Sons Oyster House, Solomons; (410) 326–2878

Kings Landing Park, Huntingtown; (410) 535–2661

Old Jail Museum, Leonardtown; (301) 475–2467

One-Room Schoolhouse, Port Republic; (410) 586–0482

Patuxent Naval Air Test and Evaluation Museum, Lexington Park; (301) 863–7418

St. Andrews Episcopal Church, California; (301) 994–1037 or www.eaglenet.com/andrews

Smallwood's Retreat, Marbury; (301) 743–7613

Calendar of Annual Events in Southern Maryland

March
Maryland Days, St Mary's City; (800) 762–1634 or (301) 862–0990

April
Celtic Festival and Highland Gathering, St. Leonard; (410) 257–9003 or www.geocities.com/rainforest/7130

Earth Day Family Open House, St. Leonard; (410) 586–9700

Gardenfest, Solomons; (410) 544–4526

John Wilkes Booth Escape-Route Tour, Clinton; (301) 868–1121

Maryland Archaeology Month, statewide; (410) 514–7661

Sunrise Service, Point Lookout State Park; (301) 872–5688

May
African-American Community Day, St. Leonard; (410) 535–2730

International Museum Day, Solomons; (410) 326–2042

Patuxent Family Discovery Day, Solomons; (410) 326–2042

Spring Festival, Cedarville State Forest; (301) 888–1410 or (800) 784–5380

Welcome Summertime Memorial Day Weekend, Chesapeake Beach; (410) 257–2735

June

Blue and Gray Days, Point Lookout State Park; (301) 872–5688

Children's Day on the Farm, St. Leonard; (410) 586–8501

Confederate POW Commemoration, Point Lookout State Park; (757) 427–5065

County Heritage Festival, Leonardtown; (301) 884–3024

House and Garden Tour, North Beach; (410) 257–6539

Midsummer Village Faire, St. Mary's; (800) 762–1634 or (301) 862–0990

July

Family Day on the Bay, Chesapeake Beach; (301) 855–8351 or (410) 257–2735

Sharkfest, Solomons; (410) 326–2042

Solomons July Fourth Celebration, Solomons; (410) 326–4251

Tidewater Archaeology Dig, St. Mary's City; (800) 762–1634 or (301) 862–0990

August

Bayfest, North Beach; (301) 855–6681

Jousting Tournament, Port Republic; (410) 535–1710

September

Calvert County Fair, Prince Frederick; (410) 535–0026

Labor Day Weekend, Chesapeake Beach; (410) 257–2735 or (301) 855–8351

October

Blessing of the Fleet, Colton's Point; (301) 769–2222

Charles County Wine Festival, La Plata; (301) 645–0558 or (800) 766–3386

Grand Militia Muster, St. Mary's City; (800) 762–1634 or (301) 862–0990

Haunts of Smallwood, Marbury; (301) 888–1410 or (800) 784–5380

Patuxent River Appreciation Days Festival, Solomons; (410) 326–2042

Point Lookout Ghost Walk, Point Lookout State Park; (301) 872–5688

St. Mary's County Oyster Festival, Leonardtown; (301) 863–5015

November

Lighthouse Open House, Point Lookout State Park; (301) 872–5688

Road Rally, North Beach; (301) 855–6681 or (410) 257–9618

Veterans Day Parade, Leonardtown; (301) 475–9791

Eastern Shore

Welcome to the Eastern Shore, the southern part of the ***Del-MarVa Peninsula*** (*DEL*aware, *MAR*yland, and *V*irgini*A*), This is where you see as well as hear about those unfamiliar boats, the skipjack, the bugeye, and the bungy. You will also see "June bugs," the thousands of kids who invade the ocean beaches and boardwalks every summer to work at jobs and on tanning.

Explore and enjoy the dissimilarities you will find within a few short miles. Stop by a library to see a mural painted by an artist who became so popular that the library could not afford another mural like it. Find budding artists at the Dorchester Arts Center. Try a new beer, search for bald eagles and great blue herons, mingle with area residents at the general store, and see centuries-old homes that have not needed restoration because they have been so well maintained over the years. Ride the ferryboats, eat at some of the best seafood restaurants in the country, examine the fine local examples of duck-decoy carving, and take a peek at some of the prettiest passenger boats and ferryboats being built these days.

Take time to locate the Mason-Dixon line; it surprises most people that the line not only separates Pennsylvania and Maryland, but it also delineates the Delaware–Maryland border. Last but not least, get some sand between your toes and contemplate the treasures of America in Miniature. On the eastern side of the Chesapeake Bay lies the Eastern Shore, a very distinct and separate entity from the "western shore." People here are dedicated to the ways of the watermen and to the riches the land can bring, although farming here means just about anything that grows (except tobacco).

At the eastern end of the William Preston Lane Jr. Memorial Bridge—the Chesapeake Bay Bridge—is Kent Island, where the first European settlement in Maryland was founded in 1631. When the settlers came, they found the Nanticoke and Choptank tribes, which are now immortalized by Indian lore exhibits and two rivers named after the tribes.

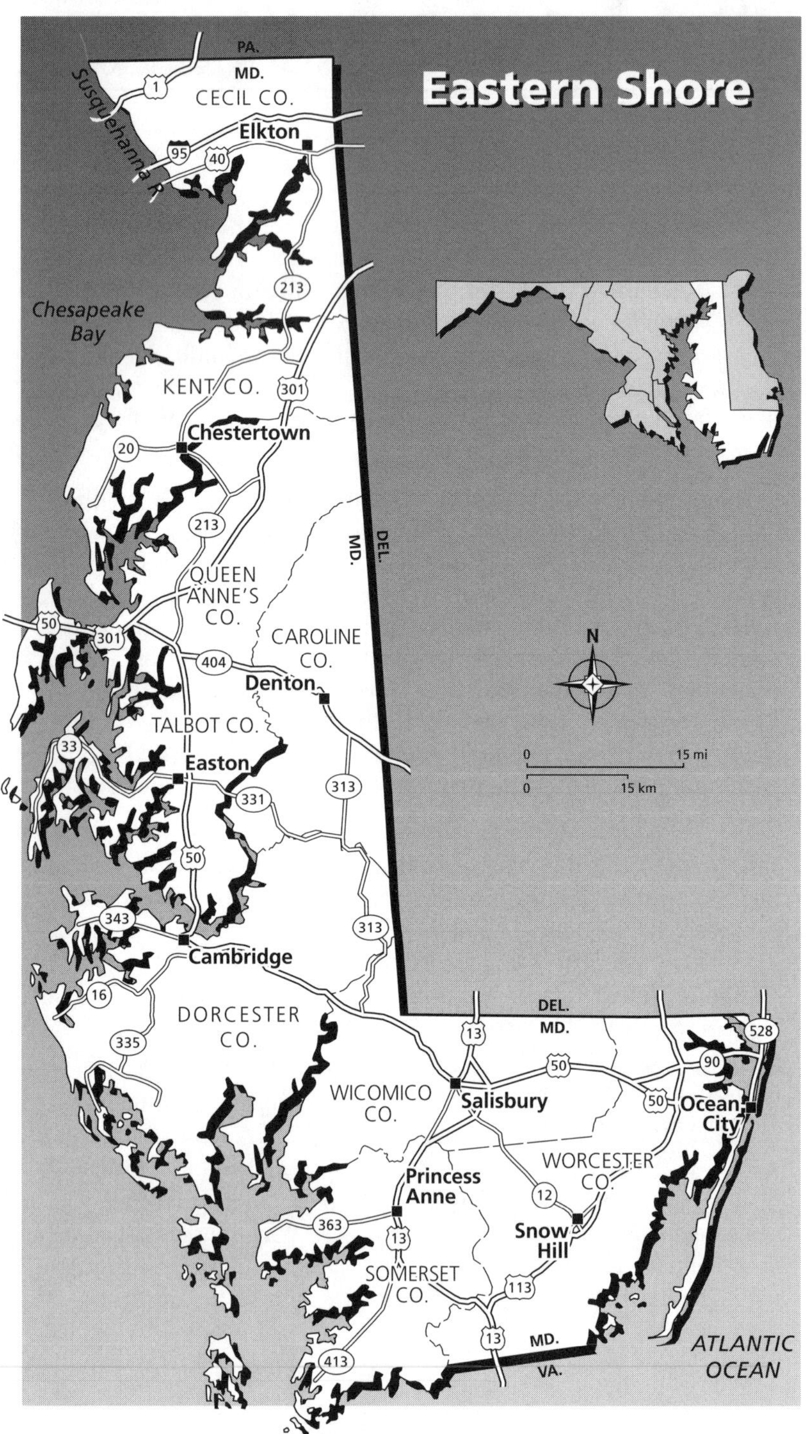

Eastern Shore
PA.
MD.
CECIL CO.
Susquehanna R.
Elkton
1
95
40
213
Chesapeake Bay
KENT CO.
301
Chestertown
20
213
QUEEN ANNE'S CO.
50
301
404
CAROLINE CO.
Denton
MD.
DEL.
TALBOT CO.
33
Easton
331
313
50
343
313
Cambridge
16
DORCESTER CO.
335
DEL.
MD.
13
50
90
528
WICOMICO CO.
Salisbury
50
Ocean City
WORCESTER CO.
Princess Anne
12
363
Snow Hill
13
SOMERSET CO.
113
13
MD.
VA.
413
ATLANTIC OCEAN
N
0
15 mi
0
15 km

History surrounds the bay's little towns and 500 sheltered harbors. The bay is home to boat-builders, sailors, fishermen (10,000 fishermen earn their livelihood from the bay), and sportsmen. The waterways are often as secluded as in the days when pirates and buccaneers hid in the bays and inlets. Some say there may still be buried treasure stashed in the sand dunes. At other times the waterways can compete with traffic-bound interstate freeways for congestion.

Judy's Favorite Attractions on the Eastern Shore

Blackwater National Wildlife Refuge

Eastern Shore Early Americana Museum

Plumpton Park Zoo

Ward Museum of Wildfowl Art

Wye Oak State Park

Hunters flock here every fall, for this is a major stop for migrating birds on the Atlantic flyway. To conserve and protect those birds that are not so abundant, nearly $2 million have been raised for conservation projects along the flyway.

On the flat-as-a-pancake terrain are farmlands, stately manors, and, once again, small towns. It seems that most of Maryland is filled with small towns. And, fortunately, the towns of the Eastern Shore are always sponsoring festivals celebrating the richness of the land or the sea.

My Eastern Shore excursion starts at the top of the bay and works its way down and to the east, over to the Atlantic Ocean.

Cecil County

Starting at the top of the state, at the head of the Chesapeake Bay, we begin at Cecil County.

Trivia

Located in the northeastern corner of Maryland, midway between Baltimore and Philadelphia, Cecil County is the only Maryland county which is considered part of the Wilmington, Delaware, New Jersey, and Maryland primary metropolitan statistical area.

One of the state's remaining covered bridges is at ***Fair Hill,*** which was a 7,000-acre estate owned by William DuPont Jr. The entire Maryland portion, more than 5,000 acres, was purchased by the state as a Natural Resource Area. In the northern reaches of the property, near the Pennsylvania border, is the 1850s covered bridge.

Ed Walls manages ***Fair Hills Natural and Environmental Center,*** a facility located in the northern half of the 5,600-acre Fair Hill Natural Resources Management Area in northeastern Cecil County. The headquarters building was formerly used by William DuPont Jr. as his hunting lodge and is next to a covered bridge over Big Elk Creek. There are two Mason-Dixon line markers on the property.

This is an outdoor education school with programs designed to encourage awareness, understanding, and appreciation of the natural world, our natural resources, and the impact of people on the environment. The indoor and outdoor classrooms are open Monday through Friday from 8:30 A.M. to 5:00 P.M. and on occasional weekends and evenings for members of the Fair Hill Environmental Foundation Inc. (a private, nonprofit support group) and for groups by reservation.

Program subjects might include bird identification, wildflowers, marsh studies, landscaping, animal designs for survival, aquatic studies, basic entomology, clean water watch, ecology, forestry, and soil studies.

The Fair Hill Nature and Environmental Center is at 630 Tawes Drive, Elkton. Call (410) 398–4909 for additional information.

Across Route 273 is the ***steeplechase track at Fair Hill***, an exact replica of Aintree, where England's Grand National is held. Since it opened in 1933 there have been a number of steeplechase races annually, and the May and October events are the only steeplechase races in the United States that permit pari-mutuel wagering. Fair Hill is also the home of the National Steeplechase and Hunt Association, which moved from Belmont, New York, in June 1989.

The ***Mitchell House*** is a two-and-a-half-story stone dwelling believed to have been built in 1764 (based on a fireback date), though it has had considerable alterations since then; it is the location of the ***Fair Hill Inn***. The house has been a Revolutionary War hospital (run by its owner, Dr. Abraham Mitchell) for Continental soldiers, a hotel, a post office, and a store.

Anthony Graziano purchased it from the state of Maryland in 1978 when it was in dilapidated condition, and he has proudly restored it. Now the house is a fine restaurant that features an Italian continental menu but specializes in Maryland seafood. Just perusing the menu, which includes Veal Imperial (a Fair Hill delight), pasta marinara (scallops, shrimp, clams, and mussels served over pasta), and seafood Beatrice (lobster tail, scallops, shrimp, and crabmeat cooked with brandy, flamed with Pernod, for two), is enough to encourage *buon appetito.*

The Fair Hill Inn is open for lunch Tuesday through Friday from 11:30 A.M. to 2:30 P.M., for dinner Tuesday through Sunday from 4:30 to 9:00

P.M., and for Sunday brunch from 11:30 A.M. to 2:30 P.M. Reservations are advised; call (410) 398–4187. The inn is located at the junction of Routes 273 and 213, Fair Hill 21921.

South of Fair Hill is Elkton, and if you have seen such movies as *The Manchurian Candidate, Guys and Dolls, The Philadelphia Story, Pillow Talk,* and *Solid Gold Cadillac,* then you have heard people talking about eloping to Elkton or going to "that town in Maryland" to get married. Until the late thirties the town of Elkton was known as the Marriage Capital of the World. Some 10,000 people a year were wed here, and one assumes most of them were eloping. They came to Elkton because it was the first county seat south of New York and other northeastern areas that did not require a waiting period or blood test before the ceremony was performed.

Only one wedding chapel remains, the ***Little Wedding Chapel***. This is where Babe Ruth and Joan Fontaine were married (no, not to each other), among dozens of notables, and this is where nearly 1,000 couples are still married each year. Stop by to talk with Barbara Foster and hear some of her many stories, witness a wedding or two, or plan for your own nuptials to be held here.

The Little Wedding Chapel is located at 142 East Main Street, Elkton 21921. The phone number is (410) 398–3640.

Detouring a little before heading down the Eastern Shore, for we are on a romantic subject, we can visit the other covered bridge (or "kissing" bridge) in Cecil. ***Gilpin's Falls covered bridge*** has a 119-foot span and a 13½-foot roadway, and it is adjacent to Route 272 over Northeast Creek, ½ mile north of Bayview. Reportedly, the bridge's arches were made from single timbers, which were curved to shape by balancing them on stumps and pulling their ends down. The bridge was constructed in the 1850s, abandoned in the 1930s, and left to disintegrate until 1959, when it was restored. Traffic along Route 272 bypasses the bridge, which is within a few yards of the roadway.

Gilpin's Falls covered bridge is on Route 272, 5 miles north of the town of North East, or 2 miles north of I–95.

Now, head west just a little more to visit the ***Day Basket Factory.*** Established in 1876 in the town of North East, the factory still makes oak splint baskets the old-fashioned way. Shortly after the Civil War, Edward and Samuel Day came to North East from Massachusetts to make their baskets because the wood was plentiful, the transportation was good, and the demand for their wares, particularly from cotton pickers, was great. Business boomed, and during World War I the factory had thirty-five people on its payroll turning out 2,000 baskets a week. In November 1989 Robert and Virginia McKnight, Dean Richwine, Theodore Lambert III, and Gary Sorrelle bought the factory. There are four or five basket makers there who produce old-time baskets, from lunch and market styles to fruit and bread baskets.

Depending on the wood supply, hobbyists will be pleased to know they have pliable number 1 oak strips, hand-split in any dimension, for chair seats or baskets or whatever you need. You can watch the process (you must be at least eighteen) Monday through Friday 8:30 A.M. to 4:00 P.M. (the shop is open from 10:00 A.M. to 6:00 P.M. Monday through Saturday in the summer and until 5:00 P.M. in the winter, but there are no workers in the factory on Saturday). Please call ahead (410–287–6100) to let them know if you want a tour. The factory is located at the corner of Irishtown Road and Mauldin Avenue, North East 21901.

Plumpton Park Zoo, the second-largest zoo in Maryland, is a rural zoological garden that features plants as well as exotic and native animals, including emu, wallabies, llamas, bison, Persian sheep, Chinese deer, miniature donkeys, pygmy goats, wild turkeys, and Australian black swans in a country setting.

Eighteenth-century buildings and ruins are on the grounds, including the 1734 mill that houses the gift shop. The zoo has an adopt-an-animal program, with prices ranging from $25 for an Amazon parrot or Australian black swan to $250 for a giraffe or a Siberian tiger, with options in between.

Plumpton Park Zoo is open from 10:00 A.M. to 5:00 P.M. daily. Admission

Water Power

The Susquehanna River separates the western border of Cecil County from the eastern border of Harford County. At one time there were two covered bridges crossing the Susquehanna River, but the last one was flooded with the construction of the **Conowingo Hydroelectric Plant**. *Built in 1928, Conowingo is one of the largest hydroelectric plants in the northeast, if not in the country, and the biggest fish lift in the United States. The enormous dam forms a freshwater lake 14 miles long, impounding some 105 billion gallons of water. It is a noted freshwater fishing spot. There's a public swimming pool, open from Memorial Day through Labor Day. Public tours used to be offered, but they were canceled as of June 1999.*

is $6.00 for adults, $5.00 for seniors (sixty and older), and $3.00 for children (two to twelve). Group tours are available by reservation. Contact the zoo at 1416 Telegraph Road (Route 273), Rising Sun, 21911 or call (410) 658–6850.

Heading south some more is Chesapeake City, where you'll come across the ***Chesapeake and Delaware Canal.*** On October 17, 1829, it made water transportation in the northern part of the bay even more important. At that time the canal had four locks, but the Corps of Army Engineers lowered the canal to sea level in 1927.

Receiving considerably less publicity than the C&O Canal, the 13-mile C&D Canal cuts off some 350 miles of water navigation for ships going between Philadelphia and Baltimore, and the 22,000 vessels that use it annually make it one of the busiest waterways in the world.

A museum in Chesapeake City, located next to the canal, reviews its history. The museum is open Monday through Saturday from 8:00 A.M. to 4:15 P.M. and Sunday from 10:00 A.M. to 6:00 P.M. It is closed on Sunday from Thanksgiving through Easter. Call (410) 885–5622 for more information.

I find the other, or north, side of the canal equally interesting. During the ride or walk across the bridge, 135 feet in the air, you can see the canal's course for miles. From the north side you can see the pilots on their pilot boats going to and from the ships navigating the canal. Stop by the Pilot House for information and a schedule on ships coming through.

For additional information write to Tourism Coordinator, Cecil County Chamber of Commerce, 1 East Main Street, Elkton 21921, or call (800) CECIL–95.

Kent County

Kent County has the largest proportion of farmland to total acreage of the Upper Eastern Shore counties, yet it is bordered on the north by the Sassafras River, on the south by the Chester River, and on the west by the Chesapeake Bay, so you can understand its multiple focal points. There might be an Old-Fashioned Fourth festival in Rock Hall, an Eastern Shore fish fry, and a Kent County Watermen's Association workboat race and docking course competition, all on the same summer weekend. After the harvest, it is time for snow goose and deer hunting. For those who prefer architectural history to land and water sports, Chestertown, the county seat of the smallest county in the state, is said to be the tenth-favorite historic place in America because of the large number of restored eighteenth-century homes.

When driving through Kent County, it is wonderful to take time to see local sites, such as the picturesque view of waterfront homes at Chestertown; the Eastern Neck National Wildlife Refuge; the Geddes-Piper House, a Philadelphia-style town house; the Kitty Knight House; the 3,000-acre wildlife research and demonstration area known as Chesapeake Farms (former Remington Farms); the Rock Hall Museum and the water; and Washington College, the tenth-oldest college in this country, which George Washington helped found.

On the second and fourth Saturdays of the month, ***Harry Rudnick and Sons*** auctions antiques, furniture, glass, china, Oriental rugs, and almost everything else anyone wants to sell. Frank Rudnick, the son of the late Harry Rudnick, says, "We have dealers, local people, and antique-shop owners, and they come from Pennsylvania, Maryland, Delaware, Virginia, D.C.—all over."

The auction starts at 9:00 A.M. and continues to about 4:00 or 4:30 P.M. "We sell about eight hundred, nine hundred, a thousand items a day," says Rudnick. Whenever there is a sale, the lunchroom is open for breakfast and lunch and the menu changes every week. "Some days," adds Rudnick, "the women prepare spaghetti, fried chicken, or turkey, and there's hamburgers, hot dogs, and homemade soup."

Harry Rudnick and Sons is on Main Street, P.O. Box 190, Galena 21635. Call (410) 648–5601.

At the ***Kent Museum*** are indoor and outdoor exhibits of farm machinery from the last two centuries. The county gave a group of local farmers one hundred acres, twenty-five acres of which they ran on a volunteer basis to help defray the museum's operating costs. The museum was started about two decades ago, and people from the area and as far away as Pennsylvania have donated equipment to it. Two early farm tractors mark the entrance, so you can't miss it.

Inside and outside the 40-by-150-foot building are exhibits on equipment used in planting and harvesting corn, wheat, soy, and other grains. You will see threshers, tools from pre-industrial days, and modern-day combines and reapers. Other exhibits explain the work done by hand planters, automated corn planters, and tractors (the earliest tractor on display is a 1947 model).

On the first Saturday in August is a threshing dinner. Of course, if you just happen by at other times of the year when they are planting or otherwise tending to the fields, you can watch them at work then, too.

No admission is charged, but contributions are accepted. Kent Museum is open 10:00 A.M. to 4:00 P.M. the first and third Saturday of the month from April through September, and it is located on Route 448 at Turner's Creek Public Landing, near Kennedyville. Call John Clendaniel at (410) 778–3257 or Mrs. William Payne at (410) 348–5721 for additional information.

Bicycle tours are popular in Kent County, and the chamber of commerce has prepared a booklet, *The Kent County Bicycle Tour,* for your information. Included are nine routes developed by the Baltimore Bicycling Club that range from 11 to 81 miles in length.

As an example, the Pomona Warm-Up is "eleven miles of gently winding country roads with great views of the Chester River. A country store located at Pomona is a good eat or drink stop." The Pump House Primer is "eighty-one miles of gently rolling to flat riding through northern Kent County and on to Cecil County's historic Chesapeake and Delaware Canal Pump House Museum at Chesapeake City. Highlights are the Sassafras River, the museum, the C&D Canal, and Cecil County's beautiful horse farms." Note that you must walk your bike across the Sassafras River bridge. In addition to tourism information, specific directions, maps, and a listing of restaurants, hotels, motels, campgrounds, and bed-and-breakfast establishments are available.

For additional county information write to Kent County Chamber of Commerce, 400 South Cross Street, Chestertown 21620, or call (410) 778–0416.

Queen Anne's County

The ***Old Wye Grist Mill*** is the oldest business in Queen Anne's County, in operation since 1664, 1671, or 1680, depending on whose reports you read. At least three mills have been located in this area for more than 300 years, giving the town of Wye Mills its name. Among its historic claims is the fact that ground cornmeal from this mill was purchased by Robert Morris, financier of the American Revolution, to be used as provisions for George Washington's army at Valley Forge in 1778.

Preservation Maryland, an organization to preserve the state's history and culture, has had the pleasure of working on this mill, which is particularly fascinating because as new equipment was developed, the old equipment was not hauled away or discarded. Therefore, there is a continuum of equipment to show the progress of milling over the years. The organization has completed work on the hydraulics and done most of the interior restoration and soon will transfer ownership to the Friends of Wye Mill. During your visit you can try your skill at Maryland's pre-industrial crafts, such as weaving, broom making, and hand milling. Also, depending on the season, you can buy cornmeal and a variety of flours—buckwheat, whole wheat, and, sometimes, rye.

The Wye Mill is open weekends, 11:00 A.M. to 4:00 P.M., April through December, and by appointment at other times. There is no admission charge, but they do ask for a donation. The mill is on Route 50, south of Route 662. The mailing address is P.O. Box 277, Wye Mills 21679, or you can contact the mill at (410) 827–6909 or 685–2886.

Queen Anne's is known for its sprawling countryside and 900 farms, its terrific access to the bay and bay tributaries, and the genteel lifestyle it promotes. Kent Narrows, formerly known for its horrendous weekend beach traffic jams, has become a minor destination of its own, with plenty of historic sites, fine boating, golf, and dining.

The meeting place of the Eastern Shore since 1955, however, has been ***Holly's Restaurant,*** noted for having the best milkshakes in the state. The tables are wooden and devoid of such frills as tablecloths, the waitresses are friendly, and the servings are enormous. You will find Holly's off Route 50 in Grasonville. Call (410) 827–8711.

Birdlife photographers and observers will enjoy the ***Horsehead Wetland Center*** and the adjacent captive wildfowl collection in Grasonville. Surrounded by more than 300 acres of natural beauty, the center has a fascinating and colorful flock of wildfowl, including ducks, geese, and swans, and nearby are deer, red foxes, river otters, and bald eagles living in the brackish marsh, pine forest, shrub habitat, meadow, and shallow water impoundment. Special screening allows you to quietly enter blinds so you can observe wildlife without disturbing it. Nature trails, wetland boardwalks, the observation towers, and viewing blinds offer a variety of ways to see the wildlife and a panoramic view of Chesapeake Bay.

The Wildfowl Trust of North America, founded in 1979, is responsible for the center, and you can be sure of programs, guided walks, workshops, a wetland festival, and lectures promoting stewardship of our dwindling wetland resources. A gift shop and a shaded picnic area are also on-site.

Horsehead Wetland Center is 1/2 mile from Route 18, off Perry Corner Road. Admission is $3.00 for adults, $2.00 for senior citizens, and $1.00 for children. Dogs are not permitted. The center is open 9:00 A.M. to 5:00 P.M. Wednesday through Sunday. It is closed Independence Day, Thanksgiving, Christmas, and New Year's Day. For more information write to the Executive Director, The Wildfowl Trust of North America, P.O. Box 519, Grasonville 21638, or call (410) 827–6694.

Trivia

St. Michaels was named after the Episcopal parish established in 1677, named for St. Michael the archangel.

For more tourism information write to Queen Anne's County Office of Tourism, 3100 Main Street, Grasonville 21638. Call (410) 827–4810.

Talbot County

Tourists coming through this area—about 100,000 each year going to St. Michaels—stop to see the Chesapeake Bay Maritime Museum, the Customs House, the Robert Morris Inn, and Tilghman Island (with a meal at Harrison's Chesapeake House). The Chesapeake Bay Maritime Museum receives by far the most tourists, and well it should.

But there are two small, privately owned museums that may also be worth your time. Millie Curtis' ***Museum of Costume*** in St. Michaels contains some unique displays. On exhibit are gowns worn by former presidents' wives, pantaloons worn by Mrs. Abraham Lincoln, and a vest worn by Clark Gable in *Gone With the Wind.*

The Town that Fooled the British

St. Michaels is known as the "Town That Fooled the British," and although the tale may be apocryphal, it has been around for so long that people will swear on their mothers' graves that it's true. So you will hear that during the War of 1812 this town, "was an important shipbuilding center of privateers, blockade runners and naval barges. This activity caused an attempt by the British naval forces to destroy the shipyards and the boats under construction. On the morning of August 10, 1813, a number of British barges manned by marines shelled the town and attacked a fort on the harbor side. Residents, forewarned, had hoisted lanterns to the masts of ships and in the tops of the trees causing the cannons to overshoot the town. This first 'blackout' was effective and only one house was struck. It is known as the 'Cannonball House.' St. Michaels is now known as 'The Town that Fooled the British.'"

Rooms are filled with ornate nineteenth- and early twentieth-century gowns. Curtis has been accumulating her collection since 1940. She has been known to greet guests wearing one of her costumes. Also of interest is the setting, representing life as it was for the wealthy and the not-so-wealthy. Ms. Curtis herself is a wealth of information and a fascinating conversationalist, so you might want to plan a little extra time to enjoy your trip to the past.

The white frame house was erected by shipbuilder and sea captain Lewis Tarr in 1843. It is restored, so you can see the original pine floors, the board-and-batten doors, and other aspects of the architecture.

The Museum of Costume is open weekends 11:00 A.M. to 4:00 P.M., April through November. The suggested donation is $2.00. Children under ten are admitted free. The address is 400 St. Mary's Square, St. Michaels 21663. Call (410) 745–5154.

The St. Mary's Square Museum exhibits items of significance to the local history and culture, not just of St. Michaels, but of the land between Tilghman and Royal Oak, called the Bay 100—that portion of land that could be defended by one hundred armed men. Two buildings, originally part of a steam and gristmill, are used for this museum, one of them dating from 1820 and one from 1860. The latter is referred to as the "Teetotum" building because it looks like the shape of a child's four-sided top of that name. In the 1820 building are artifacts from 1800 to 1850; in the kitchen area are items from 1850 to 1900; and in the Teetotum room are articles from colonial days to about 1950.

This museum was opened in 1964 by a group of local citizens, and although it sits on the original St. Mary's Square and is on city property, the museum is entirely self-supported. A group of twenty board members runs the operation.

The museum is open from May through October on Saturday, Sunday, and on holidays from 10:00 A.M. to 4:00 P.M. and by appointment. There is no admission charge, but donations are accepted. For additional information call (410) 745–9561.

Laura Ashley fans rejoice. Sir Bernard Ashley (who with his late wife, Laura, founded the clothing and furnishings empire) has added even more rooms to his ***Inn at Perry Cabin*** in St. Michaels. You now have a choice of forty-one individually and sumptuously decorated rooms and suites that include many Laura Ashley design touches. There's also an indoor pool and exercise room. The food is superb, the wine cellar extraordinary, and the setting as picture-perfect for a wedding as anyone could wish. Bring your boat and dock at the inn's slips. Pick up one of the inn's bicycles to explore the countryside (nice and flat, and very pastoral) or just come to relax.

From April through December, rates range from $195 to $575, including a full breakfast and afternoon tea. From January through March the rates have been known to drop. Also, frequent visitors have been treated to upgrades when available, without even asking. This is hospitality in a fine tradition. Inn at Perry Cabin is at 308 Watkins Lane, St. Michaels 21663. The phone number is (410) 745–5178.

If hot, and I don't mean weather, tempts your taste buds, then a stop in St. Michaels isn't complete until you've visited ***Flamingo Flats.*** Their motto is: "Where taste is paramount and life's too short to eat boring food." Opened in 1988, Flamingo Flats has hot sauce and salsa specialties; cigars; a tasting bar with more than 2,000 salsas, hot sauces, marinades, and barbeque sauces; more than 500 mustards; more than 75 jars with olives as a base; and hundreds of cookbooks, gifts, and jewelry items.

Among the sauces you'll find are Chile Today Hot Tamale, Gator Hammock Gator Sauce, Jump Up and Kiss Me, Lottie's Bajan Cajan, Matouk's Hot Calypso, Ring of Fire, and Rothschild's Fiery Raspberry Salsa. If you have an asbestos tongue, step up to the tasting bar and go to town. The shop specialty is its own Cannonball sauce. Cannonball is a combination of carrots, onions, lime juice, tomato, vinegar, and habanera peppers. It's a sauce more for tasting than for destroying your intestinal lining.

Flamingo Flats is located at 100 South Talbot Street, St. Michaels 21663. Call (410) 745–2053 or (800) HOT–8841.

Bed-and-breakfast establishments seem to belong in large Victorian homes, and the ***John S. McDaniel House Bed and Breakfast,*** operated by Dawn Rehbein, fits that description to a T. Built about 1890, the house has a high octagonal tower (a great sitting room), a hip-roof with dormers, and a porch that runs across the front and part of the south side of the house. Each of the eight guest rooms is spacious and bright and equipped with air-conditioning and a ceiling fan. Fortunately, the house is located within walking distance of historic Easton.

The John S. McDaniel House Bed and Breakfast is located at 14 North Aurora Street, Easton 21601. Call (410) 822–3704 or (800) 787–4667 for information and reservations.

Another wonderful lodging place in Easton is the ***Tidewater Inn and Conference Center.*** The Tidewater looks ages old and is filled with eighteenth-century furnishings, but it actually was built in 1949 and enlarged in 1953. And although the property is relatively new, you wouldn't be blamed if you felt the company of past cotillions, proms, and weddings. It's a question of whether the service, the restaurant, or the ambience wins the contest for "best" feature of this hotel. The service has been impeccable every time I've stopped by. The menu changes with the seasons, and the kitchen staff will work to prepare what you want the way you want it.

A grand time to be here is during duck season, when hunters stay; enjoy a 4:30 A.M. hunt breakfast on a chilly autumn morning, then leave before dawn to sit out in the blinds and await their prey. The hotel will arrange guide services and kennel the dogs.

Another marvelous feature of the Tidewater is its convenience to shopping, the restored 1921 Avalon Theater, and the Academy of Arts. All in all, the Tidewater Inn is a superb place to stay as a base for your Eastern Shore sightseeing. It's located at 101 East Dover Street, Easton 21601; call (410) 822–1300 or (800) 237–8775. Their Web site is www.tidewaterinn.com.

One of the ten remaining ferries in service in Maryland is the ***Tred Avon Ferry,*** which crosses Tred Avon River and connects Oxford to Bellevue. It has been operating since 1683 and is said to be the oldest "free-running"

Wye is This Oak So Famous?

You have heard that big oaks come from little acorns, and, of course, the converse is true—little acorns come from big oaks. The Maryland Forest, Park and Wildlife Service gathers the acorns, plants them, and lets them grow for a couple of years until they are established seedlings. You can purchase a Wye Oak seedling from the state for about $6.00 (plus tax if you live in Maryland). They are shipped in March in time for spring planting. They cannot be shipped to Arizona, California, Florida, Louisiana, or Oregon due to quarantine restrictions. These are the cutest little trees, no bigger in diameter than your little finger, but they produce mature-size leaves, about six or seven of them the first year. They do not grow as rapidly as, say, a maple tree, but they are of substantial size within a decade. And, who knows, 400 years from now there may be a champion tree in your yard. To order Wye Oak seedlings, write to the Nursery Manager, Buckingham Forest Tree Nursery, Harmans 21077. You must give a full street address; a post office box number is inadequate for delivery.

(not cable-connected), privately owned ferry in the country. It operates from March 1 through mid-December. The ferry schedule starts at 7:00 A.M. on weekday mornings and 9:00 A.M. on weekends and runs until sunset, except during June, July, and August, when it runs until 9:00 P.M.

It costs $4.50 for car and driver one-way and $7.00 round-trip, plus 50 cents per passenger each way. Bicycles are $1.50 each way and foot passengers are $1.00 each. This is a particularly photogenic ferry crossing at sunset, when the boats are all at their Oxford harbor moorings with their masts standing out against the skyline. (410) 745–9023.

Next to the Oxford landing is the Customs House, a replica of the original built in pre-Revolutionary War days when Oxford was an official port of entry. To reach the Tred Avon Ferry from Easton, take Route 33 and Route 333; from Bellevue take Route 33 and Route 329 to Royal Oak and follow the signs. Call (410) 745–9023 for further information.

Almost as good as a platter of crabs are the biscuits from ***Orrell House and Bakery***. Hundreds of dozens of these heavy biscuits, which started as a source of pin money for Mrs. Orrell about fifty years ago, go out to local stores and shops around the country. The recipe, which combines flour, water, salt, lard, sugar, and baking powder, originated in southern Maryland and the Eastern Shore during plantation days. It produces a biscuit that is soft and doughy on the inside and hard on the outside. There are some who say these biscuits are not any good until they feel like hockey pucks, and many swear by them as teething biscuits.

Believe me, just because they feel hard does not mean they have gone stale. A special pick is used to prick the tops of the biscuits (in an O and cross design) so they will not blister and burn.

The bakery is open on Wednesday from 7:00 A.M. to 2:00 P.M., Thursday from 2:00 to 11:00 P.M., and Friday from 7:00 A.M. to noon. The address is Orrell House and Bakery, P.O. Box 7, Wye Mills 21679. Turn right at the stoplight at Chesapeake College and drive to the famous Wye Oak Tree. Orrell House is between the oak and Wye parish. Call (410) 822–2065.

Wye Oak State Park is considered a "big little" place: The park in total size is only twenty-nine acres, but it contains the 450-year-old Maryland state tree, the Wye Oak. This tree measures a huge 37 feet in circumference and is considered to be the largest and finest of its species in the United States. The state bought the tree and one acre around it in 1939—the first time any state ever purchased one tree just to preserve it. Over time, more land was added to make this a state park. It was the first state park to be fully accessible to the handicapped, perhaps because it's so small that accessibility was easy to create. Wye Oak State Park is south of Wye Mills on Route 662.

For more tourism information write to Talbot County Chamber of Commerce, P.O. Box 1366, 805 Goldsborough Road, Easton 21601, or call (410) 822–4606.

Caroline County

Caroline County is the only Eastern Shore county not directly on the ocean or the bay, but there are calm waters, such as the Choptank and Tuckahoe Rivers and Marshyhope Creek, state parks for canoeing and fishing, and an active crabbing and fishing industry. The prime interest here is agrarian, and the crops are bountiful. Corn, soybeans, cucumbers, tomatoes, peas, beans, sweet corn, cantaloupes, peaches, and melons fill the fields and make a stop at a local produce stand an essential part of anyone's visit.

Across from the Caroline County Courthouse in Denton is the ***Museum of Rural Life***. Even county residents realize that the farming folk who have populated Caroline for the past three centuries may as well have been "consigned to a black hole of obscurity." The county has produced no national leaders, scientists, engineers, patriots, or even notorious rogues. Tombstones are the only proof that people have indeed lived here throughout the history of the United States.

Now, thanks to J. O. K. Walsh, the Denton Jaycees, the County Historical Society, and countless others, a determined effort has produced this museum, a tribute to those anonymous farming families who created Caroline County history.

The museum combines one of the original dwellings on Court House Square with new construction. There's a reception area, gallery for rotating exhibits, and an audiovisual room. The museum explores the various aspects and changes in rural life since European settlers arrived here in the 1600s. Hundreds of artifacts, documents, and photographs have been collected. You may even uncover some of the history behind the fireworks-induced conflagration of July 4, 1865.

If for some reason you can't find the answer to your Caroline County history question here, talk with Walsh. He's known as the person who "knows more about Caroline history than anyone." Call (410) 479–0274.

The historical marker next to the ***Choptank Electric Cooperative*** on

Routes 404 and 328, just west of Denton, marks the modest but historic ***Neck Meeting House***. Built in 1802 by members of the Society of Friends, the meetinghouse is believed to be the oldest house of worship in Caroline County. Most of the funds raised for the aluminum marker came from the recycling of aluminum cans by local residents.

The Choptank Electric Cooperative is refurbishing the small building, and if you would like to look inside, stop by the cooperative for the key.

The ***Slo Horse Inn*** is located in a quiet country setting on a twelve-acre horse farm between Ridgely and Denton. Owner Cat (Catherine) Sebasco says it was a horse farm featuring some of the slowest thoroughbred race horses ever born. "They were not known for winning," says Cat.

So she and husband Jesse kicked the horses out to pasture and converted the stable into four bedrooms, each with private bath, TV, coffeepot, and refrigerator. You can choose king, queen, double, or twin-bedded accommodations, or combine two rooms for a family or two couples. "It's very casual out here," she says. In fact, when Cat moved to Caroline from Washington, D.C., she felt like she was trying to "tap dance to a waltz." Now she has acclimated to the different pace and loves it.

Take Holly Road off Route 404 and continue for exactly 1⁹⁄₁₀ miles; look for a large white farmhouse, with a post-and-rail fence, on the right. Call (410) 634–2128.

Ashly Acres produced the first miniature horses to participate in an inaugural parade—former president Bush's. This nine-acre farm is owned by Robin Stallings, Karen Kilheffer, and Ashly Wayne Asbury, who breed, raise, and show quality registered miniature horses.

Trivia

According to George Sands of the Caroline County Library: "On March 24, 1981, the County Commissioners of Caroline County adopted a resolution establishing an official motto for 'Caroline the Green Garden County of Maryland.' This was carried out in conjunction with the library publication of an Agricultural Directory. The research showed that at the time Caroline County was first in Maryland in production of vegetables for markets and processing. It is among the top 3% in the U.S. in acreage of garden vegetables and at or near the top in Maryland and the nation in a number of related vegetable production areas. The term was coined by Bud Hutton."

A miniature horse is a true horse, not a pony or a dwarf, and is very gentle. According to Ashly Acres, the ancestor of the modern miniature horse was bred for the royal courts of Europe during the seventeenth century. The horses were often passed from one sovereign to another as diplomatic tokens of goodwill. When the power and wealth of the royalty began to decline, a few horses found their way into the traveling circuses of Europe. Some were used as pit ponies in the coal mines. The selective breeding process was interrupted, and the breed almost became extinct.

The American miniature horse is a scaled-down model of a full-size horse and can measure no more than 34 inches at the withers. Foals usually weigh between eighteen and twenty-five pounds and stand between 16 and 22 inches at birth. They come in all colors, and although they can be ridden by very small children, they usually are used in harness where they can easily pull a full-size adult. They function best as lovable exotic pets.

In the early 1900s a Virginian named Normal Fields imported some miniature horses with a shipment of pit ponies. He was so taken with them that he started a breeding program that continued for thirty-five years. Another Virginian, Smith McCoy, started with ten or twelve horses under 32 inches and built one of the largest miniature horse herds in the United States.

The address for Ashly Acres is R.D. 1, Box 207CC, Denton 21629. Tours for twenty-five people or more are available by appointment; call (410) 479–1159 to ask if you can join one.

Trivia

George Martinak deeded land to the state in 1961 for preservation as a recreational facility and a natural area for the enjoyment of all. It was named Martinak State Park after him.

In June 1984, in the quiet hours of an early Sunday night, a thirty-five-ton limb from Maryland's state tree crashed to the ground. Being practical, the state decided that some of the limb should be made into souvenirs, such as gavels; but 70,000 pounds of tree would make a lot of gavels. The Maryland Forest, Park and Wildlife Service sent a two-ton chunk of wood to sculptor Steven Weitzman to create the ***Wye Oak Sculpture***.

He carved the wood into a monument in his shop at Seneca Creek State Park in Gaithersburg. On April 3, 1985, his sculpture of two children leaning over a shovel in the act of planting a tree was moved to its permanent home at ***Martinak State Park,*** 2 miles east of Denton. The children, carved larger than life-size, are standing beneath a white oak tree in this 10-foot-tall statue that measures about 4½ feet from front to back.

Trivia

There are more than 240,000 acres of public land in the Maryland State Forests and Parks system, meaning there is a state forest or park within forty-five minutes of nearly every Marylander.

Martinak is bordered by the Choptank River and Watts Creek, and you can drop a line for bass, perch, sunfish, and catfish (a Maryland Chesapeake Bay Sportfishing License is required); camp in one of the sixty-three campsites for tent or trailer camping from April through October; stay in a year-round cabin; launch your boat; rent a boat; go hiking; picnic; enjoy a ball game; or recreate on the playground. You'll also be able to see the reconstructed hull of a wrecked bungy, a type of boat used on the bay in the early nineteenth century.

The park is open from sunrise to sunset daily, except Christmas week. Martinak State Park is on Deep Shore Road, off Route 404, Denton; call (410) 479–1619.

Seven miles west of Denton, off Route 404, is ***Tuckahoe State Park.*** Tuckahoe Creek meanders through this park, and a sixty-acre lake offers fishing and boating opportunities on twenty acres of open water. There are thirty-five campsites and four sites for youth groups. A central bathhouse with showers and toilet facilities is available. The Adkins Arboretum encompasses 500 acres of parkland and nearly 3 miles of walkways through the trees and shrubs. Canoes are available for rental from May to October. There are also other recreational options, including archery, hiking, a playground, a ball field, an equestrian center, hiking trails, a pet loop, and picnicking. Tuckahoe State Park, Queen Anne. (410) 820–1668.

Wye Oak Sculpture

For additional tourism information write to Caroline County

Economic Development Commission, P.O. Box 207, Denton 21629, or call (410) 479–2230.

Trivia

The Adkins Arboretum at Tuckahoe State Park, west of Denton, was conceived and funded by the late Leon Andrus of Cheston-on-Wye. He suggested that it be named in honor of the Adkins family, who has produced civic leaders for generations.

Dorchester County

When you cross the Cambridge bridge across the Choptank River, you'll see something that looks like a large skipjack. It's the ***Cultural and Visitors Center at Sailwinds Park,*** and the mistake is understandable because the center lies amidst two spectacular fiberglass sails. Sailwinds is part of the economic revitalization of Cambridge and Dorchester County; it includes a meeting place, classrooms, a festival area, and more. Such diverse events as crafts shows, flower shows, pageants, a seafood festival, a Native American powwow, and a beer festival are held there. Plans for the thirty-five–acre park, dubbed the Great American Waterfront Park, include a 300-room hotel and as the Committee of 100 say, "A softer, greener and essentially rural" version of Baltimore's Inner Harbor. Sailwinds Park is at 200 Byrn Street. (410) 228–SAIL.

Years before I thought about writing this book, I stopped at the ***Dorchester County Public Library*** and admired a wonderful mural of Eastern Shore scenes being painted by Chesapeake Bay artist John Moll. That creation has stayed in my mental and metal filing drawers all these years. Moll became familiar to James Michener when the author was researching his book *Chesapeake,* and they collaborated on a subsequent book because Michener thought the Oxford resident "not only captured the flavor of my subject but had earned the enthusiasm of those who love the Chesapeake."

Moll's lithographs are known for their faithful characterizations of the skipjacks and bay lighthouses he loved. His Christmas cards with Oxford and Annapolis scenes or Baycraft portraits are still popular, and John Moll oils hang in the permanent collection of the Eastern Academy of Arts and in the historic Robert Morris Inn in Oxford. This gives you an idea how popular the artist is whose work is on the Dorchester County Public Library walls. The address of the library is 303 Gay Street, Cambridge 21613 (410) 228–7331.

The ***Dorchester Arts Center*** was founded in 1970 and has between 400 and 500 members (mostly from the Cambridge area) including potters, photographers, quilters, stained-glass artists, and basket makers. In addition to regular classes in these and other crafts, the center has two galleries where local work is exhibited and sold. Each month a new exhibit opens with a reception. During the year, the center sponsors a variety of music, dance, and educational programs, a number of which are free to the public.

Each September the sidewalks along historic, brick High Street, with its beautiful period homes, are festooned with the best work of 125 or more of Dorchester County artists.

The center, located at 120 High Street, is open Monday through Friday from 10:00 A.M. to 2:00 P.M. and Saturday from 11:00 A.M. to 3:00 P.M. Call (410) 228–7782 for more information.

From the visual arts we move to the art of brewing, which brings us to the Cambridge microbrewery. The first batch of ***Wild Goose Amber Beer,*** billed as "The Only Beer for Crabs," was produced in early November 1989. According to brewmaster Alan Pugsley, Wild Goose tastes like a pale English ale. "Chesapeake's Own" microbrewery license allows the brewers to have a bar or restaurant for on-site ales; however, at this time they are distributing the beer only off-site. The brewery is in the former Phillips Packing House, which was, during World War II, the second-largest soup-packing house in the country (Campbell's was the first).

Tours of the brewery are available daily at 3:00 P.M. (groups should call for a tour), and it lasts about an hour, and naturally it includes a wee taste. Individuals can tour for free; groups cost about $2.50 per person.

Wild Goose Amber Beer microbrewery is at 20 Washington Street, Cambridge 21613. Call (410) 221–1121.

Another interesting tour is through the ***Brooks Barrel Company,*** one of the last remaining slack cooperages now operating in America, and the only one in Maryland. Paul Brooks founded the company in 1950, making "hand-crafted wooden barrel product . . . Nature's Way." These planters, kegs, and barrels are made of natural yellow pine from Delmarva and arrive ready to custom finish or seal to preserve their natural beauty, and some are available with FDA-approved liners with lids. Planning to grow strawberries next year? Try one of the 12-inch by 18-inch strawberry kegs with holes.

Some of the equipment goes back to the turn of the century, for the procedures haven't changed much. After touring the plant you'll realize what's involved every time you look at a candy barrel, view the miniseries made from Alex Haley's book *Queen,* or watch Robert Redford's movie *A River Runs Through It.*

Tours (which can be very noisy) are available by appointment. Brooks Barrel Company Inc. is at 5228 Bucktown Road, Cambridge 21613-1056. Call (410) 228–0790 or (800) 398–BROOKS.

Another place of interest is the birthplace of ***Harriet Tubman,*** the "Moses of her People" because of her work in the Underground Railroad that helped free more than 300 slaves. A slave herself, Tubman ran away only to return to Delmarva nineteen times to free others. During the Civil War she served in the Union army as a nurse, scout, and spy. The Harriet Tubman birthplace is on Green Briar Road. Call (410) 288–0401.

For more information about Harriet Tubman and the Underground Railroad, stop by the ***Underground Railroad: Harriet Tubman Museum***. There's a gift shop with items from such countries as Kenya and Nigeria, Native American goods, and local products.

There is no admission fee, and the museum, located at 424 Race Street, is open Tuesday through Friday from 1:00 to 5:00 P.M. and Saturday from noon to 4:00 P.M. (410) 228–0401.

South of Cambridge is the ***Blackwater National Wildlife Refuge,*** a marvelous sanctuary of more than 21,000 acres. The refuge boasts the largest nesting population of bald eagles in the East, after Florida. There is a $3.00 charge per car and a $1.00 charge per person on foot or bicycle. Besides the bald eagle and the great blue heron, you will see black ducks, the endangered Delmarva fox squirrel, and countless other animals and birds. Do stop by in November and December

Annie Oakley Lived Here

As you're driving through the area, you might stop by 28 Bellevue Avenue on Hambrooks Bay in Cambridge. For about five years, beginning in 1912, this was the home of Wild West sharp-shooter **Annie Oakley,** *designed and built by Oakley and her husband Frank Butler when they retired to Cambridge. The bungalow was typical of the period, except for a few features characteristic of the Butlers' unique lifestyle. It was purchased by a private owner in 1998, so it's doubtful they'll be having tours anymore.*

Nevertheless, it makes one wonder, why here? According to Thomas A. Flowers, the Old Honker, in his book Shore Folklore: Growing Up with Ghosts, 'n Legends, 'n Tales, 'n Home Remedies, *Oakley and Butler moved here because in her travels all over the world, she "had never seen a more beautiful spot than Hambrooks Bay." Butler was known to fish for perch in the bay, and Oakley's black-and-white bird dog Dave was known to stand so stock still that Oakley could shoot an apple off his head.*

when the Canada geese fly overhead. Bring your insect repellent in July and August.

Drive south on Route 16 to Route 335 in Church Creek, to Key Wallace Drive and the signs for the refuge. Blackwater National Wildlife Refuge is open Monday through Friday from 8:00 A.M. to 4:00 P.M. and on weekends from 9:00 A.M. to 5:00 P.M., Labor Day through Memorial Day. Call (410) 228–2677 for additional information.

The food is good where the locals gather, and one of these gathering places is on Taylor's Island at ***Taylor's Island General Store,*** just across Slaughter Creek Bridge, southwest of Cambridge. The best sandwiches and soups in the area are served here, and you will not go wrong with Erlyne Twining's crab soup, oyster chowder, chili, or lima bean soup; meat-based soups sell for $2.00 and non-meat soups sell for $1.50. The crab cakes contain a quarter-pound of crab meat each and go for $3.00. Quite a bargain.

Erlyne, her husband Perry, and their son Terry also sell ice, beer, soda, gas, and groceries and have an interesting display of "old-time stuff" from former general stores.

You will find signs that spell it TAYLORS ISLAND—usually state signs—and people who spell it Taylor's–usually the locals, because they say the land originally was called Taylor's Folly after the Mr. Taylor who bought the land. I side with the locals on this one. Taylor's Island General Store is on Route 16, Taylor's Island; (410) 397–3733.

And, as long as you're on Taylor's Island, stop by the museum, located in a 1916 school, showing local and regional antiques and memorabilia. There's no admission fee, but you have to call for an appointment. (410) 397–3338, (410) 397–3262, or (800) 522–TOUR.

Wild Blue Yonder

I have spent many hours at the Blackwater National Wildlife Refuge trying to photograph the great blue heron. It's not the refuge's fault that I haven't been successful. The great blue is there. But every time I get the tripod set and the camera focused and the timing just right, the great blue seems to sense that I'm about to get that one perfect shot, and he/she majestically strides off and flies to another part of the refuge. If I stay put, he/she doesn't return. If I try to follow him/her, the same routine happens. I know one shouldn't give human attributes to animals, but this case could be an exception.

Six miles west of Cambridge on Route 343 is Spocott Windmill, the only existing post windmill in the state for grinding grain. When you stop by you can also see a tenant farmhouse, a one-room Victorian-era schoolhouse, and a country store museum. This is a reconstructed windmill, from 1972, based on a windmill built here about 1850 by John H. L. Radcliffe, which was destroyed in the blizzard of 1888. Check with the Spocott Windmill Foundation about special events, such as Spocott Windmill Day. (410) 228–7090.

East New Market, originally Crossroads, could easily be called Churchtown or Churchville, for at each of the four entrances to the town stands a church. On Route 16 South, it is Trinity United Methodist; Route 16 North, St. Stephen's Episcopal; Route 14 West, First Baptist; and Route 14

A Bridge Too Far?

South of Taylor's Island you run into some barrier islands that achieved infamy beyond their size in the summer of 1980. Seems it was decided that a new bridge should be built over Narrows Ferry between Middle Hooper Island and Lower Hooper Island. No problem with that; the old one was a forty-year-old, one-lane, rickety, planked-pine swing bridge. But by the time planners and builders and others were involved, this concrete-and-steel span arching 27 feet above the narrow channel ended up costing more than $3 million, up from an estimate of $500,000.

Thomas A. Flowers, a county commissioner who relates in his book Shore Folklore: Growing Up with Ghosts, 'n Legends, 'n Tales, 'n Home Remedies *that his four-sentence dedication before about twenty people was picked up by Walter Cronkite, the* Los Angeles Times, People *magazine, and other noted publications. Among those commenting on this structure was Robert "Bob" C. Reid, one of my first editors, who at the time of the dedication was the Annapolis Bureau Chief of the* Frederick Post. *One of the finest writers I've ever met or read, Reid's article started, "Suddenly, there it is, rising from the swampland. It's a magnificent monument to nothing. It's like finding the Taj Mahal popping up over the next sand dune on the Sahara Desert, or the 'Love Boat' cruising down a trout stream in the mountains of West Virginia."*

And now for a few of Flowers' words of invocation. "Father, today we are gathered here to dedicate a bridge that is a monument to man's stupidity, a monument to man's waste, a monument to governmental interference and inefficiency, for there is no need for such an elaborate structure as this is and which is so out-of-keeping in the peaceful and lovely environment of South Dorchester." Needless to say, Flowers was never invited to another bridge dedication.

East, Salem German Evangelical and Reformed Church. These churches reflect the diverse denominations represented in this area.

Indians dwelled here; the first European mention of the region was in a grant to Henry Sewell dated 1659 in London, England. The first white settler is believed to have been a Quaker, John Edmondson, who came from Virginia in the 1660s to seek religious freedom. Edmondson was followed by the O'Sullivane family, and this historic district contains almost all of their early residences.

The entire town is designated a historic district, so, in addition to the churches, the town is known for its historical architecture. These homes are the core of the town's colonial architecture, but among the almost seventy-five buildings are a number from the eighteenth, nineteenth, and twentieth centuries. Many of the brick walks laid in 1884 still exist.

The East New Market Heritage Foundation sponsors an annual Candlelight Tour in late December. Call (410) 228–1000 for details.

Trivia

James B. Richardson, a master shipwright known along the waterways as "Mr. Jim," built the 1970 reproduction of the Spocott Windmill, likening it to the wooden boats he has built and repaired. The mill has canvas sails with a wingspan of 52 feet. The wide sails turn a wooden shaft and a series of wooden gears that turn the upper millstone grinding the grain against the bottom millstone. These post windmills appeared in England at the end of the twelfth century, and it's estimated that there were about eighteen post windmills in the county at one time.

For additional tourism information write to Dorchester County Tourism, 203 Sunburst Highway, Cambridge 21613, or call (410) 228–1000 or (800) 522–TOUR. Dorchester County is also on the Internet and can be reached at www.bluecrab.org/es.html, or via e-mail at dtourism@skipjack.bluecrab.org.

Wicomico County

For a long time Salisbury was known as the last great gasp going east (or the first coming west) on the way to the beach at Ocean City. Now it's a community in its own right with a world-renowned museum, a zoo that doesn't overwhelm you with its size, and some interesting shopping. You could spend your vacation here and avoid the hot, sweaty, shoulder-to-shoulder, sand- and sunblock-covered visitors catching the rays on the shore.

For an impressive look into the peninsula's past, stop by the ***Nabb***

Research Center for Delmarva History and Culture, where you can find some of the nation's oldest artifacts. Genealogists from around the world visit this center at Salisbury State University.

The center is named for Cambridge attorney Edward H. Nabb, whose forebear came to the Eastern Shore in the early eighteenth century as an indentured servant. In endowing the center with a $500,000 challenge grant Nabb, said "Let's face it. This [the Chesapeake Bay region] is where the United States began. There should really be a center somewhere here as a repository for that information."

Trivia

Edward H. Nabb, an octogenarian, has a pilot's license and is the only person on Earth to receive all three of the world's top power-boating awards: induction into the Power Boat Racing Hall of Fame and American Power Boat Association Honor Squadron; and the Medal of Honor of the Union of International Motor Boating. He was one of the last people to "read" for the bar in Maryland, attending some classes, but never officially enrolling toward a law degree. For more than forty years he has been a member of Maryland's oldest law firm, Harrington, Harrington and Nabb.

Because many settlers came up the Chesapeake before moving elsewhere, the Eastern Shore is an important national genealogical source for family history. They even have some records the Salt Lake City–based Church of Jesus Christ of Latter-day Saints genealogical resource center doesn't have. The Nabb Center has copies of the oldest continuous sets of courthouse records in the continental United States, dating from 1632.

Recognizing the center's potential, the late Wilcomb Washburn, head of the American Studies Program at the Smithsonian Institution, donated his personal library of more than 10,000 volumes before his death, and the Donner Foundation of New York has established a $75,000 Washburn memorial at the center.

The center is open Monday from 9:30 A.M. to 9:00 P.M., Tuesday through Friday from 9:30 A.M. to 4:30 P.M., and by appointment. It may be closed during school breaks, so for more information call (410) 543–6312.

The ***Country House*** in Salisbury is the largest country store in the East and delights all the senses with sounds of soothing music, the smell of potpourri and candles, and the feel of quality merchandise. You'll discover every colonial home furnishing you could wish to find as well as beautiful decorative accessories and old-time candy. Looking for that perfect something for your kitchen, bedroom, or bathroom? It should be here. You can select from an array of curtains, lighting fixtures, pottery, collectibles, furniture, shelving, rugs, baskets, and dried flowers. There are also some Victorian-style items, and the Christmas section is open year-round.

Owners Mike and Norma Delano handpick every item in the store, and they love to stop and talk with their customers. The shop is open Monday through Saturday 10:00 A.M. to 5:30 P.M.; on Friday night it's open until 8:00 P.M. From Thanksgiving to Christmas the store stays open until 8:00 P.M. Monday through Friday. You'll find the Country House at 805 East Main Street. Call (410) 749–1959 or log onto www.thecountryhouse.com.

Salisbury Pewter, formed only in 1980, is a company of dedicated workers who believe that although modern technology can be helpful, the most important part of their business is to maintain the heritage of their craft. Many of their methods have been handed down for centuries, and each piece of pewter they create is meticulously handcrafted and contains no lead. They offer a customizing service, and there is one wall with letters of appreciation from elected high officials for a series of pewter pieces created for an appreciation award. On weekdays you can see the crafters working pewter from raw product to a finished piece of art.

The shop is open Monday through Friday from 9:00 A.M. to 5:30 P.M., Saturday from 10:00 A.M. to 5:00 P.M. Call the store for Sunday hours. Salisbury Pewter is on Highway 13 North, Salisbury. The mailing address is P.O. Box 2475, Salisbury 21801; call (410) 546–1188 or (800) 824–4700 (out of state).

If you hate a zoo that rambles forever and ever and tries to be encyclopedic in its collection, you'll love the smallness and intimacy of ***Salisbury Zoological Park***. The Salisbury Zoo was founded by the city to advance animal conservation and environmental awareness. There are about 400 mammals, birds, and reptiles native to the Americas, with major exhibits of spectacled bears, monkeys, jaguars, bison, bald eagles, and a wonderful waterfowl collection.

The snug twelve-acre facility embraces a branch of the Wicomico River and has plenty of shade trees, exotic plants, and wildlife, making for a cool, peaceful setting for family outings. No gift or food concessions are in the zoo, but there are plenty nearby, and picnic tables and toilet facilities are inside the park.

Located at 750 South Park Drive, admission and parking are free. Pets, however, are not permitted. The zoo is open daily from Memorial Day to Labor Day from 8:30 A.M. to 7:30 P.M. and until 4:30 P.M. the rest of the year. It is closed on Thanksgiving and Christmas days. Group guided tours are available by appointment; call (410) 546–3440, www.dmv.com/-zooed.

Of major note is the ***Ward Museum of Wildfowl Art,*** which houses what is perhaps the largest collection of decorative bird carvings in the world, including many antique decoys. The museum is named for internationally renowned waterfowl carvers and painters Lem and Steve Ward of Crisfield, Maryland. During their lifetimes they produced more than 25,000 decoys and decorative birds, which the men called "counterfeits." Their workshop has been re-created, and on display are more than one hundred fine examples of their old classic hunting decoys as well as their decoratives. Lem did most of the painting, while Steve did most of the carving. Steve died in 1976, and Lem died in 1984 at the age of eighty-eight.

The museum has changing exhibits featuring oils of wild animals or the art of the Northwest Indians. You can experience the story of this Native American art form, decoy carving, from its beginning to the present. And if you don't want to venture into the wetlands yourself with the bugs and the mud, in the museum you can experience the sights and sounds of the wetland habitat of native American wildfowl. Even the setting is close to spectacular. The waterfront setting overlooks a bird sanctuary where ducks, geese, heron, osprey, and songbirds flock, as though to perform for you. An on-site gift shop has a wide selection of wildfowl-related items.

Located at 909 South Shumaker Drive, Salisbury, the museum is open Monday through Saturday from 10:00 A.M. to 5:00 P.M. and Sunday from noon to 5:00 P.M. Guided group tours are available. Admission is $4.00 for adults, $3.00 for seniors, and $2.00 for children (K–12); members and preschoolers are free. For further information contact the Ward Foundation at (410) 742–4988.

If It Looks Like a Duck . . .

The Ward Foundation was established to save the art form of decoy carving, which has grown from the carving of working decoys designed to catch birds to the decorative carving of collector's items. The foundation's annual summer seminars at 909 South Shumaker Drive, Salisbury 21801, offer hands-on instruction by some of the most talented artists and teachers in the field, such as Ernie Muehlmatt, Pat Godin, Bill Koelpin, Bob Guge, Larry Bath, and Jim Sprankle. Intensive, weeklong sessions cover such topics as anatomy and research, shaping, texturing, burning, priming and painting, and various brush techniques. Room and board are provided on campus. For information about the seminars, contact the Ward Foundation at (410) 742–4988.

If you have ever heard the railroad expression about "high balling it down the road" and wondered what it meant, take a visit to Delmar to see the ***High Ball.*** (Delmar lies in both Delaware and Maryland; State Street straddles the border. There was a time when the two halves—two mayors, two town councils, two school systems—fought over municipal functions, but things have been patched up for some time.)

Along the tracks near State Street you will see a large white ball, which was raised on high to signify that the line was clear, giving rise to the term "high balling." A small museum is housed in the caboose next to the tracks, and it is open by appointment. Call George Truitt at (302) 846–2654.

Driving along the flat stretch of Route 54 west of Delmar near Mardela Springs, you will parallel the southern end of the north-south section of the ***Mason-Dixon line.*** One could even say this is the cornerstone of the Mason-Dixon line. A double crownstone was installed in 1768 by Charles Mason and Jeremiah Dixon to settle the boundary disputes between the Penn and Calvert families, whose coats of arms it bears. There is a small parking lot and a brick and wrought-iron pavilion protecting the stones.

Called the Middle Point monument because it marks the middle of the Delmarva Peninsula, the crownstone also is a triangulation point of the National Geodetic Survey. The stone was broken off at ground level by vandals in 1983, and another stone originally set by colonial surveyors in 1760 was defaced by removal of the Calvert coat of arms. The Maryland Department of Natural Resources and Delaware's State Boundary Commission jointly replaced the monument on October 24, 1985.

Skipjacks can be seen in the watermen's villages of Deal Island, Chance, and Wenona. Over Labor Day weekend this last fleet of working sailboats races in the Tangier Sound off Deal Island in the annual Skipjack Races.

Two ferryboats continue service in this part of Maryland, survivors of the many that once linked water-isolated communities on the Wicomico River, between Wicomico and Somerset Counties. Both are small, both are free, and both operate all year, weather conditions and tides permitting.

The ***Upper Ferry*** crosses between Allen and Route 349 and takes about three minutes. It is run year-round during daylight hours with on-demand service, except on Sunday and major holidays. The Upper Ferry is an outboard motor-propelled cable ferryboat with no name.

Skipjack

A ferry has been running here since at least 1897; the current one has a capacity of two cars plus six passengers, with a maximum vehicle size of five tons gross weight. Bicycles are permitted.

The Upper Ferry runs daily from March through September from 7:00 A.M. to 6:00 P.M. and 7:00 A.M. to 5:00 P.M. the rest of the year. (410) 548–4873.

The ***Whitehaven–Mt. Vernon Cable Ferry***, called the Whitehaven Ferry, is 6 miles downriver from the Upper Ferry and connects Whitehaven to Widgeon; it has been operating since 1690. The modern ferryboat, the *Som-Wico,* takes about five minutes for a crossing and can hold three cars plus ten passengers. Bikes are permitted.

Whitehaven is the oldest incorporated town on the river and once was a vital deepwater port and shipbuilding area. Both ferries are run by the Wicomico County Road Department. Call (410) 548–4872 for more information.

Contact Lewis R. Carman, Tourism Director, at the Convention and Visitor Bureau, P.O. Box 2333, Salisbury 21802-2333, for further details on tourism, or you can call (410) 548–4914 or (800) 332–8687.

Worcester County

The town of Berlin in Worcester (pronounced like "rooster") County has no connection to the city in Germany; instead, it is a corruption of Burley Inn, the name of the site on which it was constructed. A guided map for a ***Berlin walking tour*** includes a town park and monument dedicated to Comm. Stephen Decatur, a native of Berlin. The oldest homes were built during the Federal period, later homes adopted the Victorian style, and twentieth-century homes are typified by the "bungalow." The walking tour brochure can be picked up at local Berlin businesses.

A typical Federal-style post-and-beam house is the ***Taylor House Museum.*** It was built about 1825 and now is used as the town museum. The gable-front house features a Palladian window with Victorian glass, restored wood graining, and a magnificent front doorway with butterfly medallions, sunbursts, and fluted, engaged columns. The house was supposed to be destroyed and replaced by a new post office and parking lot, but it was saved in 1981 by the Berlin Heritage Foundation. With $100,000 in private donations from the community, the house was restored from its dilapidated condition.

Although Robert J. Henry, who was instrumental in bringing the railroad to Berlin, lived in the house, the most famous occupant was Calvin B. Taylor, the founder of the Calvin B. Taylor Banking Company, which is still in existence. Much of the house and appointments are original to the times that various occupants lived in the house, including C. B. Taylor's bank desk, with its hidden doors on the side and front.

The Taylor House is at 208 North Main Street at the intersection with Baker Street, across from the Stevenson Methodist Church in Berlin. The house is open Monday, Wednesday, Friday, and Saturday, mid-May through September from 1:00 to 4:00 P.M. and for special events, such as concerts. Call (410) 641–1019. There is no admission charge.

In the middle of the historic district is the ***Atlantic Hotel,*** a faithfully restored 1895 Victorian hostelry that was rescued from the depths of distress to become this showpiece, named to the National Register of Historic Places in 1980. Each of the sixteen guest rooms (each with private bath) is beautifully furnished with antiques and is unique in its decor. Rich green and burgundy, delicate rose and aqua, deep mahogany tones, tassels, braid, lace, and crochet help transport you to a gentler time and quieter pace.

A parlor—for reading, letter writing, or conversation—is on the second

Atlantic Hotel

floor. If you must have a television in your room, the hotel staff is quite willing to provide one for you. Continental breakfast is provided. The dinner menu changes periodically to reflect seasonal availabilities, but you might find lobster sauté, stuffed scallops, sole paupiettes, a seafood sampler, or selections "from the land." One interesting offering, either as an appetizer or as part of the sampler, is the coconut shrimp, which is jumbo shrimp dredged in coconut, pan-fried golden brown, and finished with a sweet pepper and mango chutney.

Stephen Jacques is general manager and chef, and you should not be surprised if he comes to your table to personally tell you what is on the menu for the day.

The Atlantic Hotel Inn and Restaurant is located at 2 North Main Street, Berlin 21811. Call (410) 641–3589 for information or reservations.

Seven miles east of Berlin is ***Assateague Island National Seashore*** and the Assateague State Park, reached by Route 611. Nearly two million people visit this seashore annually. A two-room visitors center is open for interpretive classes and exhibits, which include a small "touch tank" of marine life. During a visit here you can take a guided walk; view a demonstration on how to catch blue crabs, clams, and ribbed mussels (mighty tasty steamed or sautéed in butter); or join a naturalist at the Old Ferry Landing to explore the 3/4-mile width of Assateague Island. You will travel by foot and bike or car from the salt marsh to the pounding surf, discovering relationships between the various barrier island life zones.

The famed ***Chincoteague ponies*** can be seen on Assateague, for two herds of the wild ponies make their home here. The herds are separated by a fence at the Maryland–Virginia state line. Managed by the National Park Service on the Maryland side, horses are often seen around roads and campgrounds. The horses sold at auction every July are on the Virginia side. No road connects the two states within the park. Supposedly, the horses are descended from domesticated stock that grazed on the island as early as the seventeenth century; Eastern Shore planters put them here to avoid mainland taxes and fencing requirements. Smaller than horses, these shaggy, sturdy ponies are well adapted to their harsh seashore environment. Marsh and dune grasses supply the bulk of their food, and they obtain water from freshwater impoundments or natural ponds.

Although they appear tame, they are unpredictable and can inflict serious wounds by kicking and biting. The Park Service strongly recommends that you do not pet or feed the ponies.

While at the park, you may see great blue herons, snowy egrets, dungins, American widgeons, black-crowned night herons, peregrine falcons, and numerous other birds on the Maryland side, but they are more easily seen on the Virginia side.

Legend has it that Edward Teach (Blackbeard the Pirate) kept one of his fourteen wives, a base of operations, and buried treasure on Assateague.

The Assateague Island National Seashore is open daily from 9:00 A.M. to 5:00 P.M.; 7206 National Seashore Lane, Berlin. Call (410) 641–1441 or visit the Web site at www.nps.gov. The Assateague State Park, 7307 Stephen Decatur Highway, can be reached at (410) 641-2120, ext. 20.

The ***Viewtrail 100*** signs you will see on secondary state and county roads mark a scenic bicycle trail, which is maintained by the Worcester 4-H Older Youth. You can join the trail in Berlin as it sweeps down to Pocomoke City, past the access to Furnace Town, Nassawango Creek Cypress Swamp, Milburn Landing on the north bank of the Pocomoke River, Mt. Zion One-Room School Museum, and many other interesting attractions.

The ***Pocomoke River*** is the northernmost swamp river on the East Coast, and along its banks are cypress trees (used to make our country's first ships) and Spanish moss. Here you can view eagles, egrets, hawks, and vultures, as well.

Another trail, the ***Beach to Bay Indian Trail,*** is a self-guided driving trail that goes from Crisfield on the Chesapeake Bay in Somerset County up to Princess Anne, Pocomoke City, Snow Hill, Berlin, and

Ocean City. It was opened in the spring of 1988 and is jointly sponsored by Somerset and Worcester Tourism, Ocean City, the State of Maryland, and the departments of Transportation, Natural Resources, and Housing and Community Development. For more Maryland bike trail information, call (410) 333–1663. For travel information about Ocean City, call (800) 62–OCEAN.

A carved-wood relief sculpture in polychrome, called **The Power of Communication**, hangs over the postmaster's door in the Pocomoke City Post Office. Perna Krick of Baltimore executed the commission in 1940. The figure of an Indian with an airplane reflects the history of the area, from Indian tradition to the development of communication, from primitive methods to present-day service.

Ms. Krick was born in Ohio in 1909 and attended the Dayton Art Institute. She studied under J. Maxwell Miller at the Rinehard School of Sculpture in Baltimore, receiving two European traveling scholarships. By the time she received this commission from the Federal Works Agency, her work had been exhibited at the Baltimore Art Museum, the Pennsylvania Academy of Fine Arts, and the Architectural League in New York.

One of the traditional sights around Ocean City is the airplanes flying advertising banners about 200 feet above sea level. Robert Bunting of Berlin bought a small crop duster in 1982 and started airplane advertising by flying up and down the beach with banner messages. The business is so popular that a half-dozen banner-bearing, single-engine aircraft are used for this kind of advertising. Each banner must have forty or fewer letters. Some carry marriage proposals; others tell you about the newest restaurant in town.

If you would like to have one carry your message for the world to see while the plane flies "low and slow," it will cost between $50 and $160 per banner. If you go watch the ground crew rig the planes, you will see them set the banner between two upright poles that are 6 feet apart. (It is said that if the ground crew is feeling prankish, they will close the poles only 2 feet apart.) Then the plane flies about 85 miles per hour to pick up the banner. Usually the pilot makes it on the first trip, but it has taken as many as six tries to hook a banner. You are looking at some first-class flying.

Between Memorial Day and Labor Day, each pilot logs about 500 hours, flying from 10:00 A.M. to 4:00 P.M., seven days a week, and together the pilots can fly as many as 110 banners in one day, although the average is about forty-five to fifty.

Ocean City is a family-oriented town on the ocean. It lies 7 miles north of Berlin. Thousands of college kids ("June bugs") come here every summer to work and vacation. There is plenty to do, from kite flying (probably my favorite activity), to boating, fishing, golfing, and checking to make sure the draft beer is kept at the right temperature. As with any resort, there are dozens (if not hundreds) of restaurants, eateries, bars, and food stands along the 3-mile boardwalk, and you have to try some of the famous saltwater taffy and Thrasher's french fries with vinegar.

The Ocean City restaurant that has to be a first on anyone's list is ***Phillips Crab House***. Eating at this restaurant, which was started by Shirley and Brice Phillips from Hooper's Island on Chesapeake Bay, has been an Ocean City ritual since 1956. The two of them have become such an institution and such an integral part of their community that they were honored in 1989 by the Ocean City Good Will Ambassadors Grand Ball.

Phillips has branched out with several locations, among them in Baltimore's Harborplace, Washington, D.C., and Norfolk. But the Ocean City location is the one to visit. It was a shingle-covered shack in the boonies when it opened. Now it is in the middle of everything that is happening and can seat 1,400 diners at one time. Despite its size, you will have to arrive early or plan to wait awhile, because there is always a line for dinner. This is where you come to eat crabs, piled in mounds on broad sheets of paper that cover tables that once held sewing machines.

And if steamed crabs, spiced shrimp, and crab cakes don't appeal to you, there is always fried chicken, Virginia baked ham served with corn on the cob, watermelon, and cole slaw. A children's menu is also available.

Phillips Crab House is at Twenty-first Street and Philadelphia Avenue, Ocean City 21842. For information call (410) 289–6821.

Those of you who served aboard the ***USS 324***, a World War II submarine that was built in 1944 and saw battle in the Java and South China Seas, will find her serving a new function as a reef off Ocean City. The *Blenny* was scuttled in 1989 about 15 miles offshore. It acts as a base for algae and soft coral growth, which will attract small fish and then larger fish, fishermen, and divers.

Ocean City is not just for summer fun. It is a year-round community that sponsors a great number of activities during the winter season, including workshops, entertainment, an annual Christmas parade, a traditional lighting and trimming of a 30-foot tree on the beach, the putting up of Christmas decorations throughout the town. Call (800) 62–OCEAN for details about this and numerous other events.

One of the unfortunate duties of Ocean City is life saving, for some people will do stupid things, and some people will be the victim of circumstances even without being stupid. The ***Ocean City Life-Saving Station Museum,*** located on the south end of the boardwalk, shows some early life-saving equipment and sands from around the world, shipwreck artifacts, antique bathing suits, models of old Ocean City hotels and businesses, photos of famous storms, and tales (not tails) of mermaids.

It's open all year, with daily hours of 11:00 A.M. to 10:00 P.M. during the summer. Admission is $2.00. Call (410) 289–4991 for off-season hours and information. www.beachinet/~ocmuseum.

A brochure about Christmas in Ocean City (as well as Berlin, Snow Hill, and Pocomoke) is available from the Ocean City Public Relations Office, P.O. Box 158, Ocean City 21842. You can call the office at (410) 289–2800.

For additional information on Worcester County, contact the Maryland Lower Shore Tourist Information Center (US Route 13 North, 144 Ocean Highway, Pocomoke City 21851; 410–957–2484) or Worcester County Tourism, P.O. Box 208, Snow Hill 21863; (800) 852–0335.

Somerset County

Every endeavor from the sublime to the ridiculous is represented at two Somerset County museums, and both museums are well documented in most state tourism brochures. These two museums may contain items about the same time, place, and people, but they sure do come out different.

Depending on your available time (you'd need at least two weeks to see and learn about the thousands of items in this collection), you will want to stop by the ***Eastern Shore Early Americana Museum*** at Route 667 and Old Westover Road, in Hudsons Corner. Pack rats and Americana lovers have Lawrence W. Burgess to thank for being a certifiable scavenger. This museum, housed in a converted poultry house, is a monument to the art of accumulation. It contains a little bit of everything, from political buttons to oyster-tonging forks. For hours, information, and an appointment, call (410) 623–8324.

On the other hand, there is the ***Governor J. Millard Tawes Historical***

Museum in Crisfield, with its exhibits pertaining to the late Maryland governor, the history and development of the Crisfield seafood industry, local art and folklore, and the life of the area from Indian times to the present.

The Tawes Museum, 3 Ninth Street, Crisfield, is open on weekends during the summer from 9:00 A.M. to 4:30 P.M. and during the winter Monday through Friday from 9:00 A.M. to 4:30 P.M. Call (410) 968–2501 for further information.

With a little time, you also might want to stop by the ***Teackle Mansion*** (used as an Underground Railroad stop by Harriet Tubman) on Sunday afternoon. This is a very elaborate example of the Federal style of architecture in 1802 and then in 1818 and 1819, erected by Littleton Dennis Teackle (1777–1848), an influential man of the early 1800s. Teackle and his wife Elizabeth Upshur Teackle (1783–1835), moved to this area from Accomack County in Virginia, shortly after they were married in 1800. Teackle was a merchant, statesman, and entrepreneur, owning agriculture and timber lands, and trading with merchants in England and the Caribbean. He established the Bank of Somerset in 1813 and served for many years in the Maryland House of Delegates.

The mansion was sold and eventually became apartments, until Maude Jeffries and her sister Catherine Ricketts founded Olde Princess Anne Days Inc. The funds this organization raised bought and restored the Mansion.

Located at 11736 Mansion Street, Princess Anne, the museum is open on Wednesday and Saturday from 1:00 to 3:00 P.M. from April through mid-December. The rest of the year it's open only on the first Sunday of the month from 1:00 to 3:00 P.M. and by appointment. Call (410) 651–2238 for information.

The Teackle mansion is also the home of the Somerset County Historical Society (410) 651–4276 from April to November.

You also might want to try some seafood, for this is the self-proclaimed ***"Seafood Capital of the World,"*** or take a ferry out to Smith Island. For both of these pleasures, you could not come to a more perfect place. As you drive down to the end of Main Street to watch the boating activity, stop for a meal at the ***Captain's Galley Restaurant***. They are not immodest when they claim to be the "home of the world's best crab cake." The crabs are caught and picked fresh daily from the Chesapeake waters, and then the meat is lightly seasoned with herbs and spices. For a real treat, try the 100 percent backfin crabmeat, fried or broiled.

Owner Rich Tonelli's soft-shell-crab sandwich is no slouch either, and during cold-weather days there is nothing better than one of their apple dumplings to warm up the insides. The local artwork is also a special treat. As you dine on delectable seafood, you can watch the watermen of the Chesapeake bring in the bounty of its waters.

Captain's Galley is at the end of Main Street, well within sight of the pavilion at the end of the city wharf. It overlooks beautiful Tangier Sound. Call (410) 968–1636 for information or reservations.

Ferries have been leaving Crisfield to the outlying Smith (the only inhabited island accessible exclusively by boat in Maryland) and Tangier Islands for years. One of the most enduring is the *Captain Tyler II*, which takes tourists to Smith Island daily from Memorial Day to September 30. This 65-foot, riverboat-style paddle wheeler was built in New York during World War II and was used as a cargo vessel for the military.

The departure time for the one-hour-and-ten-minute crossing is 12:30 P.M., and the boat leaves Smith Island at 5:30 P.M. It takes up to 150 passengers, and bicycles are permitted. The fare is $18.00 for adults and $9.00 for children six to twelve and includes free bus transportation to Rhodes Point. Contact Tyler's Cruises, Rhodes Point 21858; (410) 425–2771.

Two of Maryland's ten ferries—the Whitehaven and Upper ferries—operate between Somerset and Wicomico Counties. Check the Wicomico County section for additional details.

For further tourism information write to Somerset County Tourism, P.O. Box 243, Princess Anne 21853. Call (410) 651–2968 or (800) 521–9189 (nationwide).

PLACES TO EAT ON THE EASTERN SHORE

BERLIN
Atlantic Hotel Inn and Restaurant,
2 North Main Street,
(410) 641–3589

CAMBRIDGE
Port Side Seafood Company,
201 Trenton Street,
(410) 228–9007

CRISFIELD
Captain's Galley,
Main Street,
(410) 968–1636

EASTON
Tidewater Inn,
101 East Dover Street,
(800) 237–8775 or
(410) 822–1300

ELKTON
Fair Hill Inn,
Routes 273 and 213,
(410) 398–4187

GRASONVILLE
Fisherman's Village,
3116 Main Street,
(410) 827–8807

Harris' Crab House,
433 Kent Narrows Way North,
(410) 827–9500

Holly's,
off Route 50 at Jackson Creek Road,
(410) 827–8711

OCEAN CITY
Captain's Galley II,
12817 Harbor Road,
(410) 213–2525

Crab Alley,
9703 Golf Course Road,
(410) 213–7800

Fager's Island,
Fifty-ninth Street,
In-the-Bay,
(410) 524–5500

Harrison's Harbor Watch,
Boardwalk South overlooking the Inlet,
(410) 289–5121

Hobbit,
Eighty-first and Bay,
(410) 524–8100

Mo's Seafood Factory,
82nd Street on the Bay,
(410) 723–2500

Phillips by the Sea Restaurant,
Oceanfront at Thirteenth Street,
(800) 492–5834 or
(410) 289–9121

Phillips Crab House,
2004 Twenty-first Street,
(410) 289–6821

Phillips Seafood House,
141st Street and Coastal Highway,
(800) 799–2722 or
(410) 250–1200

Shenanigan's Irish Pub and Seafood House,
Boardwalk and Fourth Street,
(410) 289–7181

Wharf Restaurant and Lounge,
12801 Coastal Highway,
(410) 250–1001

ST. MICHAELS
Inn at Perry Cabin,
308 Watkins Lane,
(410) 745–5178

STEVENSVILLE
Hemingway's Restaurant,
(exit 37S) off Route 50,
(410) 643–CRAB

Kentmorr Restaurant and Crab House,
910 Kentmorr Road,
(410) 643–2263

TAYLOR'S ISLAND
Taylor's Island General Store,
Route 16,
(410) 397–3733

PLACES TO STAY ON THE EASTERN SHORE

Amanda's B&B Reservation Service, (800) 899–7533,
(410) 225–0001,
www.amandas-bbrs.com,
or AmandasRS.aol.com (e-mail)

BERLIN
Atlantic Hotel Inn and Restaurant,
2 North Main Street,
(410) 641–3589

CAMBRIDGE
Cambridge House,
112 High Street,
(410) 221–7700

Commodores Cottage,
215 Glenburn Avenue,
(800) 228–6938 or
(410) 228–6938

Denton
Slo Horse Inn,
11649 Holly Road,
(410) 634–2128 or
www.oldbayrealty.com/slohorse.html

Easton
McDaniel House
Bed and Breakfast,
14 North Aurora Street,
(800) 787–INNS or
(410) 822–3704

Tidewater Inn and
Conference Center,
101 East Dover Street,
(410) 822–1300 or
www.tidewaterinn.com

Ocean City
There are dozens, if not hundreds, of hotels, motels, boarding houses, apartments, bed and breakfasts, and condo units for rent in Ocean City. They are bayside or oceanside and are available only on a weekly basis (Saturday to Saturday, Sunday to Sunday), a full weekend only, or by the night. They are seasonal and year-round. For your first visit, you might want to contact the Chamber of Commerce (410–213–0552) or one of about a dozen vacation rental establishments and ask for information about this resort area, then reconnoiter for a future visit. Here is a sampling of places available and their Web sites, so you can get a feel for the place before you reserve.

Americana Hotel,
Tenth Street (boardwalk),
(800) 321–9174,
(410) 289–6271,
or www.ocean-city.com/americana.htm

Barefoot Mailman Motel,
Thirty-fifth Street
(oceanfront),
(800) 395–3668,
(410) 289–5343, or
www.ocean-city.com/barefoot.htm

Beachmark Motel,
Seventy-third Street
(oceanfront),
(800) 638–1600,
(410) 524–7300,or
www.beachmarkmotel.com

Castle in the Sand Hotel,
3701 Atlantic Avenue,
(800) 552–SAND,
(410) 289–6846,or
www.castleinthesand.com

Coconut Malorie Resort,
200 Fifty-ninth Street,
(800) 767–6060 or
www.fagers.com

Commander Hotel,
1401 Baltimore Avenue,
(888) 289–6166,
(410) 289–6166, or
www.commanderhotel.com

Dunes Manor Hotel,
2800 Baltimore Avenue,
(800) 523–2888

Harrison Hall Hotel,
Fifteenth Street
(boardwalk),
(800) 638–2106, or
(410) 289–6222

Princess Bayside
Beach Hotel,
4801 Coastal Highway,
(800) 854–9785,
(410) 723–2900, or
www.princessbayside.com

Oxford
Robert Morris Inn,
314 North Morris Street,
(410) 226–5111

Princess Anne
Washington Hotel Inn,
11784 Somerset Avenue,
(410) 651–2525

St. Michaels
Inn at Perry Cabin,
308 Watkins Lane,
(800) 722–2949,
(410) 745–2200, or
www.perrycabin.com

Smith Island
Inn of Silent Music
(Tylerton),
2955 Tylerton Road,
(410) 425–3541

Smith Island Motel (Ewell),
4018 Smith Island Road,
(410) 968–1933

Other Attractions Worth Seeing on the Eastern Shore

Annie Taylor House
Museum and Rural Life,
Denton; (410) 822–7039

Brannock Maritime
Museum, Cambridge;
(410) 228–6938

Chesapeake Bay
Maritime Museum,
St. Michaels;
(410) 745–2916 or
www.cbmm.org

Chesapeake City Historic District, Chesapeake City; (410) 885–2415

Chesapeake Pewter, Salisbury; (410) 860–6700 or (800) 228–2629

Chesapeake Railroad, Greensboro; (410) 482–2330

Church Hill Theatre, Church Hill; (410) 758–1331

Costen House and Hall Memorial Garden, Pocomoke City; (410) 957–1297 or (410) 957–1919

Customs House, Oxford; (410) 226–5760

Cypress Park Nature and Exercise Trail, Pocomoke City; (410) 957–1919 or (410) 957–1333

Dorchester Heritage Museum, Cambridge; (410) 228–1899

Durding's Store, Rock Hall; (410) 778–7957

Emmanuel Episcopal Church, Chestertown; (410) 778–3477

Fairmount Academy, Upper Fairmount; (410) 651–0351

Furnace Town Historic Site (1828–1850), Snow Hill; (410) 632–2032

Geddes-Piper House, Chestertown; (410) 778–3499

H. M. Krentz Skipjack Charter, Tilghman; (410) 745–6080

Historic Holly Tree, Perryville; (410) 642–6861 or (302) 993–0268

Julia A. Purnell Museum, Snow Hill; (410) 632–0515

Kitty Knight House, Georgetown; (410) 648–5777

Meredith House and Nield Museum, Cambridge; (410) 228–7953

Mount Zion One-Room School Museum, Snow Hill; (410) 632–0669

The Nathan of Dorchester, Cambridge; (410) 228–7141

Nutters Museum, Fruitland; (410) 546–0314

Old Trinity Church (1675), Church Creek; (410) 228–3583

107 House/Tory House, Charlestown; (410) 287–8793

Patty Cannon House, Reliance; (800) 522–TOUR

Pemberton Hall and Park, Salisbury; (410) 749–0124 or (410) 548–4900

Pocomoke Cypress Swamps, Snow Hill; (410) 632–2566

Poplar Hill Mansion, Salisbury; (410) 749–1776

Port Deposit Historic District, Port Deposit; (410) 378–2121

Queen Anne's Courthouse at Queenstown, Queenstown; (410) 827–7646

Remington Farms, Chestertown; (410) 778–1565

Rock Hall Museum, Rock Hall; (410) 778–1399

Rockawalkin School, Salisbury; (410) 742–8805

Rodgers Tavern, Perryville; (410) 642–6281

St. Francis Xavier Shrine, Warwick; (410) 275–2866

Sheriff John F. Dewitt Museum, Elkton; (410) 398–1790

Smith Island Center, Ewell; (410) 651–2292

Smith Island Cruises, Crisfield; (410) 425–2771

Stanley Institute, Cambridge; (410) 228–0401

Tangier Island Cruises, Crisfield; (410) 968–2338

Upper Bay Museum, North East; (410) 287–5909 or (410) 287–0672

Washington College, Chestertown; (410) 778–2800

Waterman's Museum, Rock Hall; (410) 778–6697

Wicomico Heritage Center, Salisbury; (410) 860–0447 or (410) 543–0651

Calendar of Annual Events on the Eastern Shore

February
National Outdoor Show, Golden Hill; (410) 228–5413

March
Artists of the Chesapeake, Centreville; (410) 758–2520

Elkton Salutes St. Patrick, Elkton; (410) 398–1528

St. Patrick's Day Parade and Festival, Ocean City; (410) 289–6156

April
Delmarva Birding Weekend, throughout the Eastern Shore; (800) 852–0335

Main Street Stroll, Elkton; (410) 398–1528

Martinak Spring Fest, Denton; (410) 820–1668

Maryland Archaeology Month, statewide; (410) 514–7661

Maryland International Kite Festival, Ocean City; (410) 289–7855

Nanticoke River Shad Festival, Vienna; (410) 873–2102

Oxford Day, Oxford; (410) 226–5730

Salisbury Dogwood Festival, Salisbury; (410) 749–0144

Spocott Windmill Day, Lloyds; (410) 228–7090

War World Championship Wildfowl Carving, Ocean City; (410) 742–4988, ext. 106

May
Antique Aircraft Fly-in, Cambridge; (410) 228–5530

Bridge Walk Rendezvous, Stevensville; (410) 643–8530

Chestertown Tea Party Festival, Chestertown; (410) 778–0416

Colonial Highland Gathering and Scottish Games, Elkton; (302) 453–8998

Janes Island Native American Pow Wow, Crisfield; (410) 623–2660

Kent Island Days, Stevensville; (410) 827–4810

Memorial Day Street Fest, Elkton; (410) 398–4999

Memorial Day Weekend, Berlin; (410) 641–4775

Mid-Atlantic Maritime Festival, Talbot; (410) 820–8606

Springfest, Ocean City; (410) 250–0125

White Marlin Boardwalk Parade and Craft Festival, Ocean City; (410) 289–1413

June
Bay Country Music Festival, Centreville; (410) 827–4810

Berlin Village Fair, Berlin; (410) 641–4775

Cypress Festival, Pocomoke; (410) 957–1919

Elkton (Marriage Capital of the World), Elkton; (410) 398–7007

Galena Art Festival, Galena; (410) 648–6959

North East Flag Day Ceremony, North East; (410) 287–5801

Queen Anne's County Waterman's Festival, Grasonville; (410) 827–4810

Rock Hall Annual Rockfish Tournament, Rock Hall; (410) 639–2662

Tilghman Island Seafood Festival, Tilghman; (410) 886–2677

July
Annual July Fourth Extravaganza and Fireworks, Elkton; (410) 398–4999

Bay Country Festival, Cambridge; (410) 228–7762

Caroline County Fair, Denton; (410) 479–4030

Chestertown Fireworks, Chestertown; (410) 778–0500

Fourth of July Fireworks Jubilee, Ocean City; (410) 250–0125

Greek Festival, Ocean City; (410) 524–0990

Kent County Fair, Tolchester; (410) 778–0767

North East Water Festival, North East; (410) 392–0155

Ocean City Tuna Tournament, Ocean City; (410) 213–1121

Oceana Waiter/Waitress Charity Cup Race, Ocean City; (410) 250–5512

Rock Hall Fireworks and Fourth of July Celebration, Rock Hall; (410) 778–0146

Sassafras Boat Parade, Galena; (410) 648–5510

Talbot County Fair, Easton; (410) 822–1244

August

Beach Polka Party, Ocean City; (410) 524–6440

Betterton Day Parade, Betterton; (410) 788–0416

Caroline Summerfest, Denton; (410) 479–3721

Crab Days, St. Michaels; (410) 745–2916

Crab Feast and Seafood Festival Parade, Port Deposit; (410) 378–5786

Dorchester Chamber Seafood Feast-I-val, Cambridge; (410) 228–3575

National Hard Crab Derby and Fair, Crisfield; (410) 968–2500

Wesley Chapel Annual Fish Fry, Rock Hall; (410) 778–6046

Wheat Threshing, Steam and Gas Engine Show, Federalsburg; (410) 754–8422

White Marlin Open, Ocean City; (410) 289–9229, (800) OC–OCEAN, or www.whitemarlinopen.com

Worcester County Fair, Snow Hill; (410) 632–1972

Wye Field Day, Queenstown; (410) 827–8056

September

African-American Heritage Festival, Berlin; (410) 641–3255

Annual Benefit Boat Auction, St. Michaels; (410) 745–2916

Autumn in Delmar Country Craft Fair, Delmar; (800) 239–6645 or (410) 228–6645

Beachcomber Fun Run, Ocean City; (410) 289–6834

Berlin Fiddlers' Convention, Berlin; (410) 641–4775

Candlelight Walking Tour of Chestertown, Chestertown; (410) 778–3499

Chestertown Jazz Festival, Chestertown; (410) 348–5528

Eastern Shore Fall Festival Championship Jousting Tournament, Ridgely; (410) 482–2176

Fall Festival, Elkton; (410) 392–2743

Johnny Appleseed Festival, Elkton; (410) 398–1349

Maryland Coast Day, Berlin; (410) 629–1538 or (410) 213–BAYS

Maryland State Surfing Championships, Ocean City; (410) 213–0515

Pemberton Colonial Fair, Salisbury; (410) 548–4900

Polkamotion-by-the-Ocean, Ocean City; (410) 787–8675

Port Deposit Heritage Day, Port Deposit; (410) 378–2121

Sunfest, Ocean City; (410) 250–0125

Sunfest Kite Festival, Ocean City; (410) 289–7855

Traditional Boat Festival, St. Michaels; (410) 745–2916

Tuckahoe Outlaw Days, Denton; (410) 479–1183

Wetlands Fest, Grasonville; (410) 827–6694

Yesterdays, North East; (410) 287–2658

OCTOBER

Autumn Walk at Leaf Thyme, Elkton; (410) 398–5566

Berlin Fall Festival, Berlin; (410) 641–1064

Chesapeake Celtic Festival, Snow Hill; (410) 632–2032

Elkton Halloween Parade and Pumpkin Carving Contest, Elkton; (410) 398–0550

Fall into St. Michaels, St. Michaels; (800) 660–9471

Ghost Walk, Chesapeake City; (410) 885–2025

Harvest Festival, North East; (410) 287–2658

Haunted House, North East; (410) 287–5333

J. Millard Tawes Oyster and Bull Road, Crisfield; (410) 968–2501

Martinak Fall Fest, Denton; (410) 820–1668

Mid-Atlantic Small Craft Festival, St. Michaels; (410) 745–2916

Ocean City Oktoberfest, Ocean City; (410) 524–6440

Olde Princess Anne Days, Princess Anne; (410) 543–2100 or (800) 521–9189

Queen Anne's County Seafood Funfest, Stevensville; (410) 643–8530

Tilghman Island Day, Tilghman; (410) 886–2677

Upper Shore Decoy Show, North East; (410) 287–2675

U.S. Offshore Powerboat Race, Ocean City; (410) 289–2800 or (800) OC–OCEAN

NOVEMBER

Day Basket Factory Open House, North East; (410) 287–6100 or (800) 382–3105

OysterFest, St. Michaels; (410) 745–2916

Pocomoke City Parade, Pocomoke City; (410) 957–1919

Waterfowl Festival, Easton; (410) 822–4567

Winterfest of Light, Ocean City; (410) 250–0125

DECEMBER

Nineteenth Century Candlelight House and Walking Tour, Chesapeake City; (410) 885–5377

Ocean City Parade, Ocean City; (410) 524–9000

Delaware

The ***DelMarVa Peninsula*** (*DEL*aware, *MAR*yland, and *V*irgini*A*) has always been that to me. It would never have occurred to me to question whether it should have or at some other time might have been VaMarDel or MarVaDel or some other variation of the three states. Wade B. Fleetwood, who wrote a column about the people and places of the Eastern Shore, did question it, and now so have I. We have drawn no conclusion. It could be from north to south, or alphabetical, or political. I don't know. The only positive thing my research has given me is that it was referred to as that as early as 1870 when the fourteen counties of the Eastern Shore (three in Delaware, nine in Maryland, and two in Virginia) were discussing separate statehood. Why fight tradition?

Trivia

British captain Samuel Argall landed in a sheltered bay off the Atlantic Ocean during a ferocious storm in 1610. He named the bay De La Warr, after Thomas West, the governor of Virginia, a man who never had and never would step foot in the state. The name was shortened to Delaware and applied to the river that feeds the bay, and to the Native Americans who lived there.

So, if the Delaware of DelMarVa comes first, why does this book list Maryland first? Because. *Maryland: Off the Beaten Path* was here first, and it wasn't until the third edition that it expanded its scope.

Poor Delaware is just too tiny to claim its own volume. I know, someone out there is bound to say, "Well, all of Delaware is off the beaten path," and to a great extent that is very deliciously true. Nancy Sawin, a famed Delaware illustrator, has caught the state and the peninsula in many of her books. Her books can be difficult to find, but they're a treasure of information about everything from outhouses to swamps to lighthouses.

Trivia

Delaware is the second smallest state in the nation (Rhode Island is the smallest), making it about half the size of Los Angeles (CA) County.

Despite Delaware's diminutive size, the Delaware Estuary is the major staging area for 80 percent of the snow geese in the Atlantic Flyway. Delaware also is known as the state without sales tax, and there are a number of outlet stores and malls, particularly at Rehoboth Beach (what else are you

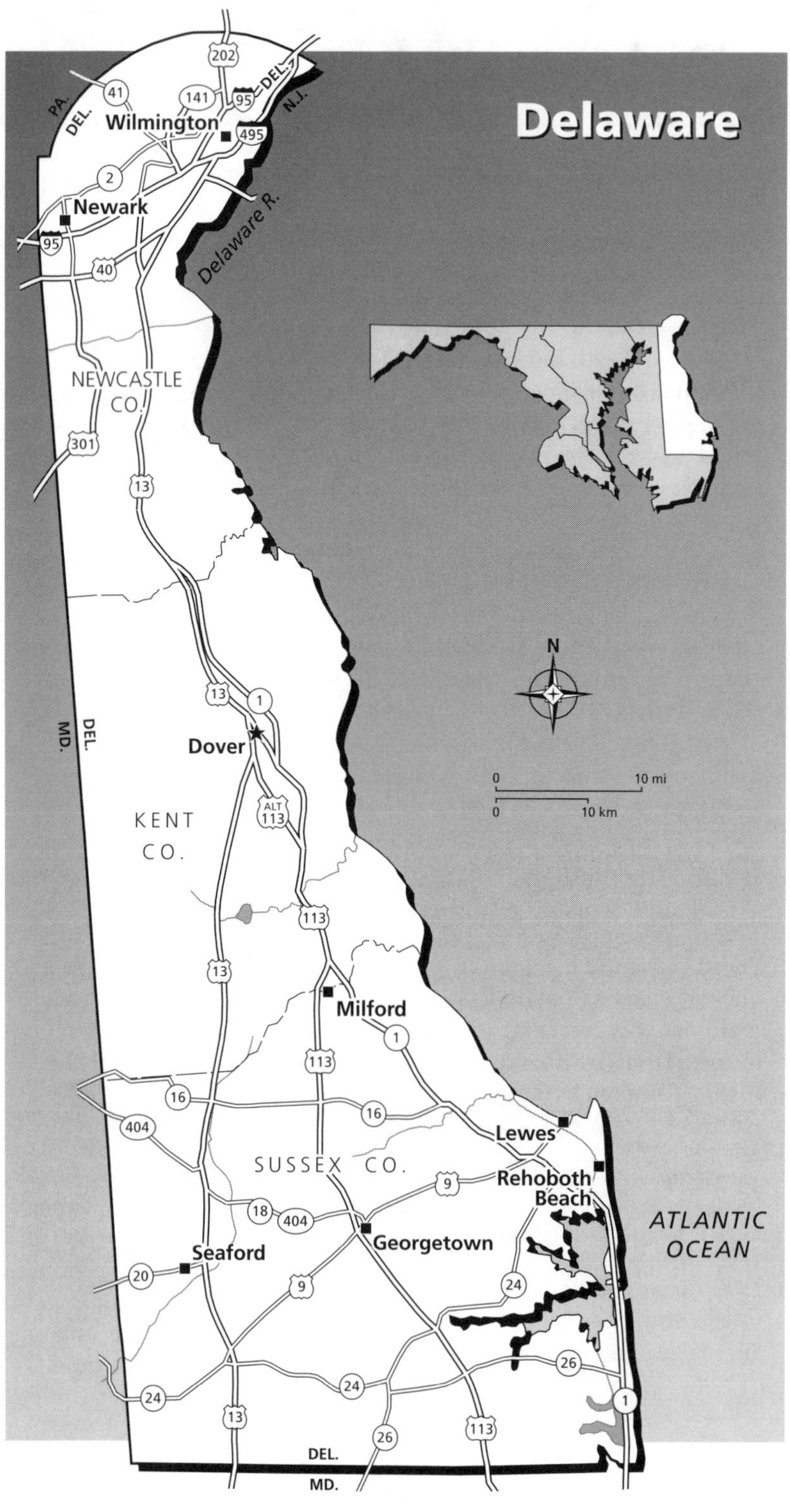
Delaware
PA.
DEL.
N.J.
Wilmington
Newark
Delaware R.
NEWCASTLE CO.
KENT CO.
SUSSEX CO.
Dover
Milford
Lewes
Rehoboth Beach
Georgetown
Seaford
ATLANTIC OCEAN
MD.
DEL.
N
0
10 mi
0
10 km
202
141
95
495
41
2
40
301
13
1
ALT 113
113
16
404
18
9
20
24
26

Judy's Favorite Attractions in Delaware

Delaware Agricultural Museum and Village
Dover Air Force Base
Trap Pond State Park
Zwaanendael Museum

to do besides shop on a rainy day during your vacation?).

Everywhere you turn in Delaware there's a delightful treasure, whether it's watching children getting on a school bus, eyes and body filled with excitement and anticipation, or the changing song patterns of rain falling pitter patter on the car roof, interrupted by the overhanging trees dropping huge glops of water. The scenic ponds created to supply energy to the dozens of grist- and lumber mills are too perfect to be captured by mere artists or mere words. They have to be experienced firsthand. And the friendliness of everyone you meet is just too precious to appreciate in just one visit. You may have to move to Delaware and spend a lifetime in this Small Wonder and the First State (to ratify the Constitution).

Among the many things that are Delaware and about which Delaware so rightly and proudly boasts is the fact that there's no sales tax. That's why you'll find so many outlet stores and other good shopping venues.

New Castle County

Starting from the north of Delaware, we begin in Wilmington, the largest city in the state, and branch out and then south. Wilmington was laid out in 1731 by Quakers and was an important shipping center. Early in the 1800s, Eleuthère Irenée du Pont and his two sons moved into the area, and seeing the abundant waterpower potential, started their gunpowder business. Their influence on the development of the city and surrounding area can not be overstated. Eventually the DuPonts would be responsible for building public schools and creating some of the most incredible museums and museum settings.

Trivia

Delaware is also known as the Diamond State, because it was considered a "jewel" among states due to its strategic location.

Draped on either side of the Brandywine Creek that runs from the heart of Wilmington are Brandywine, Alapocas, and Rockford Parks. ***Brandywine Park*** was designed by Frederick Law Olmstead, creator of New York City's Central Park and the National Zoo in Washington, D.C. There's a playground here, a zoo, and the Josephine Garden, with its Japanese cherry trees.

A little farther north is the ***Delaware Art Museum,*** with one of the country's most important assemblages of English pre-Raphaelite paintings in

Trivia

Downtown Wilmington, near the Amtrak station, is the site of a Wyland mural. Wyland was born in 1956 in Detroit, Michigan, and saw his first grey whales migrating off the California coast when he was fourteen. He started painting whales and dolphins two years later, and by 1974 he had painted his first mural, an Alps mountain scene in Royal Oak, Michigan. This Wilmington painting, called Whaling Wall XLIV, Marine Mammals, *was done in 1993. It's located between Shipley and Market Streets on Martin Luther King Boulevard.*

the Bancroft collection. American artists also are represented, and a hands-on section is great for children to learn about art.

Located at 2301 Kentmere Parkway, the museum is open Tuesday through Saturday 10:00 A.M. to 5:00 P.M. and Sunday noon to 5:00 P.M. The museum is closed on New Year's, Thanksgiving, and Christmas days. The admission for adults is $5.00, seniors over sixty, $3.00, and students with identification, $2.50. Call (302) 571–9590.

There are other special places to visit, and the ***Hagley Museum*** is one of them. Set on 240 landscaped acres at the original DuPont mills, there are numerous exhibits showing the maturation of this country's economic growth.

When you consider how explosive gunpowder is, you can look at the architecture and design of the mills with great appreciation. The three side walls farthest from the water were made of heavy stone. The side wall along the creek was made of wood. When the inevitable explosion took place, it would blow out the less-sturdy wooden wall into the creek. This prevented the force of the explosion blowing out walls that would have otherwise damaged other buildings nearby.

The Hagley is open daily 9:30 A.M. to 4:30 P.M. from mid-March to December 31, and weekends 9:30 A.M. to 4:30 P.M. the rest of the year. The Hagley is closed Thanksgiving, Christmas, and New Year's Eve days. Admission is $9.75 for adults, $7.50 for seniors and students, and $3.50 for children. A family rate is available at $26.50. Call (302) 658–2400.

Next to the Hagley is the ***Delaware Toy and Miniature Museum,*** with more than one hundred dollhouses and rooms, antiques, and newly crafted miniatures, which document European and American history from the eighteenth century forward.

Trivia

The Blue Hen chicken was adopted as Delaware's state bird on April 14, 1939, but its history as a symbol of the state dates from Revolutionary War days. The men of Capt. Jonathan Caldwell's company, recruited from Kent County, brought their fighting game chickens with them, and when the men weren't fighting the enemy they amused themselves with cock fights. The reputation for the tenacity of the cocks in their fights spread throughout the army, and the men of Delaware, equally tenacious, were compared to the fighting Blue Hens.

Within the collection are dolls, toys, trains, boats, and planes. Among the features are toys by Bliss, Hubley, Ives, A. C. Gilbert, Schoenhut, and McLoughlin. A permanent Victorian Christmas parlor is a particularly nostalgic scene, even if you never experienced one. There's no better way to connect the generations than by discussing the reminiscences of earlier times as prompted by the Nuremberg kitchens, the dollhouses, and period toys. If you like art in miniature, this is the place to visit.

A reference library and, of course, a museum sales shop are available for the incurable (myself included).

The Toy and Miniature Museum is located on Route 141. Admission is $5.00 for adults, $4.00 for those who are sixty-two and older, and $3.00 for those younger than thirteen. Reservations are required for a guided tour. The museum is open Tuesday through Saturday from 10:00 A.M. to 4:00 P.M. and Sunday from noon to 4:00 P.M. It is closed on Monday. (302) 427–TOYS (8697).

Other highlights of the Wilmington area are Old Swedes Church, Nemours Mansion and gardens, and, most definitely, the Winterthur Museum.

A little north of Wilmington is the anomaly of modern government known as ***Arden***. It was one of three towns (along with Ardentown and Ardencroft, which would come later) created under the principles conceived by Philadelphia-born economist Henry George and his Theory of Single Tax. Born in 1839, George proposed that land only should be taxed, thereby creating the concept of the "single tax." Thus, in 1895 a group of single taxers from Philadelphia invaded Delaware with their political evangelism. Frank Stephens, a Philadelphia sculptor, with the help of architect Will Price and soap manufacturer Joseph Fels, acquired a Brandywine farm of 160 acres and started the village of Arden. It continues to this day as a single-tax entity.

Utopian in nature, the community also incorporated the artistic ideas of William Morris and the Arts and Crafts Movement, the Garden Cities planning ideas of Ebenezer Howard, and some social theories of Petr Alekseevich Kropotkin (1842–1921). Many of the homes are tiny, for they were summer places, but there definitely is a mix of new and old, fancy and ramshackle, set on varying locations on varying-sized lots.

The three villages are surrounded by woodlands, including the Naaman's Creek natural area, designated as one of "Delaware's Outstanding Natural Areas." There are two things that drive the residents of Arden: the ***Arden Club*** and the ***Arden Community Recreation Association***.

Trivia

Old Swedes Church in Wilmington, built in 1698, is the oldest Protestant church still in use in the United States. The pipe organ was built by the Austin Company of Hartford, Connecticut, and has sixteen stops and sixteen ranks of pipe, for a total of 913 pipes.

Music, dance, theater, visual arts, and such crafts as pottery and ironwork are still highly valued in the three Ardens.

There is not much for the tourist to "see" in the way of historic buildings or museums, so you have to look at their activities calendar, scheduling your visit for the contra dancing/square dancing every month, the Arden Fair (the Saturday before Labor Day), the Shakespearean productions (*Twelfth Night* and *Macbeth* were presented in 1996) in the little (130-seat) outdoor theater on the Arden Green, and the Candlelight Music Dinner Theater in Ardentown that has shows throughout the year. Call (302) 475–2313 for information.

Old New Castle is filled with colonial-era homes and buildings that the Rockefeller Foundation initially wanted to restore as a living museum of colonial America. However, the locals raised such a fuss that the Rockefellers went to Williamsburg, Virginia, instead. Rather than reconstructing the history represented at Williamsburg, New Castle exudes the past from every brick and slather of mortar. It was here that William Penn set foot in North America for the first time. From those Quaker beginnings, the town became a trade center through shipping. A disastrous fire leveled the business area in 1824, but the town was restored when the railroad came through less than a decade later. Then the railroad was re-routed into Wilmington, and the town has sat there ever since.

Among the houses that are open for your inspection and journey into the past are the Amstel House, the Dutch House, and the George Read II House and garden. You can also tour the restored Court House, or just spend a lazy afternoon on the green.

The ***Amstel House*** dates from the 1730s and was the home of colonial governor Nicholas Van Dyke. The furnishings show how life was during the colonial period, and includes a complete colonial kitchen. Yeah, we know George Washington was everywhere, and that includes attending a wedding here. Amstel House is at

Trivia

The only Revolutionary War battle fought in Delaware was the Battle of Cooch's Bridge (east of Newark), on September 3, 1777. It's said the new thirteen-star flag was first unfurled during this battle, a delaying action to slow the British advance toward Philadelphia. The area in which the Battle of Cooch's Bridge took place can be seen from a 90-foot observation tower in Iron Hill Park, west off SR 896 via Welsh Tract Road or Old Baltimore Pike.

Fourth and Delaware Streets, and it's closed in January and February. (302) 322–2794.

In the ***Dutch House*** you are touring what is thought to be the oldest brick house in Delaware. Constructed in the late seventeenth century, it has been restored and contains wonderful decorative arts and historical items. It's located at 32 East Third Street; (302) 322–2794.

Both the Amstel and Dutch houses are open from March through December, Tuesday through Saturday 11:00 A.M. to 4:00 P.M. and Sunday 1:00 to 4:00 P.M. They're open on weekends the rest of the year but closed on holidays. Admission to each is $2.00 for adults and $1.00 for children under twelve, or you can get a combination ticket for $3.50 for adults and $1.50 for children.

George Read was one of the signers of the Declaration of Independence and the U.S. Constitution, and his son's home, called the ***George Read II House,*** was built over a seven-year period starting in 1797. It's a superb illustration of Federal-style architecture, and you'll note the carved woodwork, fanlights, silver door hardware, and period furnishings as you tour through the twelve rooms (three of which are in the Colonial Revival style). A Philadelphia-style adaptation of a Victorian garden, designed in 1847, decorates the side and back yards. You have a choice of touring this home on your own or calling for an appointment for a guided tour. If you have the time, I recommend the latter.

Trivia

New Castle was the original state capital of Delaware. In 1777 Dover was named the new capital. Delaware is one of four states in the country where the initial letter of the capital is the same as the initial letter of the state. The others are Honolulu, Hawaii; Indianapolis, Indiana; and Oklahoma City, Oklahoma.

From March through December the George Read II House, at 42 The Strand, is open Tuesday through Saturday 10:00 A.M. to 4:00 P.M. and Sunday noon to 4:00 P.M. It's open on weekends in the winter but closed on holidays. The admission is $4.00 for adults, $3.50 for seniors and children thirteen to twenty-one, and $2.00 for children six to twelve. Call (302) 322–8411.

Surely you've noted that the top of the Delaware border, where it meets Pennsylvania, is the arc of a circle. The spire at the top of the ***New Castle Court House*** is the center point of the 12-mile radius that marks that arc. Although New Castle was the colonial capital of Delaware from 1732 to 1777, the courthouse is now restored to its 1804 appearance. Flags of the Netherlands, Sweden, Great Britain, and the United States represent the various governments that have had jurisdiction over New Castle.

Located at 211 Delaware Street, between Market and Third Streets, it's open Tuesday through Saturday 10:00 A.M. to 3:30 P.M. and Sunday 1:30 to 4:30 P.M.; closed on state holidays. There is no admission charge. Call (302) 323–4453 or (800) 441–8846.

If there's time, stop by the ***hexagon-shaped Old Library Museum*** (40 East Third Street), the Old Presbyterian Church, and the Original Ticket Office. Then reward yourself with a picnic stop at the green. Located on Delaware Street, between Third and Market Streets, it was laid out by Peter Stuyvesant in 1655.

Trivia

Iron Hill, just south of Newark, is the home of one of the highest hills in the state (which isn't saying much), and on a clear day, from the top of the Iron Hill Tower, you can see four states: New Jersey, Pennsylvania, Maryland, and, of course, Delaware.

Another delightful little town is ***Hockessin,*** just outside of Wilmington. As noted in the Delaware part of the introduction, one of the pleasures of the DelMarVa is the chance to pick up a Nancy Sawin book; she's done at least eleven, including *Delaware Sketchbook, Backroading Through Cecil* (MD) County, *Between the Bays* (Delaware and Chesapeake), and even one on outhouses entitled *Privy to the Council Seats of Yore,* with sketches of a variety of "necessary" buildings from lean-to to Alpine chalet to one that was fenced and shingled to one that had four columns on its porch.

One of my great delights is driving through the state and trying to spot the objects Ms. Sawin has drawn. Sawin was born in Wilmington in 1917, and when she retired in 1974 from a life in education, she started writing and illustrating books on local history. Her home is adjacent to Sandford School, where she had been teacher, coach, and headmistress. She refers to her home as a "semimuseum of early 'Americana'," and some of the items therein are for sale.

Visitors are welcome, but please call first. Nancy C. Sawin, 147 Sawin Lane, Hockessin; (302) 239–2416.

As you're driving around this area you may want to try the ***Back Burner*** restaurant. They have delicious seafood and meat entrees and friendly and attentive service. It's a small space, and people from Wilmington make a special drive "to the country" for the food. The Back Burner is at 425 Old Lancaster Pike; (302) 239–2314.

Trivia

Locals who jog through Hockessin know there's an old gardener on Evanson Road who has nailed a basket to a tree on his property that is right next to the road. Every summer day there are fresh tomatoes, zucchini, chilis, and various other delights for any passersby to grab.

For additional information write to the Wilmington Convention and Visitors Bureau, 1300 Market Street, Suite 504, Wilmington 19801 or call (302) 652–4088. You can also contact the New Castle Visitors Bureau, Box 465, New Castle 19720; (302) 322–8411 or (800) 748–1550.

Kent County

Kent, the middle of the three Delaware counties, has Dover as its focus. This is the home of the Dover Air Force Base and some Amish families (with their attendant farmers' markets and horse-drawn buggies); it is also the county seat. It's a hubbub of activity and constant change. Here you'll also find such unusually named places as Slaughter Beach, Seven Hickories, Dutch Neck Crossroads, and Little Heaven and an abundance of protected open spaces where you can explore what nature has left for you and the people of Delaware have kept protected for you.

Some of the information presented here is thumbnail in nature because it's easy to find your way around such places as Dover; other areas are a little more difficult to uncover and receive a little bit more attention.

The ***State House*** in Dover is the second-oldest continuously used statehouse (the one in Annapolis, Maryland, is first), and this restored 1792 structure has period furnishings and an exhibit of artifacts and historical items. Included in the tour is information about legislative and judicial activities, and how these actions affected the population, including slaves and free blacks. (302) 739–4266.

Free guided tours start from the Delaware Visitor Center and the private, nonprofit ***Sewell C. Biggs Museum of American Art,*** which is located behind the statehouse. Biggs, a native of Middletown, collected art from the eighteenth century to modern times and donated it to this museum, which is named in his honor. This building is made of brick and cast iron and was one of the first fireproof buildings in the state.

Trivia

The Delaware State Seal was adopted on January 17, 1777, and contains the coat of arms. It also shows a farmer, corn, and a wheat sheaf (signifying the agricultural vitality of the state), a ship (symbolizing New Castle County's shipbuilding industry), a militiaman with his musket (honoring the role of the citizen-soldier to the maintenance of American liberties), an ox (representing animal husbandry), and water (for the Delaware River).

The State House is located at South State Street, on the east side of the green. The entrance is at 406 Federal Street. There is no admission charge, and it is open Tuesday through Saturday from

10:00 A.M. to 4:30 P.M. and Sunday from 1:30 to 4:30 P.M. Call (302) 739–4266. The Biggs Museum, 406 Federal Street, is open Wednesday through Saturday from 10:00 A.M. to 4:00 P.M. and Sunday from 1:30 to 4:30 P.M. (302) 674–2111.

If you're at the State House, then you're in the ***Capital Green***, which was laid out in 1722 and is lined with historic buildings and is the very ground upon which the United States Constitution received its first signature in 1787. From here, also, Delaware's Continental Regiment mustered for the Revolutionary War, and from here they marched to join Washington's army. Political rallies still are held here, and in May there's Old Dover Days, with many private homes and buildings open to the public. If you're taking a guided tour, be sure to ask your leader about the woman who sent poisoned candy to her lover's family, resulting in the death of at least one person. This isn't a modern revenge happening; it took place in the 1890s.

Trivia

Because Delaware was the first state to ratify the Constitution, on December 7, 1787, it is always the first state in such national events as a presidential inauguration.

At the ***Hall of Records,*** near Legislative Hall, is the public archives for the state. This is where you can find the original 1682 charter of King Charles II and William Penn's order for the platting of Dover.

The Hall of Records is at Legislative Avenue and Duke of York Street; no charge. It's open Monday through Friday from 8:30 A.M. to 4:15 P.M. Closed on holidays. Call (302) 739–5314.

While in Dover, a must stop—if you're a fan of the TV show *Homicide* or other police-based shows, or your reading preferences tend toward procedurals—is the ***Delaware State Police Museum and Education Center,*** for this state-of-the-art educational facility provides an opportunity to learn the history of the Delaware State Police law enforcement methods, a look at a 911 command and control console, and to see uniforms and weapons on display. There are exhibits about substance abuse, highway safety efforts, and a variety of other important topics, with talks presented by specially trained troopers and volunteers. You can also catch a close-up view of patrol cars and motorcycles.

Located at the State Police Headquarters Complex, 1425 North DuPont Highway, the museum is open Monday through Friday (except state holidays) from 11:00 A.M. to 3:00 P.M. and the third Saturday of each month. There is no admission charge. (302) 739–7700.

So, your life is filled with CDs—for music, for computer programs, and who knows what else? Your children have never even known an eight-track, much less heard of a Victrola. Now's the time to correct that. Stop by the ***Johnson Victrola Museum*** in Dover to see this tribute to Eldridge Reeves Johnson (a Delaware native who was an inventor, businessman, and philanthropist), the inventor and founder of the Victor Talking Machine Company (1901). Designed to look like a 1920s store, the museum has an extensive collection of phonographs, records, and memorabilia related to the company, including an original oil painting of "Nipper," the dog who listened to "His Master's Voice."

Trivia

The Lincoln Collection at the University of Delaware contains more than 2,000 items relating to the public and private lives of Abraham Lincoln.

The museum is open Tuesday through Saturday from 10:00 A.M. to 3:30 P.M. There's no admission charge (donations are accepted) to the museum, located at Bank Lane and New Street. (302) 739–4266.

Go north of Dover about 2 miles and you'll see the ***Delaware Agricultural Museum and Village,*** covering 200 years of the agrarian heritage of Delaware, with dairy and poultry farming objects, horse-drawn equipment, and tractors from 1670 through the 1950s. There's a barbershop, farmhouse, general store, one-room schoolhouse, sawmill, train station, and blacksmith and wheelwright shops, all representing structures from the Civil War to the turn of the twentieth century.

Trivia

Wilmington was a major iron- and steel-working center where the entire suspended superstructure of the Brooklyn Bridge was manufactured.

Some of the programs that have been featured are "A More Abundant Life: Rural Delaware and Culture in New Deal Art," "The Ten Ton Tomato Club and Other Tales," and "Christmas on the Farm." Special events include "Fall Harvest Festival" and "A Farmer's Christmas."

The museum and village are about 2 miles north of Dover, at the junction of US Routes 13 and 13 alt. They're open Tuesday through Saturday 10:00 A.M. to 4:00 P.M. and Sunday 1:00 to 4:00 P.M. from April through December. The rest of the year they're open Monday through Friday from 10:00 A.M. to 4:00 P.M. Closed on holidays. Admission fees are $3.00 for adults, $2.00 for seniors sixty and older and for children from six to seventeen. Call (302) 734–1618.

Head south of Dover for about 4 miles if aviation is your passion. One of the more exciting places to visit is the ***Dover Air Force Base,*** particularly during the open house dates. That's when you'll see dozens of C5As or the

Trivia

Each C5A or C-5 Galaxy, the largest cargo airplane in the world, at Dover Air Force base is big enough to hold several football fields.

C-5 Galaxy. Community Appreciation Days are held the third Saturday of each month from April through November, and some of the special exhibitions include a fire attack on an aircraft by the base fire department, an explosive ordnance robot demonstration, a security police K-9 demonstration, and a silent drill team (probably my favorite). The Aero club offers low-cost airplane rides.

I know you've seen a lot of historic buildings around here, but this is probably the first time you've seen a World War II hangar that's listed on the National Register of Historic Places. It was the site of the Army Air Force's rocket test center and is now the home of the museum.

Also on display at the base museum is a collection of vintage planes from 1941, including a C-47 Gooney Bird and a B-17G. Other World War II artifacts also are on display.

The museum is open Monday through Saturday 9:00 A.M. to 4:00 P.M. and is closed on holidays. There is no admission charge. Best of all, photography is encouraged! Dover Air Force Base is on US Route 113, and the museum is at 1301 Heritage Road. Call (302) 677–5938.

South of the air force base is the ***John Dickinson Plantation,*** the boyhood home of John Dickinson, who in 1778 drafted the Articles of Confederation, for which he was known as the "Penman of the Revolution." His 1740s brick home and the reconstructed outbuildings are typical of eighteenth-century plantation architecture and lifestyle, with the added benefit that the home is furnished with family pieces and period antiques.

From March through December it is open Tuesday through Saturday

Trivia

The Delaware Bay area is home to the largest population of **horseshoe crabs,** *which date from 250 million years ago. Actually related to scorpions, ticks, and land spiders, rather than crabs, they are not considered dangerous to humans. They grow when they molt (usually sixteen times until they become full-size adults), increasing in size by about one-fourth each time. During the high tides of the new and full moon, in the spring, thousands of horseshoe crabs descend on the Delaware Bay shoreline to spawn. Horseshoe crab eggs are important food for migratory shorebirds passing over the Delaware Bay during the spring mating season.*

10:00 A.M. to 3:30 P.M. and Sunday 1:30 to 4:30 P.M. It is closed on holidays. There is no admission charge, and guided tours are offered. The John Dickinson Plantation is on Kitts Hammock Road. Call (302) 739–3277.

Just southeast of Dover, in ***Magnolia,*** is the "town sign" that states: THIS IS MAGNOLIA, THE CENTER OF THE UNIVERSE, AROUND WHICH THE WORLD REVOLVES. Magnolia is noted as being one of those little peninsula towns that has not lost its personality in this modern age. The house you'll be looking at when you see this sign is the John B. Lindale House, a Victorian with really neat twin towers. It is a private residence, but you can still admire it.

In Leipsic, east of Smyrna, is an area that grew from the fur trapping and shipping trades of the early nineteenth century. You'll enjoy a visit here if you stop by the nearly 16,000-acre ***Bombay Hook National Wildlife Refuge,*** where you're sure to spot plenty of ducks, geese, and shorebirds during migrating season (more than one and a half million shorebirds traverse Delaware in the annual migration in late May and early June) and other wildlife year-round.

You can drive along the 12-mile loop or hike on the nature trails and climb the observation towers for a panoramic view. The refuge is open daily from dawn to dusk, and a visitors center is open daily during the summer and on weekdays during the winter. The admission to the refuge is $4.00 per private vehicle or $2.00 if you're on foot or coming in by bike. (302) 653–6872.

Trivia

Because of Delaware's liberal incorporation laws, more than half the country's Fortune 500 *companies have filed incorporation papers in the state.*

Another tribute to agriculture can be found in Harrington at the ***Messick Agricultural Museum,*** with its extensive display of farm implements of the early twentieth century. You'll see automobiles, a covered wagon, various engines, horse-drawn plows and vehicles, tools, tractors, and trucks. There's also an early-twentieth-century kitchen and smokehouse.

The museum, located on Walt Messick Road, is open Monday through Friday from 7:30 A.M. to 5:00 P.M. and by appointment on weekends and holidays. There is no admission fee. (302) 398–3729.

There are a number of annual events in Harrington, including the Crab Feast in late August, Heritage Day in late September, and the Delaware State Fair in late July. This is a real old-fashioned state fair which still has strong agricultural roots and has not been "citified."

The town of ***Smyrna*** is pretty small, but it is growing. At the moment there's no department store, and there are a few other "big town" conveniences that are missing. But it more than makes up for what it lacks in charm. Actually, Smyrna is a historic town that straddles the two counties of New Castle and Kent. The line of demarcation is Duck Creek, located on the north side of the town.

Trivia

Swedish immigrants built the first log cabins in America in Delaware, in 1638.

On the south side, Lake Como (with a freshwater beach) is a beautiful, small lake surrounded by houses with well-manicured yards and the Delaware Home and Hospital. As one local said, "If I focus [into the past], I can see children playing with buckets and shovels in the sand, moms and dads and older kids in striped woolen swimwear walking on the beach, swimming in the cool waters, and diving off the end of the pier."

A must-stop is at ***Lewes*** (pronounced Lewis), the Delaware side of the Lewes–Cape May, New Jersey, ferry. The hour-plus ride at about $18 a car is a great way to avoid driving up the New Jersey Turnpike and then down to the beach towns of southern New Jersey or Atlantic City. (Call 302–645–6313 or 800–64–FERRY.)

But there are other reasons to come to Lewes, which is the northernmost of the coastal towns, and is actually on the Delaware Bay rather than on the Atlantic Ocean. You can't miss the ***Zwaanendael Museum*** (Valley of the Swans), a Dutch Renaissance building that is an adaptation of the town hall at Hoorn in the Netherlands. No, it wasn't brought over stone by stone, and it wasn't built three centuries ago. Instead, it was built in 1931 (the tricentennial anniversary of the founding of Lewes). Inside are exhibits of historic military and

Trivia

It's said the first "mermen" (no, not the current surfing music group) to reach American shores came from the Japanese in 1822 and that by 1842 P.T. Barnum displayed his first merman as the "Feejee Mermaid." Many fine museums own a merman specimen, but few choose to exhibit it. Therefore, because you get so few opportunities, one of the things you're sure to want to see at the Zwaanendael Museum is the merman. This one is about a foot long, and in 1941 it was loaned to the museum by a prominent local family who received it from a sea captain. The last family member died in 1985, and the museum collected $250 in donations to buy the merman from the estate. Although the museum has tried to provide the best exhibits on maritime history, the public won't let allow the removal of the merman from display.

maritime artifacts from 1631 to the War of 1812.

The Zwaanendael Museum, Savannah Road and King's Highway, is open Tuesday through Saturday from 10:00 A.M. to 4:30 P.M. and Sunday from 1:30 to 4:30 P.M. It is closed on holidays. There is no admission charge. (302) 645–9418.

Zwaanendael Museum

Also to be seen, depending on whether you want nature or history, are the ***Prime Hook National Wildlife Refuge,*** (302) 684–8419, and the ***Seaside Nature Center,*** (302) 645–6852.

At the ***Lewes Historical Society Complex*** is a furnished country store from the early years of this century, the 1798 Burton-Ingram House with period Chippendale and Empire antiques, and other historic buildings.

For curiosity's sake, stop by the ***Cannonball House*** on Front Street to see a cannonball in the foundation of the building, a souvenir of the War of 1812.

And should you be in the area on the first Saturday of November, you should stop by the Eagle Crest Aerodrome to witness the ***Punkin Chunkin' contest***. It's just what it sounds, a contest to see who can hurl pumpkins the farthest distance by the use of catapults and other odd contraptions. As this is apparently the *only* punkin chunkin' contest anywhere, these people are setting world records.

For information contact the Lewes Chamber of Commerce and Visitor's Bureau at 120 Kings Highway, Lewes 19958; (302) 645–8073 or www.punkinchunkin.com.

For additional information contact the Kent County Tourism Corporation, 9 East Lockerman Street, Box 576, Dover 19903, (302) 734–1736, or the Delaware Tourism Office, 99 Kings Highway, Box 1401, Dover 19903, (302) 734–1736.

Sussex County

Even if you've never heard of Sussex County, you've most likely heard of Rehoboth Beach and possibly even Bethany Beach, even though both are billed as "quiet resorts." They are primarily residential and have been promoted as great family vacation and residential areas.

On the south side of the Fenwick Island Lighthouse is one of the original ***Transpeninsular Line Markers,*** which was erected on April 26, 1751. This stone marked the east end of the 70-mile-long line that connected the Atlantic Ocean to the Chesapeake Bay, denoting the then-southern border of Pennsylvania. Those three lower counties are now Delaware. A little more than a decade later, Mason and Dixon used the midpoint of the line when they surveyed the border between Pennsylvania and Maryland. (302) 539–8129.

Trivia

The entrance to Bethany Beach, just south of the Delaware Seashore State Park, is marked by a 26-foot Indian totem pole. This greeting to Bethany Beach was sculpted by Dennis D. Beach and installed in the spring of 1994. It replaced a carving by Peter Toth, who donated his totem in 1976. Unfortunately, Toth's totem fell victim to termites and nasty storms. Chief Little Owl, *named for a chief of the Nanticoke Indians, represents an eagle protecting an Indian by clutching him to its breast.*

The 84-foot-tall white brick ***Fenwick Lighthouse,*** with a Third Order Fresnel lens projecting light 15 miles into the ocean, was commissioned on August 1, 1859, to protect ships from venturing onto the treacherous shoals extending 5 to 6 miles out from the Delaware coastline. It was automated in 1940, then decommissioned in 1978. A public outcry brought about the reinstallation of the original light, weighing about 1,500 pounds, and it has been in service since then. It's at the eastern terminus of the Mason-Dixon line at the Delaware/Maryland border. There's a cluster of buildings here, the lighthouse, two keepers' dwellings (now in private ownership), storage sheds, and the tower. The light is listed in the National Register of Historic Buildings. The Coast Guard deactivated it in 1978, but the Friends of the Fenwick Island Lighthouse has maintained it.

Trivia

When you catch sight of a T-shirt, sweatshirt, or cap with the legend "Slower Lower Delaware," you may have difficulty tracking down who first coined this phrase. But if you want it adorning a garment, a mug, license-plate frame, gourmet coffee, and more, get to Suzie's Tavern and Restaurant in Millsboro. Loyal customers started donning them here in 1991. Suzie's is on 226 Main Street; (302) 934–8188.

The lighthouse, between Delaware Route 521 and 146th Street, is open to the public on selected days and by appointment. There's no admission charge, but donations are accepted. For more information call the Friends of the Fenwick Island Lighthouse at (410) 250–1098.

Trivia

"Woodburn," the official home of Delaware's governors, was built in 1790–1791 by Charles Hillyard and is considered one of the finest Middle Period Georgian homes in the state. Prior to being purchased by the state in 1965, the home was owned by an abolitionist, two U.S. Senators, three doctors, and a judge.

DiscoverSea is the place to visit to view hundreds of artifacts recovered from shipwrecks along the Delmarva coastline, dating from colonial days. Dedicated to preserving our maritime heritage, the museum opened in July 1995 after more than seventeen years of research and hard work. Stop by for a visit, a lecture, or a beach tour and travel to the past via this hands-on experience.

Open daily Memorial day through Labor Day from 9:00 A.M. to 9:00 P.M. and on weekends from 10:00 A.M. to 4:00 P.M. the rest of the year. There is no admission fee to DiscoverSea, which is located at 708 Ocean Highway, Fenwick Island. Call (302) 539–9366 for additional information.

If you'd like to try your hand at ***treasure hunting*** using a metal detector, the local beaches offer a potential bonanza, or at least a short entertainment. Your find may be change, jewelry, or an ancient relic, and you're particularly likely to find something after a crowded day on the beach or after a good Nor'easter. You can rent or buy a metal detector from Sea Shell City, with rentals going for about $20 for a half day and $35 for an entire day. When searching for treasure, remember, don't trespass, cover your holes, don't go across the sand dunes, don't litter, and stay out of legally protected historic or archaeological sites. If you're really considerate and others haven't been, you'll take whatever litter you may find and dispose of it. Sea Shell City is located at 708 Ocean Highway, Ocean View. (302) 539–9366.

Trivia

In 1997 the Bethany-Fenwick Area Chamber of Commerce started a January 1 **"Exercise Like the Eskimos"** *to raise funds for scholarships for area high school seniors. By 1999 they were awarding $3,000, double what was given in the past. What's involved? It's running into the Atlantic Ocean (which is about forty degrees)! This polar bear stuff has always sounded to me like a cardiologist's heaven, but that's another story. Teams and individuals are invited to participate with $30 and $10 the entry fees, respectively. Everyone registered gets a free hat. Hot chocolate and T-shirts are sold. Mangos' Oceanfront Restaurant serves a New Year's Buffet, and part of that charge benefits the scholarship. If freezing your buns off sounds like a lot of fun, call the chamber of commerce at (302) 539–2100.*

As one might expect, the town of Laurel (originally Laureltown) was so named because of the abundance of laurel bushes growing along Broad Creek. Settled in 1802, the town was the largest in Sussex County by 1859 and was once a thriving shipping center and port town. With more than 800 buildings on the National Register of Historic Places, it is the largest designated historic district in the state of Delaware. Many properties were destroyed in the "Great Fire" of 1899, but others survived. Pick up a *Walking Tour of Historic Laurel* brochure from the historical society to see some of the fascinating moments from the past.

Trivia

The first beauty contest was held in Rehoboth Beach in 1880, and Miss United States was selected, with Thomas Edison as one of the judges.

As small as Bethel and the area around it is, there are enough people to see and talk to—and even things to do and learn—that you might find ways to spend an entire day there—even a lifetime. Start with the ***Laurel-Woodland Ferry,*** more commonly called the Woodland Ferry, that crosses the Nanticoke River just as boats have done since 1793. It's the last free and last river ferry in Delaware. The *Virginia C.*, apparently named for the wife of a former captain, is a diesel-powered cable-guided ferry that can carry three cars on its six-minute ride across the river. Operated from sunup to sundown by captains John Illiston and John and Bonnie Maull, the ferry may make up to 300 trips on a busy day, saving its passengers a road trip of nearly 20 miles.

Signs on Route 78 in Laurel and Reliance, Route 490 south of Blades, and Route 80 at Seaford indicate if the ferry is running. Call (302) 629–7742.

On the western side of the Nanticoke is the town of ***Woodland,*** with a population of about one hundred people. As the Nanticoke is known for its shad and Woodland is known for its hospitality, you might want to schedule your visit for the annual spring shad supper held by the women of the Woodland Methodist Church.

While in Bethel you'll want to stop by ***Jeff Hastings' farm market*** to buy some fresh produce. He's been known to have some spectacular seedless watermelon. And just past his place is the ***Bethel Store.*** They have soft ice cream that's pretty good, costs less than a dollar for a cone, and is made with real milk, not the skimpy, thin, fat-free stuff. You have to time your tastes to the days of the week. According to Mark Shaver (who

Trivia

Emily P. Bissell (1861–1948) created the first Christmas seals when she drew pictures on stamps in 1907. She sold the stamps to raise funds to aid tubercular children.

has been connected with this family store for sixteen years), they used to have only vanilla. Then some customers started requesting chocolate, so he did that one day a week. Then they started clamoring for more. So now it's chocolate three days a week, on Monday, Wednesday, and Friday. The rest of the week it's vanilla. Shaver says they're too poor to afford two machines to make both every day. I would add that there isn't enough room in the store for two machines.

Trivia

On the Saturday after Labor Day, Miltonians (residents of Milton) clean out garages, attics, and closets, and the **Town-Wide Yard Sale** *takes place.*

Across the street is the post office, where Bettie Stoakley has been postmaster for the past sixteen years, serving 120 families. Yes, it's an old house, and as you go in you'll notice the bottom tread and riser of some stairs that used to go up to a second floor. Stoakley says it's been that way since before she arrived.

In Laurel, as well as Milton, Ridgeville, and Milford, and other places, you'll see ***murals by Jack Lewis,*** a graduate of Rutgers with a master's degree in education. You'll find them on exterior walls, in banks, in the family court in Georgetown, and even in a prison. He's been teaching art in the state for thirty years, and he participated in a Fulbright Scholarship exchange program. Basically, Lewis says, he's a watercolorist, and murals are not his chief interest. Fortunately, he has dabbled in the area murals, for our enjoyment. Call (302) 337–8840 for more information.

Trivia

The town of Milton, settled in 1672 by English colonists, was known by several names over the years, until 1807 when the town was named after the English poet John Milton.

The Laurel area is noted for at least one other bit of historical trivia. On June 21, 1904, some signals were crossed and the schooner *Golden Gate,* traveling down the nearby Broad Creek, was struck by a mail train. Luckily the train engine automatically uncoupled, so the rest of the train didn't fall into the creek. This may be the only occurrence of a train and sailing ship colliding.

The ***Spring Garden Bed and Breakfast,*** with Gwen or (Gwenie) North as your hostess, is an excellent place to use as a base for your local explorations. Her half Victorian and half colonial home has been lovingly restored and is among the buildings on the National Register of Historic Places. North's family has been in this area since the seventeenth century, and Gwen has her finger on about as much history as you'll want. She was the first winner of the Governor's State Tourism Award. There are two bedrooms downstairs and four upstairs. The gardens are particularly inviting, and Gwen grows enough herbs to offer some to her guests so they'll remember her even when they return home.

Call Spring Garden at (302) 875–7015 or (800) 797–4909. Talk to Gwen about the ***sweet potato houses,*** and if you're really interested, she'll tell you where to see some, or she'll call Kendall Jones for you, and he'll take you on a tour.

In a nutshell, or in a potato skin if you will, the life of a sweet potato is not easy. The seeds first must be started indoors in February. Then they must be transplanted to warm beds, then to the outdoors, and then harvested and dried. Sweet potatoes apparently are horrible if eaten when freshly harvested. They'll keep all winter if they're stored in a constant fifty-degree temperature. Ergo, these buildings were constructed to hold the very productive sweet potato cash crop.

The buildings are usually two to three stories tall and are long and relatively narrow. They include three or more layers of wood siding. On the exterior is a horizontal layer, followed by a diagonal layer in the center, and a vertical layer on the inside. All this helped to insulate the building, and sometimes a form of tar paper or sawdust was used between the layers to further insulate it. Inside are a series of bins, about 3 feet by 9 feet, where the potatoes were stored. Sometimes access to the bins was from a central aisle, sometimes from a perimeter walkway. A stove at one end had to be tended morning and night once the first frost had set in. The second and third floors did not butt against the walls; this

Sweet potato house

helped ventilation and ensured an even distribution of the heat to the upper and lower floors.

A blight hit the extremely labor-intensive crop in the 1940s and destroyed the industry. Now, some of the sweet potato or potato houses have been converted into office or living space. If you'd like to just drive by one, there's an excellent example across from the old Christ Church on Route 24, about a mile east of Route 13 just south of the intersection with Route 9. It's slightly different from most sweet potato houses because of the number of window it has, but you'll get the idea.

Gwen's Spring Garden B&B is one of three (soon to be more) on a ***Bike and Bed program***. This four-day/three-night inn-to-inn bike touring experience averages 30–45 miles of back roads pedaling. You'll go through small towns and past so many antiques stores that you wish you were in a car so you could cart home some of those treasures, or be glad you're on a bike and can't buy anything. You'll go past a bison farm. The package includes three nights' accommodation, hotel tax, luggage transportation from inn to inn, three breakfasts and three dinners, snacks at each inn on arrival, detailed maps with points of interest, and secure bike storage. Call Ambassador Travel at (800) 845–9939.

A second is ***Eli's Country Inn*** near Greenwood. This is a painstakingly renovated farmhouse in the country, where you literally can hear the quiet.

Two rooms downstairs are accessible, and there is plenty of room on the porches and decks for sitting around in the afternoon if you don't want to go do something. With seventy-eight-plus acres, planted with soybeans, fresh fruits, and vegetables, you can also do some gardening if

Trivia

When you try to trace Native American bloodlines from the original residents of Delaware, you have to go to Bartlesville, Oklahoma. Yes, that's where you'll locate the headquarters of the Delaware Indians. The Delaware or Lenni Lenape were a friendly tribe who gradually gave up their lands to the new settlers. They moved westward into Pennsylvania, then Ohio, then Indiana. Some even went to Canada (still occupying two small reserves in Ontario province). By 1820 they had crossed the Mississippi River into Missouri, then Kansas, and finally moved into Indian Territory in 1866. An 1867 agreement with the Cherokees allowed them to purchase land where they now reside. The Delawares are comprised of approximately 10,000 people today.

you want. The organ is original, and the home has a vacuum cleaner motor powering it.

Trivia

The sand dunes at Cape Henlopen can reach 80 feet, and the Great Dune is the highest sand dune between North Carolina's Cape Hatteras and Cape Cod in Massachusetts.

Eli's Country Inn is on Route 36, Greenwood 19950-0779. Call (302) 349–4265, (800) 594–0048, or (302) 349–9340.

Do be warned that the local Greenwood police like to park at the intersection of US Route 13 and State Route 16, just waiting for out-of-state drivers to speed by.

There's no telling where you might think you are when you go through ***Trap Pond State Park.*** This 2,000-plus acre park was once part of the large freshwater swampland of southwestern Sussex County. The pond was created in the early 1800s for a sawmill that processed the bald cypress trees from the area.

In the 1930s the federal government purchased the area and the Civilian Conservation Corps developed the recreation site. Within the park are bald cypress trees (the northernmost stand in the United States), wetlands, wildflowers, wildlife, a nature preserve, a picnic area, a playground, a primitive camping area for youngsters, more than 7 miles of hiking trails, a canoe trail (perhaps the only marked canoe trail on the Eastern

Trivia

The Kendzierski family apparently owns the only known privately owned fort in the United States. Fort Saulsbury is 6 miles east of Milford, near the town of Slaughter Beach, in the northeast corner of Sussex County. Constructed in 1917 and 1918, the location was selected as protection of the mouth of the Delaware Bay and River during World War I, and the fort was named for Delaware's U.S. Senator (1859–1871) and Attorney General (1850–1855) Willard Saulsbury Sr. The casements were 14 feet thick, steel-reinforced concrete, with 6 feet of earth on top for camouflage. Since completion came so close to the November 1918 armistice, the fort wasn't fully staffed as a defensive facility until World War II came along, and then only until Fort Miles at Cape Henlopen was completed in 1942. The fort then became a POW camp for German and Italian soldiers. The fort was deactivated on January 11, 1946, sold to the Kendzierski family, then served as a pickle processing and storage operation for the Liebowitz Pickle Company, and then was a storage spot for the Milford Salvage Company. It's unused today, but thought to be the only surviving World War I–era fort that is essentially unchanged.

Shore), camping, and a rent-a-camp program that lets you rent equipment to see if you like the experience before investing in all the gear.

Birders can spy on great blue herons, owls, hummingbirds, robins, mockingbirds, cardinals, finches, warblers, bald eagles, and pileated woodpeckers. Pets are permitted in some areas of the park, but they must be kept on a leash and attended to at all times. Bicycles and horses are permitted on designated trails.

Motorboats (electric only) are permitted in some areas of the pond and are limited to a no-wake speed of five miles per hour. Rowboats, pedal boats, and canoes may be rented in the summer. The park is part of a trash-free program, which means you carry out everything you carry in.

There is a small entrance fee during the summer and on weekends and holidays in May, September, and October. Call (302) 875–5153 or (302) 875–2392 (campground).

As you drive the 20 miles along the beach from the Maryland border to Lewes (the first town in the first state), you may notice ***seven concrete towers*** rising up about 80 feet. They've been there for a number of years, since the days when German U-boats were a threat to our shores. They belong to the state, but there have been days when people were ready to tear them down. After all, they weren't being used. But there wasn't ever enough money, so they still stood. Now, people (perhaps the same ones) have decided the towers are historic.

That means you may climb the 115 steps of the ***Cape Henlopen State Park tower*** to the top for a lovely view that stretches from the Rehoboth boardwalk to Gordons Pond, taking in the Atlantic Ocean, Delaware Bay, and the outlying salt marsh. It's open seven days a week during the summer season in good weather. It's open on weekends the rest of the year. The admission price is $2.50 for state residents and $5.00 for out-of-staters. Call (302) 645–8983.

While meandering along west of Cape Henlopen, southwest of Milford, on Route 36, if you get a yen for a little fishing, stop by ***Abbott's Mill Nature Center,*** near Milford. It's one of a number of lakes and ponds, but there are also a historic gristmill, trails meandering through pine woods and along a stream, and canoeing and fishing. There's also a nature center, and an Autumn at Abbott's Mill Festival is held the third Saturday in October. Year-round family programs, particularly for children from three to eighteen, but also for adults and families, are highlighted. For information call (302) 422–0847.

Places to Eat in Delaware

Dover
Tango's Bistro,
1570 North DuPont Highway,
(302) 678–8500

Fenwick Island
Libby's Restaurant,
Ocean Highway,
(302) 539–7379

Lewes
The Lighthouse Restaurant,
Fisherman's Wharf,
(302) 645–6271

Milford
Banking House Inn,
112 Northwest Front Street,
(302) 422–5708

New Castle
Arsenal on the Green,
30 Market Street,
(302) 328–1290

Lynnhaven Inn,
154 North DuPont Highway,
(302) 328–2041

Salty Sam's Pier 13,
130 South DuPont Highway,
(302) 323–1408

Newark
Ashley's,
100 Continental Drive,
(302) 454–1500

Rehoboth
Blue Moon,
35 Baltimore Avenue,
(302) 227–6515

Chez La Mer,
210 Second Street,
(302) 227–6494

Garden Gourmet,
4121 Highway 1,
(302) 227–4747

Victoria's,
2 Olive Avenue,
(302) 227–0615

Woody's,
2 Christian Street,
(302) 227–2561

Smyrna
Thomas England House,
1165 South DuPont Highway;
(302) 653–1420

Wilmington
Brandywine Room,
Eleventh and Market Streets, (302) 594–3156

Columbus Inn,
2216 Pennsylvania Avenue,
(302) 571–1492

Green Room,
Eleventh and Market Streets, (302) 594–3155

Places to Stay in Delaware

Note that accommodations statewide usually are full the first weekend after Memorial Day and the third weekend after Labor Day due to the NASCAR races at Dover Downs. There are dozens of hotels, condominiums, motels, apartments, houseboats, and other accommodations along the beaches of Dewey, Fenwick, Bethany, and Rehoboth. Some offer week-long (Saturday to Saturday or Sunday to Sunday) rentals, weekends, or one-night options. Some are open only seasonally. Some are on the ocean, some are several blocks away.

Claymont
Darley Manor Inn Bed and Breakfast,
3701 Philadelphia Pike,
(302) 792–2127

Wilmington Hilton,
I–95 and Naaman's Road,
(302) 792–2700

Dewey Beach
Atlantic Oceanside Motel,
1700 Highway 1,
(302) 227–8811

Bay Resort,
126 Bellevue Street,
(302) 227–6400

Dover
Sheraton Inn and Conference Center,
Dover,
1570 North DuPont Highway,
(302) 678–8500

Fenwick Island
Fenwick Towers Condominiums,
Route 1,
(302) 539–6087

Greenwood
Eli's Bed and Breakfast,
Route 36,
(302) 349–4265

Laurel
Spring Garden Bed and Breakfast, Delaware Avenue, (302) 875–7015 or (800) 797–4909

Lewes
Inn At Canal Square, 122 Market Street, (800) 222–7902 or (302) 645–8499

Montchanin
Inn at Montchanin Village, Route 100 and Kirk Road, (302) 888–2133

New Castle
Armitage Inn, Delaware Street and The Strand, (302) 328–6618

Newark
Christiana Hilton Inn, 100 Continental Drive, (302) 454–1500

William Penn Guest House, 206 Delaware Street, (302) 328–7736

Rehoboth
Boardwalk Plaza, 2 Olive Avenue, (302) 227–7169

Brighton Suites Hotel, 34 Wilmington Avenue, (302) 227–5780

Gladstone Inn, 3 Olive Avenue, (302) 227–2641

Henlopen Hotel, 511 North Boardwalk, (800) 441–8450

Wilmington
Hotel DuPont, 100 West Eleventh Street, (302) 594–3100

Sheraton Suites Wilmington, 422 Delaware Avenue, (302) 654–8300

Other Attractions Worth Seeing in Delaware

Ashland Nature Center, Hockessin; (302) 239–2334

Brandywine Park (Zoo) Wilmington; (302) 571–7747

Brick Hotel Gallery, Odessa; (302) 378–4069

Collins-Sharp House, Odessa; (302) 378–4069

Corbit-Sharp House, Odessa; (302) 378–4069

Delaware Center for the Contemporary Arts, Wilmington; (302) 656–6466

Delaware Museum of Natural History, Route 52 between Greenville and Centreville; (302) 658–9111

Delaware Park Racetrack, Wilmington; (302) 994–2521

Elsie Williams Doll Collection, Georgetown; (302) 856–9033

Fort Christina, Wilmington; (302) 652–5629

Fort Delaware State Park, Delaware City; (302) 834–7941

Hale-Byrnes House, Stanton; (302) 998–3792

Heart Education Center, Newark; (302) 633–0200

Historic Houses of Odessa, Odessa; (302) 378–4069

Immanuel Episcopal Church, New Castle; (302) 328–2413

Iron Hill Museum of Natural History, Newark; (302) 368–5703

Kalmar Nyckel Foundation, Wilmington; (302) 429–7447

Lincoln Collection of the University of Delaware, Wilmington, (302) 573–4419

Nanticoke Indian Museum, Millsboro; (302) 945–7022

Nemours Mansion and Gardens, Wilmington, (302) 651–6912

Old Drawyer's Church, Odessa; (302) 378–4069

Old Dutch House, New Castle; (302) 322–2794

Old St. Anne's Episcopal Church, Middletown (no phone)

Port Penn Interpretive Center, Port Penn; (302) 834–0431

Rockwood Museum, Wilmington; (302) 761–4340

Treasures of the Sea Exhibit, Georgetown; (302) 856–5700

Wilmington & Western Railroad, Wilmington; (302) 998–1930

Wilmington Maritime Center, Wilmington; (302) 984–0472

Wilson-Warner House, Odessa; (302) 378–4069

Winterthur Museum, garden and library, Winterthur; (302) 888–4600 or (800) 448–3883

Woodburn, Dover; (302) 736–5656

Calendar of Annual Events in Delaware

February

Annual Delaware Antiquarian Book Show/Sale, Wilmington; (302) 655–3055

Valentine Tea, Rockwood Museum, Wilmington; (302) 761–4340

Wilmington International Exhibition of Photography, Newark; (302) 478–6392

March

Annual Chocolate Festival, Rehoboth Beach; (302) 227–8259

Annual ICCD St. Patrick's Day Parade, Wilmington; (302) 45–IRISH

St. Patrick's Tea, Rockwood Museum, Wilmington; (302) 761–4340

April

Earth Day Celebration of Brandywine Zoo, Wilmington; (302) 571–7850

Easter Egg Hunt, Bethany Beach; (302) 539–8011

Easter Promenade, Rehoboth; (800) 441–1329 or (302) 227–2233

Governor's Annual Easter Egg Hunt, Dover; (302) 739–5656

Great Delaware Kite Festival, Lewes; (302) 645–8073

Spring Fling at the Brandywine Zoo, Wilmington; (302) 571–7850

May

A Day in Old New Castle, New Castle; (302) 322–5744

Annual Winterthur Point-to-Point Races, Wilmington; (800) 448–3883

Blessing of the Fleet, Lewes; (302) 645–5297

Delmarva Hot Air Balloon Festival, Milton; (302) 684–8404

Milford Memorial Hospital Fair, Milford; (302) 422–3904

Old Dover Days, Dover; (302) 734–1736

Spring Annual Surf Fishing Tournament, Fenwick Island; (302) 539–2100 or (800) 962–7873

Wilmington Garden Day, Wilmington; (302) 428–6172

June

Delaware State Fair, Harrington; (302) 398–3269

Delmarva Chicken Festival, Millsboro; (302) 937–6777

Lewes Garden Tour, Lewes; (302) 645–8073

July

Annual Cottage Tour, Rehoboth Beach; (302) 227–8408

Annual State Fair, Dover; (302) 398–3269

Fourth of July Parade, Bethany Beach; (302) 539–8011

Haneef's Annual Artisan Festival and Parade, Wilmington; (302) 657–2108

July Fourth Celebration, Dover; (302) 734–7513

July Fourth Fireworks, Newark; (302) 366–7036 or (302) 366–7060

Old-Fashioned Independence Day Celebration, Laurel; (302) 422–3904

Rehoboth Beach Fireworks, Rehoboth Beach; (302) 227–2772

AUGUST

African-American Festival, Seaford; (302) 628–1908 or (302) 337–8230

Arden Fair, Arden; (302) 475–3126 or (302) 475–3912

Creekside Bluegrass Festival, Laurel; (302) 875–3658

Delaware State News Sand Castle Contest, Rehoboth Beach; (302) 741–8204 or (302) 741–8210

Garrison Days, Delaware City; (302) 834–7941

Old Canal Fest, Delaware City; (302) 832–1890

Old Sussex Day, Trap Pond State Park; (302) 834–7941

Wyoming Peach Festival, Wyoming; (302) 697–2966

SEPTEMBER

Brandywine Arts Festival, Wilmington; (302) 656–8364

Seaford Towne and Country Fair, Seaford; (302) 629–9690

OCTOBER

Autumn Jazz Festival, Rehoboth Beach; (800) 29–MUSIC

Boast the Coast, Lewes; (302) 645–8073

Bridgeville Apple-Scrapple Festival, Bridgeville; (302) 337–8771

Sea Witch Halloween Festival and Fiddlers' Convention, Rehoboth Beach; (302) 227–2233 or (800) 441–1329

NOVEMBER

World Championship Punkin' Chunkin' Festival, Lewes; (302) 645–8273

Yuletide at Winterthur, Wilmington; (800) 448–3883

DECEMBER

Yuletide in Odessa, Odessa; (302) 378–4069

Index

D

E

F

G

H

N

O

P

T

U

V

W

Z

About the Author

Judy Colbert is a longtime resident of Maryland. An award-winning freelance writer and photographer, Judy's articles and photographs have appeared in such publications as *Washingtonian, Maryland, AAA World, American Health, Home & Away, Self,* and *Frequent Flyer.* She has appeared on *Good Morning America* and Arthur Frommer's *Almanac of Travel.*

Other titles that Judy has authored include *The Spa Guide* and *Virginia: Off the Beaten Path,* both published by The Globe Pequot Press.